HANDBOOK
❖
NUMBER FIVE

A Problem Solver's Handbook

A guide to Intermediate Mathematical Olympiads

Andrew Jobbings

The United Kingdom Mathematics Trust

A Problem Solver's Handbook

© 2013 United Kingdom Mathematics Trust

All rights reserved. No part of this publication may be reproduced or transmitted in any form or by any means, electronic or mechanical, including photocopy, recording, or any information storage and retrieval system, without permission in writing from the publisher.

Published by The United Kingdom Mathematics Trust.
Maths Challenges Office, School of Mathematics, University of Leeds, Leeds, LS2 9JT, United Kingdom
http://www.ukmt.org.uk

First published 2013

Reprinted 2014

ISBN 978-1-906001-19-3

Printed in the UK for the UKMT by Charlesworth Press, Wakefield.
http://www.charlesworth.com

Typographic design by Andrew Jobbings of Arbelos.
http://www.arbelos.co.uk

Typeset with LaTeX.

The books published by the United Kingdom Mathematics Trust are grouped into series.

❖

The EXCURSIONS IN MATHEMATICS series consists of monographs which focus on a particular topic of interest and investigate it in some detail, using a wide range of ideas and techniques. They are aimed at high school students, undergraduates and others who are prepared to pursue a subject in some depth, but do not require specialised knowledge.
1. *The Backbone of Pascal's Triangle*, Martin Griffiths
2. *A Prime Puzzle*, Martin Griffiths

❖

The HANDBOOKS series is aimed particularly at students at secondary school who are interested in acquiring the knowledge and skills which are useful for tackling challenging problems, such as those posed in the competitions administered by the UKMT and similar organisations.
1. *Plane Euclidean Geometry: Theory and Problems*, A D Gardiner and C J Bradley
2. *Introduction to Inequalities*, C J Bradley
3. *A Mathematical Olympiad Primer*, Geoff C Smith
4. *Introduction to Number Theory*, C J Bradley
5. *A Problem Solver's Handbook*, Andrew Jobbings

❖

The PATHWAYS series aims to provide classroom teaching material for use in secondary schools. Each title develops a subject in more depth and in more detail than is normally required by public examinations or national curricula.
1. *Crossing the Bridge*, Gerry Leversha
2. *The Geometry of the Triangle*, Gerry Leversha

❖

The PROBLEMS series consists of collections of high-quality and original problems of Olympiad standard.
1. *New Problems in Euclidean Geometry*, David Monk

❖

The YEARBOOKS series documents all the UKMT activities, including details of all the challenge papers and solutions, lists of high scorers, accounts of the IMO and Olympiad training camps, and other information about the Trust's work during each year.

Contents

Series Editor's Foreword   vii

Preface   ix

1 Introduction   1
    1.1 The aim of this book 1
    1.2 Intermediate Olympiads in the UK 2
    1.3 Preparing for an Olympiad 2
    1.4 The layout of the book 5
    1.5 Further reading 6

2 Algebra   7
    2.1 General guidance 7
    2.2 Basic equations 12
    2.3 Simultaneous equations 16
    2.4 Sequences 22
    2.5 Miscellaneous problems 28

3 Geometry   33
    3.1 General guidance 33
    3.2 Angles 35
    3.3 Pythagoras 43
    3.4 Area and perimeter 50
    3.5 Touching circles 58
    3.6 Coordinates 64
    3.7 Three dimensions 69
    3.8 Miscellaneous problems 73

4	**Integers**	**77**
	4.1 General guidance	77
	4.2 Digits	79
	4.3 Divisibility	83
	4.4 Factors and equations	88
	4.5 Miscellaneous problems	93
5	**Combinatorics**	**101**
	5.1 General guidance	101
	5.2 Counting	103
	5.3 Placement	107
	5.4 Miscellaneous problems	113

Appendix A Cayley, Hamilton and Maclaurin   **117**

Appendix B Answers to questions in the examples   **121**

Appendix C Solutions to the exercises   **123**

   Exercise 2.2 123
   Exercise 2.3 131
   Exercise 2.4 143
   Exercise 2.5 145
   Exercise 3.2 152
   Exercise 3.3 167
   Exercise 3.4 176
   Exercise 3.5 191
   Exercise 3.6 198
   Exercise 3.7 201
   Exercise 3.8 208
   Exercise 4.2 220
   Exercise 4.3 224
   Exercise 4.4 228
   Exercise 4.5 234
   Exercise 5.2 245
   Exercise 5.3 248
   Exercise 5.4 252

Sources of the problems   **261**

Index   **265**

Series Editor's Foreword

This book is part of a series whose aim is to help young mathematicians prepare for competitions at secondary school level. Here the focus is on the Cayley, Hamilton and Maclaurin papers, which are aimed at pupils aged 13–16. Like other volumes in the Handbooks series, it provides cheap and ready access to directly relevant material. All these books are characterized by the large number of carefully constructed exercises for the reader to attempt.

I hope that every secondary school will have these books in its library. The prices have been set so low that many good students will wish to purchase their own copies. Schools wishing to give out large numbers of copies of these books, perhaps as prizes, should note that discounts may be negotiated with the UKMT office.

London, UK   GERRY LEVERSHA

About the Author

Andrew Jobbings gained both his BSc and his PhD in mathematics from Durham University. He taught mathematics for 28 years, including 14 years as Head of Department at Bradford Grammar School, before founding the publishing business Arbelos.

With a keen interest in providing mathematics enrichment activities, Andrew helped to establish the IMOK suite of competitions in 2002. He devises problems for the UKMT and is involved with many other UKMT projects. He has regularly chaired a problems group for the European Kangaroo contest and gives Royal Institution masterclasses.

Preface

The problems on IMOK Olympiad papers are intended to be different. They probably look unusual, so that it is not immediately obvious how to solve them, in contrast to a typical question from a school text-book. Furthermore, there is no set syllabus content, unlike an examination such as GCSE. However, the mathematics involved in the solutions should be familiar to most good pupils of appropriate age, though the problems may appear unfamiliar.

Though solutions to each year's problems are provided in the 'official' solutions booklet, these have been worked on by a group of people to produce a polished result and are not intended to be 'model' solutions. There is no attempt to show how a solution might be discovered, nor all the work that was done on scrap paper!

This book aims to provide an informal guide, either for potential candidates, or for any other pupils wishing to tackle problems of a more challenging nature. In particular, the discussions of sample problems aim to show how anyone might attack a problem which may be quite unlike anything they have ever seen before.

Acknowledgements

Many people have been involved either in setting up the IMOK Olympiads in 2002 or in running them since. All of them deserve thanks for their help and support over the first ten years of the competition. I am pleased to have this opportunity to thank the following in print:

- Chris Robson, who was instrumental in getting the project started;
- Dean Bunnell, James Cranch, Tony Gardiner, Patricia King and Gerry Leversha, who have acted as team leaders, overseeing the marking of each paper and writing solutions;

- ❖ Dean Bunnell, James Cranch, Mary Teresa Fyfe, Tony Gardiner, Howard Groves, Terry Heard, Gerry Leversha, Steve Mulligan, Andy Parkinson and Mary Read, who have been members of the problems group;
- ❖ all those who have contributed problems;
- ❖ Adam McBride, Peter Neumann, Sylvia Neumann and Bill Richardson, who have helped prepare and scrutinise the papers and solutions;
- ❖ the UKMT staff, the markers and all others who have helped to make the IMOK Olympiads a success.

I should also like to thank Daisy Gomersall, who most helpfully commented from a student perspective on an early draft of this book, and Gerry Leversha, whose guidance as editor has been invaluable.

Above all I should like to acknowledge the ingenuity and imagination of those who have devised, selected and polished the problems: if this book has any value, it accrues from the quality of their work.

Baildon, Shipley, UK   ANDREW JOBBINGS

Chapter 1

Introduction

1.1 The aim of this book

Many countries set Mathematical Olympiads at the 'Senior' level. Some countries also set Olympiads at a younger level—roughly ages 14 to 16—and this book aims to provide guidance to candidates for these papers. This book is aimed especially at pupils, but may also be useful to teachers in schools.

A lot of pupils with high skill levels may feel unprepared for an Olympiad paper, especially regarding the presentation of solutions, and may not be confident in their ability to solve unfamiliar, hard, problems. Some pupils may be lucky and have a teacher who can help, or they may be involved with the admirable mentoring scheme administered by the UKMT. Others may be left to work on their own, using whatever resources they can access, such as websites.

An Olympiad paper consists of mathematical *problems*: no question should be a matter of routine, and for all questions some insight is usually required to make progress. There is no fixed syllabus content, though it is assumed that candidates will have good skills based on familiarity with standard school work at the appropriate level. For this reason a book based solely on subject knowledge would have limited use. The emphasis of this book is therefore on "know-how" rather than on knowledge. Nevertheless, along the way some reminders are given about key facts which are assumed to be familiar.

The book is written with the pupil reader in mind. Just as for any mathematics book, the reader is advised to have a pencil and paper handy, and to be prepared to use them whenever something is unclear!

1.2 Intermediate Olympiads in the UK

In the UK, Mathematical Olympiads are provided by the United Kingdom Mathematics Trust (the UKMT).

The Intermediate Mathematical Olympiad and Kangaroo (IMOK) is the follow-on round of the Intermediate Mathematics Challenge (IMC), for pupils in the age range 14 to 16. The most successful 500 or so pupils in the IMC are invited to take one of the three Olympiad papers:

Paper	Age
Cayley	–14
Hamilton	14–15
Maclaurin	15–16

Each of these Olympiad papers consist of six challenging problems. The earlier problems tend to be easier; the last two are more demanding. Candidates are expected to hand in full written solutions. The IMOK Olympiad papers used between 2003 and 2012 form the basis of this book.

After the IMOK every candidate receives a booklet containing all the papers and solutions, as well as other information. The most recent booklet is available for purchase from the UKMT.

The names of three notable British mathematicians were chosen for the papers. You will find far more information about them in appendix A.

1.3 Preparing for an Olympiad

When faced with unusual or challenging problems, what is needed above all is perseverance, the desire to keep trying until some progress is made. In an Olympiad there will be plenty of time to try the problems and keep worrying away at them until one of them yields up its secrets. Success is rarely a question of extra knowledge, more one of know-how.

Some general guidance about taking a paper is given below. In the following chapters some additional guidance is given, relevant to the work of that chapter, and sample Olympiad problems are discussed in detail, in an attempt to explain some of the thought processes you might go through when tackling them. Reading through these discussions carefully will help to prepare you, but they are not intended to be complete solutions.

However, the best preparation is practice. That is why all previous IMOK Olympiad problems are included in this book, so that you have plenty of questions to try. The guidance given in each section should help you to attempt the problems in the following exercise. Only refer to the solutions when you have succeeded in finding a solution yourself, or if you make little progress even after spending some time thinking about the problem.

Taking the paper

Few candidates will do all the problems on the paper and doing three or four fully is exceptional. You should aim to solve one or two questions first, then if time allows go on to others. The early problems tend to be easier, the later ones harder, so it is fairly clear where to start!

Two hours should give you plenty of time. So do not be afraid of spending time on one question and doing a lot of rough work. But do remember to allow time to write out your solution to each question in a clearly explained way. Few marks are awarded whenever a candidate just hands in an 'answer', or a jumble of rough working. Indeed, you are instructed *not* to hand in rough working.

General guidance on writing solutions

The later chapters of this book contain a lot of guidance about how to write your solutions. Nevertheless, there are a few additional general points which you may find helpful.

You are not expected to write polished solutions, though the examiners are always pleasantly surprised by the quality and ingenuity of some pupils' work. What you need to do is set out the steps in your solution in a clear and logical manner, so that the marker can readily follow your mathematical argument.

It is helpful to lay out your solution line-by-line, with each new assertion beginning on a new line. You should also remember to include clear diagrams where necessary; it is better to have too many diagrams than too few.

Do not expect the marker to do your work for you, which means that you should present calculations explicitly. For example, if you are looking at a lot of cases (which is not usually a good idea, see later) you should give detailed working for each of them.

Finally, you should be aware that answers obtained by inexact methods will receive little credit. For that reason you should avoid approaches like scale drawing. Similarly, calculations which involve converting exact numbers such as π, $\sqrt{2}$ or even $\frac{1}{3}$ to approximate decimals like 3.14, 1.414 or 0.33 are also wasted effort. One reason that calculators are forbidden is to help you to avoid doing this.

Dealing with a lot of cases

Why is dealing with a lot of cases such a bad idea?

Suppose, for example, you are asked to find all three-digit positive integers with some property. The naive approach would be just to consider all such numbers in turn, starting at 100 and ending at 999. This is a bad strategy for two reasons.

Firstly, bearing in mind the advice given above, you need to show the working for each number, explaining why it does, or does not, satisfy the required property (ticks and crosses are not enough). That is a lot of work.

Secondly, and more importantly, it is easy to make a mistake, either by leaving some numbers out, or including some extra ones, or by making errors in the calculations. The markers are likely to penalise such mistakes very heavily, since the strategy is only a good one if it is carried out completely accurately.

Such a high-risk strategy can be avoided by using some mathematics, either to reduce the number of cases, or, even better, to eliminate the need to look at any cases at all. In our example, you might be able to prove that numbers of the required form are, say, all squares; then you would only need to consider 100, 121, ..., 361, though this is still rather a long list. Better still, suppose you were able to prove that numbers of the required form are all squares of prime numbers; then the list would shrink to just seven numbers: 11^2, 13^2, 17^2, ..., 31^2.

As a rule of thumb, if you find yourself dealing with more than about ten cases, then you should spend some time trying to find a better method.

Chapter 1: Introduction 5

1.4 The layout of the book

This book contains all the problems that were set for the first ten years of the IMOK Olympiads, that is, 2003 to 2012. The problems have been divided into categories, according to the techniques required in their solution. Some problems fall into more than one category; in such cases the problem has been placed in the most appropriate section.

Each category is covered by a section of the book, which includes:

> key mathematical facts;
>
> techniques for solvers, indicated by the symbol ✦;
>
> an example—a discussion about a sample question;
>
> reminders about the presentation of full written answers, indicated by the symbol ✧;

Each section ends with an exercise of problems for the reader to tackle.

Age level and difficulty

In order to give an indication of the age level and degree of difficulty of each section, a table such as

Cayley 6   Hamilton –   Maclaurin 2 3 5

shows where the problems in that section appeared in the original papers. The table above, for example, shows that the topic appeared at question 6 (possibly more than once) on a Cayley paper, did not appear on Hamilton, and occurred at 2, 3 and 5 on Maclaurin.

In each exercise, the problems appear roughly in ascending order of difficulty. A letter is shown alongside each problem, indicating which paper the problem has been taken from: C for Cayley; H for Hamilton and M for Maclaurin. A few problems appeared on more than one paper, in which case only the first is indicated.

Solutions

Solutions to all the problems in the exercises are given in appendix C; these are based on those given in the official solutions booklets.

You are strongly advised to try the questions first before looking at the solutions. Give yourself time, use paper and pencil, and make a determined effort to solve each problem in your own way. Only after you have found your own method, or when you really need some help, should you turn to the solution given here. But then you will have a better understanding of the problem, and so will be able to appreciate the solution much more.

In many cases a problem has more than one method of solution. You may find a solution which you think is better than any of those given here, or you may find one which you prefer for other reasons. Be reassured: any valid solution, well presented, will receive full credit in an Olympiad. And the ability to discover a different solution is a good indicator that you have the potential to do well.

1.5 Further reading

A useful list of books and other resources can be found on the web-site: *AMC's Math Club*. The Mathematical Association of America and American Mathematics Competitions. URL: http://amc.maa.org/mathclub/index.shtml

For a modern source of the geometrical results needed at this level, see the first parts of: Gerry Leversha. *Crossing the Bridge*. UKMT, 2008. ISBN: 978-1-906001-06-3

For a book dealing with the Junior Olympiad, which contains much good advice also relevant to the Intermediate level, see: Tony Gardiner. *More Mathematical Challenges*. Cambridge University Press, 1997. ISBN: 978-0-521-58568-2

Chapter 2

Algebra

Problems involving algebra are common in Olympiads. Some problems are clearly algebraic since they explicitly contain algebraic notation. Other problems may appear at first sight to be only arithmetical—they only contain numbers—but in fact these are implicitly algebraic, in that a solution by algebra is possible and may even be preferable.

You may be able to find a direct way (that is, without algebra) to solve a problem of the latter sort, but the method may be hard to write up clearly, and it may be difficult to convince someone that nothing has been omitted. In such cases, using an algebraic approach will almost certainly help you to provide a clear solution, without any gaps.

Some problems that appear to be geometrical may also lend themselves to an algebraic approach.

2.1 General guidance

Notation

The statements of some problems already include unknown quantities, such as a, b and c, or x and y. To solve other problems you may need to introduce your own algebraic notation.

> ✧ When introducing letters as algebraic symbols, you should always specify what each letter stands for.

In mathematics, algebraic letters usually represent numbers rather than physical quantities.

✧ If you adopt an algebraic approach you should take account of the units whenever you introduce a letter.

For example, you might write "let the length of the rectangle be ℓ m", so that ℓ is a number and the equation $\ell^2 = 36$ makes sense.

This convention has several useful consequences:

(a) an algebraic expression such as x^3 is just a number, so there is no need to worry about what units the cube of some quantity like speed might have;
(b) expressions such as $4y^3$ and y may be combined; $4y^3 + y$ is just the sum of two numbers;
(c) algebraic equations are statements connecting numbers and their solutions are numbers.

Finally, you should avoid the temptation to introduce a separate symbol for everything in sight—this does not usually prove helpful!

✧ When introducing algebraic notation, consider carefully which quantities to represent by a letter. In particular, avoid introducing more symbols than necessary.

The meaning of solve

When a problem asks you, say, to 'solve' an equation, it means that you should find *all* the solutions.

For example, to solve the equation $a^2 = 4$, it is not sufficient to say 'the solution is $a = 2$'. Though $a = 2$ is indeed a solution, there is another solution, namely $a = -2$. The best way to avoid missing solutions is to use a general method such as factorisation: in this case we would rearrange the equation in the form $a^2 - 4 = 0$, so that $(a-2)(a+2) = 0$.

✧ Be aware that 'solve' means 'find *all* the solutions of'.

Nature of the solutions

In some problems you may be told, for example, that the required solutions are positive, or that they are integers. If no such restrictions are given, then you should assume that the solutions may be any real number.

⬥ You should not make any assumptions about the nature of the solutions of algebraic equations, unless such conditions are given in the question.

Note that questions in which the unknowns are given to be integers are discussed in chapter 4.

Deriving equations

Some algebraic problems explicitly give you equations to work with. In others, you need to derive one or more equations yourself. When you do so, it may be tempting just to write down your equation without attempting to explain where it has come from—you should overcome that temptation!

⬥ When you derive an equation you should always explain where the terms in the equation come from.

Proving given equations

Sometimes a problem gives you an equation and asks you to prove it. In such cases you will need to think carefully about how to set out your work.

What you should never do is start from the given equation and prove that something true, $0 = 0$, say, follows. Doing this would merely show that $0 = 0$ follows from the required equation, and since true results can follow from false ones we are none the wiser about the truth of the desired equation.*

There are several ways to avoid this logical flaw. It is often best to consider separately the expressions on the left-hand side and the right-hand side of the equation that you are asked to prove. Either show how one side can be rearranged to give the other, or show that each of them can be rearranged to give a third expression.

⬥ When asked to prove a given equation, think carefully about how to set out your work. In particular, do not start from the given equation.

---

*Here is an example of a true statement following from a false one: suppose that $2 = -2$; we may square both sides of the equation to give $4 = 4$.

Labelling equations

When you have several equations, there is a risk that you do not explain how you manipulate them, so that your solution is not presented clearly. In such cases it may be helpful to label each equation, so that you can refer to it directly by its label.

- ✧ When you manipulate equations, be sure to explain what you have done, and to which equation(s). Labelling the equations is a good way to make an explanation clear.

Simplifying

Sometimes you can make an algebraic problem easier by choosing your method or notation carefully, so that intermediate expressions are less complicated. Whatever method you use, you can always help yourself by simplifying expressions as you proceed.

- ✧ Aim to simplify as you go along. For example, where appropriate, factorise expressions rather than expanding them, or combine algebraic fractions into a single fraction.

Division by zero

The rules of arithmetic do not allow you to divide by zero. This has two consequences when dealing with algebra.

Firstly, if an algebraic fraction arises in your work, you should consider whether the denominator may be zero. This might lead to some special cases which need to be considered separately. For example, if the fraction $\frac{a}{b-2}$ arises in your working, then you will need to consider what happens when $b = 2$, because then the fraction is undefined.

Secondly, though it is possible to divide both sides of an equation by the same non-zero quantity, you should not divide both sides by a quantity which may be zero. So you should avoid dividing by an expression which contains one or more variables, because the expression may itself be zero. In such cases, it is almost always better to use a method involving factorisation. For example, to solve $a^2 = 4a$, rather than dividing by a (which may be zero), it is better to rewrite the equation in the form $a^2 - 4a = 0$, then factorise to obtain $a(a - 4) = 0$, giving $a = 0$, or 4.

Chapter 2: Algebra

⬥ Be aware that division by zero is not permitted. Whenever you wish to divide by an expression, determine whether that expression might be zero. If so, use a method involving factorisation.

Checking

When solving any mathematical problem it is a good idea to check that your answers actually work for the original problem. This is especially true when solving problems in algebra: it is not enough just to check an equation you have derived, because you may have made a mistake in the process of deriving that equation.

⬥ Always check your answers in the original question, not just in an equation that you have derived.

And, of course, be sure you have actually answered the question that was asked. For example, if your choice of symbol does not represent what you were asked to find, then you probably need to do a final calculation.

⬥ Remember to confirm that you have answered the given question.

We return to the issue of checking in section 2.5.

Patterns and proof

A common procedure when solving some algebraic problems is to look at some simple cases, in order to get a feel for the problem. Indeed, you may be able to "spot" a pattern in the results you obtain. Though this can help you to understand the problem, it does not constitute a proof that the pattern is always there—what you need to do is find a proof which shows that your suspected result is always true.

⬥ When you make use of a pattern you should explain in a general way why the pattern continues for ever; it is not sufficient just to show the first part of the pattern and assume that it continues in the same form.

Special cases

Even when you can prove a general result, there may be some special cases where the result, or your proof, fails. Be on the alert for these.

⟡ When you have derived a general result, you should determine whether there are any particular cases for which your reasoning does not apply. For such cases you may be able to find another line of reasoning, or you may be able to show that the result does not hold in that particular circumstance.

2.2 Basic equations

Cayley 1 2 3 4 5 6   Hamilton 1 3 5   Maclaurin 1 5

You should be familiar with the standard methods of simplifying algebraic expressions, and with the methods of solving the following standard types of equation:

(a) linear equations such as $5g = 7 - 6g$;
(b) simultaneous linear equations such as

$$3a + 4b = 2$$
$$7a - 3b = 17.$$

For simultaneous equations, you should be able to adopt either of the two standard approaches, elimination or substitution, as appropriate.

Techniques

✦ When no algebraic symbols are given in a question, consider letting a letter stand for some quantity. Often a good quantity to choose is whatever you are asked to find in the question.

⟡ Remember the advice in the section Notation on page 7.

Example 2.2

Before the last of a series of tests, Sam calculated that a mark of 17 would enable her to average 80 over the series, but that a mark of 92 would raise her average mark over the series to 85.

How many tests were there in the series?

Chapter 2: Algebra

Discussion

We are asked to find the number of tests, so let the number of tests be n.

> ◈ Remember the advice in the section NOTATION on page 7. Here we avoid introducing any more letters, unless we find later that we need to.

Now we can find the total of Sam's marks in all the tests by multiplying the average by the number of tests. From the information in the first of Sam's calculations, we see that the total of the marks is $80 \times n$, that is, $80n$. However, this total has been achieved by adding a final mark of 17. Hence the total of the marks before the final test is $80n - 17$.

By considering the second of Sam's calculations in a similar way, we see that the total of the marks before the final test is $85n - 92$.

We have now found two expressions for the total of the marks before the final test, so that
$$85n - 92 = 80n - 17.$$

> ◈ Remember the advice in the section DERIVING EQUATIONS on page 9. Here we have carefully explained where each of the terms comes from.

The above equation may be rearranged to give
$$5n = 75$$
and therefore
$$n = 15.$$

We conclude that there were 15 tests in the series.

> ◈ Remember the advice in the section CHECKING on page 11. Here we check that 15 actually does fit the facts given in the problem.

Exercise 2.2

C 1. The edge length, in centimetres, of a solid wooden cube is a whole number greater than two. The outside of the cube is painted blue and the cube is then cut into small cubes whose edge length is 1 cm. The number of small cubes with exactly one blue face is ten times the number of small cubes with exactly two blue faces.
Find the edge length of the original cube.

C 2. An aquarium contains 280 tropical fish of various kinds. If 60 more clownfish were added to the aquarium, the proportion of clownfish would be doubled.
How many clownfish are in the aquarium?

C 3. When two congruent isosceles triangles are joined to form a parallelogram, as shown in the first diagram, the perimeter of the parallelogram is 3 cm longer than the perimeter of one of the triangles.
When the same two triangles are joined to form a rhombus, as shown in the second diagram, the perimeter of the rhombus is 7 cm longer than the perimeter of one of the triangles.
What is the perimeter of one of the triangles?

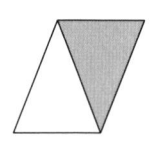

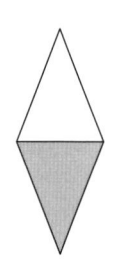

C 4. Two different rectangles are placed together, edge-to-edge, to form a large rectangle. The length of the perimeter of the large rectangle is $\frac{2}{3}$ of the total perimeter of the original two rectangles.
Prove that the final rectangle is in fact a square.

C 5. At dinner on a camping expedition, each tin of soup was shared between 2 campers, each tin of meatballs was shared between 3 campers and each tin of chocolate pudding was shared between 4 campers. Each camper had all three courses and all tins were emptied. The camp leader opened 156 tins in total.
How many campers were on the expedition?

M 6. Five numbers are arranged in increasing order. As they get larger the difference between adjacent numbers doubles.

The average of the five numbers is 11 more than the middle number. The sum of the second and fourth numbers is equal to the largest number.

What is the largest number?

C 7. Walking at constant speeds, Eoin and his sister Angharad take 40 minutes and 60 minutes respectively to walk to the nearest town.

Yesterday, Eoin left home 12 minutes after Angharad. How long was it before he caught up with her?

H 8. An $s \times s$ square, where s is an odd integer, is divided into 1×1 unit squares. All the unit squares along the edges and the two diagonals of the $s \times s$ square are discarded.

Find a fully simplified expression, in terms of s, for the number of unit squares remaining.

C 9. Mij the magician has a large bag of red balls and a large bag of green balls. Mij wanders round the audience selecting volunteers, asking each volunteer to remove two balls, one from each bag, until $\frac{2}{5}$ of the red balls and $\frac{3}{7}$ of the green balls have been removed. The balls remaining in the bags are then emptied into a bucket.

What fraction of all the balls does the bucket contain?

C 10. A mathematician has a full one-litre bottle of concentrated orange squash, a large container and a tap. He first pours half of the bottle of orange squash into the container. Then he fills the bottle from the tap, shakes well, and pours half of the resulting mixture into the container. He then repeats this step over and over again: filling the bottle from the tap each time, shaking the mixture well, and then pouring half of the contents into the container.

Suppose that on the final occasion he fills the bottle from the tap and empties it completely into the container. How many times has he filled the bottle from the tap if the final mixture consists of 10% orange squash concentrate?

H **11.** (a) What is the angle A between the hands of a clock at two o'clock?

(b) What is the next time after this that the angle between the hands is equal to A?

M **12.** At six o'clock, a spider starts to walk at a constant speed from the hour hand anticlockwise round the rim of the clock face. When it reaches the minute hand, the spider turns round and walks round the rim in the opposite direction at the same constant speed, reaching the minute hand again after a further 20 minutes

What time does the clock read when the spider reaches the minute hand for the second time?

2.3 Simultaneous equations

Cayley 2 3   Hamilton 1 3 4 6   Maclaurin 2 3 4 6

You should be familiar with standard methods of solving simultaneous equations, notably substitution and elimination. The second of these is usually the most promising approach when faced with harder equations—a method which enables one or more unknowns to be eliminated will often quickly lead to a solution.

The basic method of eliminating an unknown is to add or subtract multiples of equations; other methods involve factorising, for which some standard factorisation results can be helpful:

Fact 2.3.A

(i) $a^2 - b^2 \equiv (a-b)(a+b)$.

(ii) $a^2 + b^2$ *does not factorise*.

Chapter 2: Algebra

Fact 2.3.B
(i) $a^3 - b^3 \equiv (a-b)(a^2 + ab + b^2)$.
(ii) $a^3 + b^3 \equiv (a+b)(a^2 - ab + b^2)$.

Fact 2.3.C
(i) $a^4 - b^4 \equiv (a-b)(a+b)(a^2 + b^2)$.

Note that we have used the sign '$\equiv$' here, meaning *is identically equal to*, or *is equivalent to*, rather than the sign '=', meaning *is equal to*. This need not worry you unduly; we have simply used it to indicate that the results are true *in general*, that is, for all values of a and b, not just for some particular values.

Techniques

Some problems are clearly simultaneous equations in disguise—they have been "dressed up" in some context, but involve relationships between several quantities, such as ages, heights, or prices.

- ✦ Consider converting a word problem into an algebraic one by introducing letters to represent unknown quantities.

- ✧ Remember the advice in the section NOTATION on page 7.

You may find that the naive approach of substituting directly from one equation into another, where this is possible, leads to some ungainly expressions. Sometimes when this happens you just need to persevere.

- ✧ Remember the advice in the section SIMPLIFYING on page 10.

However, it is always worth checking to see whether there is a different approach which avoids the complicated algebra. You will also need to search for another approach when the basic methods of elimination or substitution fail.

- ✦ Look to see whether a different approach helps, such as finding the sum of three equations, or factorisation.

Example 2.3

Solve the simultaneous equations

$$p + pr + pr^2 = 28$$
$$p^2r + p^2r^2 + p^2r^3 = 224.$$

Discussion

We shall discuss two different approaches to solving these equations. Both approaches lead to the same intermediate result, after which the solutions are the same.

First approach—elimination We notice that multiplying every term of the first equation by pr makes the left-hand sides of the two equations the same:

$$p^2r + p^2r^2 + p^2r^3 = 28pr \qquad (2.1)$$
$$p^2r + p^2r^2 + p^2r^3 = 224. \qquad (2.2)$$

✧ Remember the advice in the section Labelling equations on page 10. Here we explain carefully what we have done, and label our equations so that we can refer to them easily.

We can then subtract equation (2.2) from equation (2.1) to eliminate all the terms on the left-hand side, giving

$$0 = 28pr - 224,$$

from which we deduce that $pr = 8$.

We may now continue as described later, but first we discuss another approach.

Second approach—factorisation and substitution We notice that on the left-hand side of each equation we can take out a common factor:

$$p(1 + r + r^2) = 28 \qquad (2.3)$$
$$p^2r(1 + r + r^2) = 224. \qquad (2.4)$$

Then we can rewrite equation (2.4) as

$$pr \times p(1 + r + r^2) = 224$$

and substitute from equation (2.3) to give

$$pr \times 28 = 224,$$

from which we deduce that $pr = 8$.

Continuation of both approaches With either approach we know that $pr = 8$, or equivalently that $p = \frac{8}{r}$. (We may divide by r because we know that $r \neq 0$. Can you see why?) We can substitute this into the first given equation in order to eliminate p and thereby obtain an equation for r:

$$\frac{8}{r} + 8 + 8r = 28.$$

Note that we could instead eliminate r and obtain an equation for p.

After a little simplification we obtain the quadratic equation

$$2r^2 - 5r + 2 = 0,$$

which can be solved to give two values for r:

$$r = 2 \text{ or } r = \tfrac{1}{2}.$$

All that remains is to find the corresponding values of p. The simplest equation to use for this purpose is $pr = 8$, which shows that each value of r corresponds to exactly one value of p:

$$\text{when } r = 2, \ p = 4;$$
$$\text{when } r = \tfrac{1}{2}, \ p = 16.$$

✧ When giving solutions to simultaneous equations, you should be careful to show clearly how the values of the variables correspond. Here it is *not* appropriate to give the answers in the form

$$r = 2 \text{ or } \tfrac{1}{2}, p = 4 \text{ or } 16$$

since this allows the possibility of four solution pairs.

Finally, we can check that both these answers work in the original equations given in the question.

✧ Remember the advice in the section CHECKING on page 11.

Exercise 2.3

C 1. Mars, his wife Venus and grandson Pluto have a combined age of 192. The ages of Mars and Pluto together total 30 years more than Venus's age. The ages of Venus and Pluto together total 4 years more then Mars's age.
Find their three ages.

H 2. If Julie gave £12 to her brother Garron then he would have half the amount that she would have. If instead Garron gave £12 to his sister Julie then she would have three times the amount that he would have.
How much money do they each have?

C 3. Three loaves of bread, five cartons of milk and four jars of jam cost £10.10.
Five loaves of bread, nine cartons of milk and seven jars of jam cost £18.20.
How much does it cost to buy one loaf of bread, one carton of milk and one jar of jam?

H 4. James, Alison and Vivek go into a shop to buy some sweets.
James spends £1 on four Fudge Bars, a Sparkle and a Chomper. Alison spends 70 p on three Chompers, two Fudge Bars and a Sparkle. Vivek spends 50 p on two Sparkles and a Fudge Bar.
What is the cost of a Sparkle?

H 5. On Monday, the cost of 3 bananas was the same as the total cost of a lemon and an orange.
On Tuesday, the cost of each fruit was reduced by the same amount, resulting in the cost of 2 oranges being the same as the total cost of 3 bananas and a lemon.
On Wednesday, the cost of a lemon halved to 5 p.
What was the cost of an orange on Monday?

Chapter 2: Algebra

M 6. Find all integer values of x and y that satisfy the following equations:
$$x^2 + y^2 = x - 2xy + y$$
$$x^2 - y^2 = x + 2xy - y.$$

H 7. Four positive integers a, b, c and d are such that:

the sum of a and b is half the sum of c and d;
the sum of a and c is twice the sum of b and d;
the sum of a and d is one and a half times the sum of b and c.

What is the smallest possible value of $a + b + c + d$?

M 8. Solve the simultaneous equations
$$\frac{5xy}{x+y} = 6$$
$$\frac{4xz}{x+z} = 3$$
$$\frac{3yz}{y+z} = 2.$$

M 9. Solve the equations
$$x + xy + x^2 = 9$$
$$y + xy + y^2 = -3.$$

H 10. Find all solutions to the simultaneous equations
$$x^2 - y^2 = -5$$
$$2x^2 + xy - y^2 = 5.$$

M 11. Solve the simultaneous equations
$$x + y = 3$$
$$x^3 + y^3 = 9.$$

H 12. The heights of four friends, Anna, Bob, Claire and Duncan, are all different and the sum of their heights is 6 m 72 cm. Anna is 8 cm taller than Claire, and Bob is 4 cm shorter than Duncan. The sum of the heights of the tallest and shortest of the friends is 2 cm more than the sum of the heights of the other two.

Find the height of each person.

M 13. Find all real values of x and y that satisfy the equations
$$x^4 - y^4 = 5$$
$$x + y = 1.$$

2.4 Sequences

Cayley 4   Hamilton 3 4   Maclaurin 1

You should be familiar with the basic idea of a sequence as an ordered list of terms. Each term in a sequence may be defined by a formula, or a rule connecting it to other terms.

Questions at Intermediate Olympiad level usually do not require any knowledge of special sequences, though you should be aware of simple examples such as:

Fact 2.4.A
(i) *The sequence of* triangle numbers *is* $1, 3, 6, 10, \ldots, \frac{1}{2}n(n+1), \ldots$.
(ii) *The* Fibonacci sequence *is* $1, 1, 2, 3, 5, 8, \ldots$, *where each term after the second is the sum of the previous two.*

You should also be aware that:

Fact 2.4.B *The sum of the first n natural numbers is* $\frac{1}{2}n(n+1)$, *that is,*
$$1 + 2 + 3 + \cdots + n = \frac{n(n+1)}{2}.$$

Note that fact 2.4.B may also be seen as a result about the triangle numbers.

Chapter 2: Algebra

Techniques

- Looking at a few specific examples may help you to understand a problem, but general results cannot be proved from examples, so make sure that you give a proof that applies generally.
- Introduce some algebraic notation to help prove general results. Useful quantities to consider include:
  - (a) two terms, such as the first two, or the last two, or the first and last;
  - (b) the first term and the difference between the second and first terms.

Example 2.4

The first two terms of a sequence are the numbers 1, 2. From then on, each term is obtained by adding 1 to the previous term and then dividing by the term before that. Thus the third term is obtained by adding 1 to the second term and then dividing by the first term.

(a) Write down the first five terms.
(b) Calculate the sixtieth term.
(c) What happens if other non-zero numbers are chosen for the first two terms, but the rule for calculating the next term remains the same?

Discussion

(a) Using the rule for calculating the next term we find

$$\text{the third term} = \frac{2+1}{1} = 3,$$

$$\text{the fourth term} = \frac{3+1}{2} = 2$$

$$\text{and the fifth term} = \frac{2+1}{3} = 1.$$

Therefore the first five terms are 1, 2, 3, 2, 1.

(b) We may have suspicions about what is happening, but we cannot *deduce* anything from these first five terms, so we need to investigate further.

✧ Remember the advice in the section PATTERNS AND PROOF on page 11.

Continuing to calculate terms, we obtain
$$\text{the sixth term} = \frac{1+1}{2} = 1$$
$$\text{and the seventh term} = \frac{1+1}{1} = 2.$$

We have found two consecutive terms which are the same as two earlier consecutive terms, in this case the first and second. But the rule for calculating the next term depends only on the previous two, so that the eighth term will be the same as the third, the ninth will be the same as the fourth, and so on; whichever term we consider (after the seventh) will repeat an earlier term. We deduce that the sequence will repeat in blocks of five—every fifth term is the same:

$$\underline{1,\ 2,\ 3,\ 2,\ 1,}\ \underline{1,\ 2,\ 3,\ 2,\ 1,}\ \underline{1,\ 2,\ 3,\ 2,\ 1,}\ \ldots.$$

Hence the sixtieth term is equal to the fifth term, namely 1.

Note that we have *not* calculated any later terms after the seventh; we have deduced what later terms are by showing in a general way that the sequence repeats.

(c) There is little point in looking at further numerical examples; what we need is a general result, so let the sequence start $a, b, \ldots$.

✧ Remember the advice in the section NOTATION on page 7.

Using the rule for calculating the next term of the sequence, we find that the third term is $\frac{b+1}{a}$, so the first three terms are

$$a,\ b,\ \frac{b+1}{a}.$$

Adding 1 to the third term we obtain
$$\frac{b+1}{a} + 1 = \frac{b+1+a}{a},$$
so that the fourth term is
$$\frac{b+1+a}{a} \div b = \frac{a+b+1}{ab}$$

and hence the first four terms are

$$a,\ b,\ \frac{b+1}{a},\ \frac{a+b+1}{ab}.$$

Adding 1 to the fourth term we obtain

$$\frac{a+b+1}{ab} + 1 = \frac{a+b+1+ab}{ab}.$$

Notice that the numerator of this expression factorises

$$a+b+1+ab = (a+1)(b+1),$$

so the fifth term is

$$\frac{(a+1)(b+1)}{ab} \div \frac{b+1}{a} = \frac{(a+1)(b+1)}{ab} \times \frac{a}{b+1}$$

$$= \frac{a+1}{b}.$$

✧ Remember the advice in the section SIMPLIFYING on page 10. Here we simplify each of the terms as we go along, writing it as a single algebraic fraction, then factorising and cancelling if possible.

Continuing in the same way, the sixth term is

$$\frac{a+b+1}{b} \div \frac{a+b+1}{ab} = \frac{a+b+1}{b} \times \frac{ab}{a+b+1}$$

$$= a$$

and the seventh term is

$$(a+1) \div \frac{a+1}{b} = (a+1) \times \frac{b}{a+1}$$

$$= b.$$

The sixth and seventh terms are the same as the first and second, so we are now in the same position as in part (b): we have found two consecutive terms which are equal to two earlier consecutive terms. Because the rule for calculating each term depends only on the previous two, whichever term we consider (after the seventh) will repeat an earlier term. We deduce that the sequence always repeats a block of five terms irrespective of the starting two numbers:

$$a,\ b,\ \frac{b+1}{a},\ \frac{a+b+1}{ab},\ \frac{a+1}{b},\ a,\ b,\ \frac{b+1}{a},\ \frac{a+b+1}{ab},\ \frac{a+1}{b},\ \ldots\ .$$

However, we do need to be a little more careful since not all values of a and b are allowed. The rule for calculating the next term involves dividing by an earlier term, hence no term of the sequence can be zero, which means that there are some restrictions on the values of a and b. Can you determine what those restrictions are?

✧ Remember the advice in the section SPECIAL CASES on page 11.

Note that the sequence may also exhibit other patterns for particular values of a and b, though it will always still be the case that every fifth term is the same. For example, it is possible to choose a and b so that the sequence is constant, with *all* the terms the same.

Exercise 2.4

C 1. The first two terms of a sequence are the numbers 1, 2. From then on, each term is obtained by dividing the previous term by the term before that. Thus the third term is obtained by dividing the second term, 2, by the first term, 1.

   (a) Write down the first five terms.

   (b) Calculate the fiftieth term.

   (c) What happens if other non-zero numbers are chosen for the first two terms, but the rule for calculating the next term remains the same?

H 2. The first and second terms of a sequence are added to make the third term. Adjacent odd-numbered terms are added to make the next even-numbered term, for example,

$$\text{first term} + \text{third term} = \text{fourth term}$$
$$\text{and} \quad \text{third term} + \text{fifth term} = \text{sixth term}.$$

Likewise, adjacent even-numbered terms are added to make the next odd-numbered term, for example,

$$\text{second term} + \text{fourth term} = \text{fifth term}.$$

Given that the seventh term equals the eighth term, what is the value of the sixth term?

H 3. This question concerns sequences which are formed in the following way: each term after the first term is equal to

$$1 - (1 \div \text{the previous term}).$$

For example, if the first term is 5 then

$$\text{the second term is } 1 - (1 \div 5) = \tfrac{4}{5},$$
$$\text{the third term is } 1 - \left(1 \div \tfrac{4}{5}\right) = -\tfrac{1}{4},$$

and so on.
   (a) Find the first six terms of the sequence whose first term is 3.
   (b) What are the first six terms of the sequence whose first term is x? (You should try to simplify expressions as much as possible.)
   (c) What is the product of the first 100 terms of the sequence with first term x?

M 4. The first term of a sequence is not equal to 1. Each term after the first is equal to "(3 more than the previous term) divided by (1 less than the previous term)".
   (a) What values of c make the sequence recur forever, in the form $c, c, c, c, \ldots$?
   (b) Is it possible for any term of the sequence to be equal to 1?

2.5 Miscellaneous problems

Cayley 5   Hamilton 3 4 5   Maclaurin 2 3 4

We gather here some questions that do not fit naturally into the earlier sections of this chapter.

Many of these problems lead to harder algebra. Indeed, for some of them you will need to be familiar with methods of simplifying and combining algebraic fractions. You may also need to be familiar with methods of solving quadratic equations, in particular, solution by factorisation.

Checking solutions to equations

Beyond the standard good practice given in the section CHECKING on page 11, there are sound mathematical reasons why solutions of equations should be checked.

The reason this is necessary is as follows. In most cases your argument will show that, if certain equations are true, then the solution can only be a member of a particular set. This is fine as far as it goes, but what it does not do is show that every member of that set is actually a solution to the equations—some may not be. So it is necessary to check each one, in order to show that your list does not contain any extra, spurious, answers.

Note that in elementary school algebra such checking is usually not expected, because it is *assumed* that all the solutions found are actually solutions of the given equation(s). In many cases this assumption is valid, but it is easy to invent more complicated equations where it fails, such as equations involving square roots.

It is good practice in Olympiad papers not to make assumptions, especially since checking is often very easy. In any case, a check may also reveal that you have made a mistake.

For all these reasons you are advised to get into the habit of checking your answers.

> ✧ When solving equations, you should always verify that your list of answers is correct by checking that each of them satisfies the original equation(s).

Note that there is an alternative method of writing out a solution: it is actually sufficient to check that the argument used in producing the

Chapter 2: Algebra

answers is reversible. Of course, this may not be possible. Even if it is possible, however, it is a good habit to carry out a check as a matter of course.

Example 2.5

The Principal of Abertawe Academy plans to employ more teachers. If she employs 10 new teachers, then the number of pupils per teacher will be reduced by 5. However, if she employs 20 new teachers, then the number of pupils per teacher will be reduced by 8.

How many pupils are there at Abertawe Academy?

Discussion

We are asked to find the number of pupils, but if we let this number be p, it is difficult to see how to relate the information given in the question to p.

The question refers to two other quantities: the number of teachers and the number of pupils per teacher. If we also let the number of teachers be t, then we should be able to relate the number of pupils per teacher to p, t and the information given.

> ✧ Remember the advice in the section NOTATION on page 7. Here we felt it necessary to introduce a second letter, but we should try to avoid using any more.

The number of pupils per teacher is currently $p \div t$.

If the Principal employs 10 new teachers, there will be $t + 10$ teachers altogether, so that the number of pupils per teacher will be $p \div (t + 10)$. Since the number of pupils per teacher would then go down by 5 we deduce that

$$\frac{p}{t+10} = \frac{p}{t} - 5. \tag{2.5}$$

Similarly, if the Principal employs 20 new teachers, then the number of pupils per teacher will be $p \div (t + 20)$ and we deduce that

$$\frac{p}{t+20} = \frac{p}{t} - 8. \tag{2.6}$$

We now have two equations in the two unknowns p and t, so we should have enough material to solve the problem. Because the equations involve algebraic fractions, we simplify by 'clearing the denominators'. We do this for each equation by multiplying every term by an appropriate expression.

Multiplying equation (2.5) by $t(t+10)$, we obtain

$$pt = p(t+10) - 5t(t+10) \tag{2.7}$$

and multiplying equation (2.6) by $t(t+20)$, we obtain

$$pt = p(t+20) - 8t(t+20). \tag{2.8}$$

Equations (2.7) and (2.8) may be rearranged to give

$$5t(t+10) = 10p \tag{2.9}$$

and

$$8t(t+20) = 20p. \tag{2.10}$$

We wish to find p, but it is easier to find t first: we may eliminate p using the fact that $20p = 2 \times 10p$, which means that equation (2.9) is half equation (2.10). As a result we deduce that

$$5t(t+10) = 4t(t+20)$$

and we may now divide both sides by t (which is not zero) to give

$$5(t+10) = 4(t+20).$$

◆ Remember the advice in the section DIVISION BY ZERO on page 10. Here we check that t is not zero.

Finally, expanding the brackets and collecting terms we obtain $t = 30$. We may use any appropriate equation to find p, for example, equation (2.9), from which we obtain $p = 600$.

We may now easily confirm that our results—600 pupils and 30 teachers—fit the conditions given in the question.

Hence there are 600 pupils at Abertawe Academy.

◆ Remember the advice in the sections CHECKING on page 11 and CHECKING SOLUTIONS TO EQUATIONS on page 28.

Chapter 2: Algebra

Exercise 2.5

H **1.** The shape shown in the diagram (not to scale) has a perimeter of length 72 cm and an area equal to 147 cm².

Calculate the value of a.

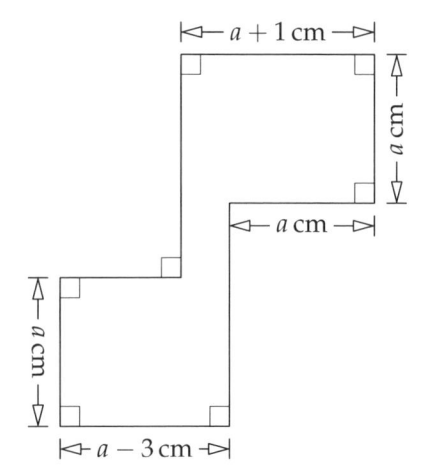

H **2.** Kelly cycles to a friend's house at an average speed of 12 km/h. Her friend is out, so Kelly immediately returns home by the same route.

At what average speed does she need to cycle home if her average speed over the whole journey is to be 15 km/h?

M **3.** An *arithmetic* sequence is one in which the difference between successive terms remains constant (for example, 4, 7, 10, 13, ...).

Suppose that a triangle is right-angled and has the property that the lengths of its sides form an arithmetic sequence. Prove that the sides of the triangle are in the ratio 3 : 4 : 5.

M **4.** I have 44 socks in my drawer, each either red or black. In the dark I randomly pick two socks, and the probability that they do not match is $\frac{192}{473}$.

How many of the 44 socks are red?

C **5.** Two candles are the same height. The first takes 10 hours to burn completely whilst the second takes 8 hours to burn completely.

Both candles are lit at midday. At what time is the height of the first candle twice the height of the second candle?

H **6.** In my town, 10% of the dogs think they are cats and 10% of the cats think they are dogs. All the other cats and dogs are perfectly normal.

    When all the cats and dogs in my town were rounded up and subjected to a rigorous test, 20% of the animals thought they were cats. What percentage of them really were cats?

H **7.** Inzamam runs twice as fast as he walks. On Monday, when going to school, he walked for twice the time for which he ran. On Tuesday, doing the same journey, he ran for twice the time that he walked and was six minutes quicker than on Monday.

    On Wednesday, he walked all the way to school. How long did it take him?

M **8.** On Utopia Farm, Farmer Giles has a field in which the amount of grass always increases by the same amount each day. Six cows would take three whole days to eat all the grass in the field; three cows would take seven whole days to eat all the grass in the field.

    Assuming that each of Farmer Giles' cows eats the same amount of grass per day, how long would one cow take to eat all the grass in the field?

M **9.** Find all real values of x that satisfy the equation

$$(1+x)^4 - 2(1-x)^4 = (1-x^2)^2.$$

Chapter 3

Geometry

There are more questions in this chapter than in any other chapter in the book. This is not a surprise since the geometrical context lends itself very well to problems of Olympiad style. However, there is some overlap with chapter 2, Algebra, because there are geometry problems which require the solver to use an algebraic method such as 'let angle ... be $x°$', or 'let side ... have length a cm'.

3.1 General guidance

Diagrams

Whereas geometry problems at Senior Olympiad level usually do *not* include a diagram, the tradition at Intermediate level is mixed: a diagram may or may not be provided.

Your solution should always include a diagram for reference, whether or not one is given in the question; apart from any other reason, you may wish to add additional labels. It is rare for anyone to criticise a solution for having too many diagrams!

- ✧ The purpose of your diagrams is to convey information, so be sure to draw diagrams clearly and label them carefully. A pencil, a ruler and a pair of compasses will help you to produce clear diagrams.

- Be prepared to draw more diagrams as your understanding of the problem develops.

- The convention for labelling polygons is that vertices are referred to in consecutive order as you proceed around the perimeter, along the edges.

For example, 'quadrilateral $ABCD$' means that A, B, C and D occur in order around the quadrilateral, so that the sides are AB, BC, CD and DA.

Notation

Some geometrical problems are perhaps best approached by introducing algebraic notation. There is more guidance about using algebraic notation in chapter 2.

- When introducing letters as algebraic symbols, you should always specify what each letter stands for.

- When trying an algebraic approach, you should aim not to use more letters than is really necessary.

- In mathematics, algebraic letters usually stand for numbers rather than physical quantities, so that equations connect numbers. If you adopt an algebraic approach you should take account of the units whenever you introduce a letter.

For example, you might say "let the angle be $x°$" so that x is just a number.

Naming triangles

When dealing with related triangles, such as those which are congruent or similar, it is a good idea to name the triangles with the correct order of vertices, so that the corresponding sides and angles can be read off conveniently.

- Name related triangles using the correct order of vertices.

Using standard facts

When solving a geometric problem you will need to make use of standard facts. In a full written solution, you should indicate to the reader the most important facts that you have used.

 ⟡ Mention the key geometrical facts you use at each stage.

Working towards a given result

In some problems the required result is given in the question. In such cases, when giving a full written solution, it is more important than ever to ensure that your solution is complete.

 ⟡ When you are working towards an answer which is given in the question, ensure that you show all the steps in your working and explain your reasoning carefully.

3.2 Angles

CAYLEY 1 2 3 5   HAMILTON 2   MACLAURIN 2

You should be familiar with basic facts about angles: angles on a straight line, the angles connected with parallel lines, and angles in a triangle.

A result which is often more useful than 'the angle sum of a triangle' concerns the exterior angle of a triangle:

Fact 3.2.A *The exterior angle of a triangle is equal to the sum of the opposite interior angles.*

So in figure 3.1 we have $x = p + q$.

You should also be familiar with the result that the base angles of an isosceles triangle are equal. The converse result may be helpful if you are trying to prove that two lengths are equal:

Fact 3.2.B *If two angles of a triangle are equal, then the sides opposite those angles are equal.*

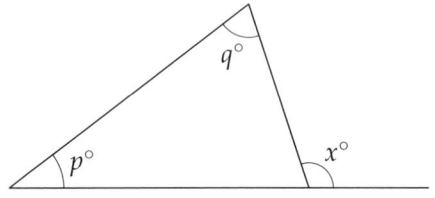

Figure 3.1: Exterior angle of a triangle

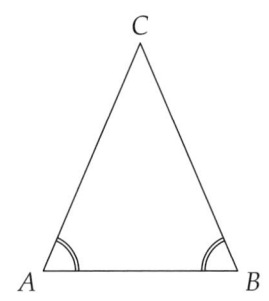

Figure 3.2: Sides opposite equal angles

So if $\angle A = \angle B$ in figure 3.2, then we conclude that $CA = CB$.

Note that we should not refer to triangle ABC as isosceles until *after* we have used the result—only then do we know that the sides are equal.

You will, of course, know the sizes of the angles of an equilateral triangle and of a rectangle. The simplest result to use when dealing with the angles of a general polygon concerns the exterior angles:

Fact 3.2.C *The sum of the exterior angles of a polygon is 360° (figure 3.3).*

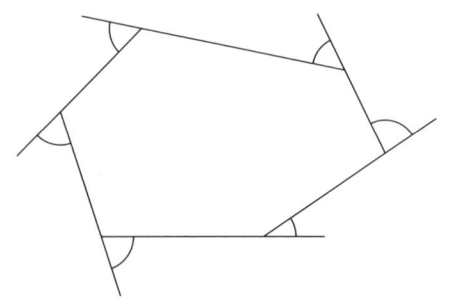

Figure 3.3: The exterior angles of a polygon

Since the exterior angles of a *regular* polygon are equal, we may deduce the following fact straight away:

Fact 3.2.D *Each exterior angle of a regular polygon with n sides is equal to* $360° \div n$.

Techniques

You may be tempted to work your way around the diagram, finding the value of every possible angle. The temptation should be resisted! Such an unstructured approach is not only inefficient, there is also a risk that it leads to a poorly presented solution—many of the steps may be left unexplained, or, worse, hidden somewhere on a diagram.

✧ Remember the advice in the section DIAGRAMS on page 33.

A far better approach is to try to find a chain of reasoning which will lead from the facts given in the problem to the required result, and only to evaluate the angles essential to that argument. The first of the following techniques may help you to find such a chain of reasoning.

✦ Ask yourself the questions:

"What am I given?"

"What am I asked to prove?"

✦ When asked to prove that two lengths are equal, see whether you can use 'sides opposite equal angles' (fact 3.2.B).

✦ Consider using algebra, especially if no specific angles are given in the question.

Example 3.2

In the diagram (which is not to scale), AQ bisects $\angle RQP$, AR bisects $\angle KRP$ and $\angle QPR = 80°$.
What is the size of $\angle QAR$?

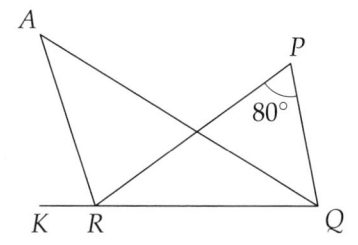

Discussion

For convenience, let us draw a new diagram including all the information given in the question (figure 3.4).

✧ Remember the advice in the section DIAGRAMS on page 33.

We see that it is not possible to find any other angles straight away—we are only told the actual value of one angle.

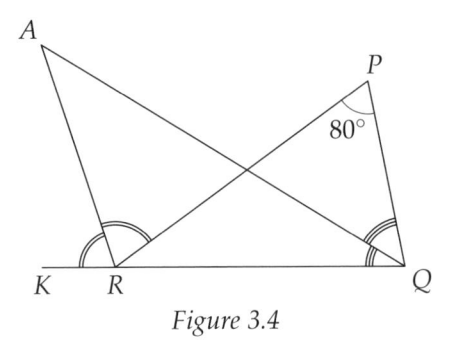

Figure 3.4

Taking the advice given above, let us try using some algebra. The usual approach would be to let the value of the angle we are asked to find be $x°$, say, as shown in figure 3.5.

✧ Remember the advice in the section NOTATION on page 34. Here we use $x°$ (rather than just x) so that x is a number, without units.

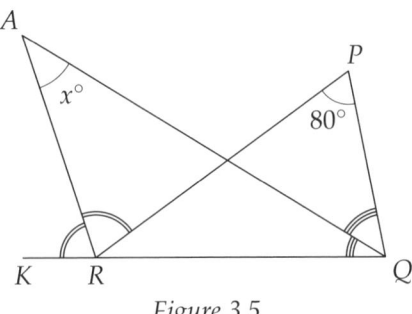

Figure 3.5

However, this still does not allow us to find any other angles, even in terms of x, so we need to try something else. We shall use the label $r°$

for each of the two equal angles at R, and $q°$ for those at Q, as shown in figure 3.6.

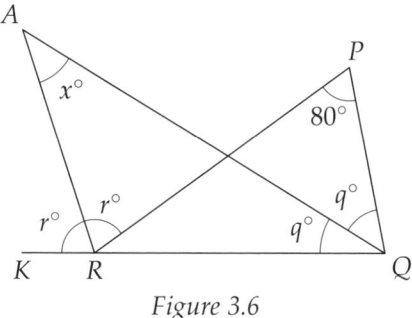

Figure 3.6

✧ Remember the advice in the section NOTATION on page 34. Normally it is not a good idea to introduce a lot of different letters, but in this case it is actually helpful, provided we are careful.

Now we should be able to connect all these angles. Indeed there are a lot of equations we could write down, but how can we be systematic? Well, it would be a good idea to try and connect them without involving *any* other angles. For example, using 'the exterior angle of a triangle' for triangle ARQ, we obtain the equation

$$r = x + q. \tag{3.1}$$

✧ Remember the advice in the section USING STANDARD FACTS on page 35. In this case we explicitly refer to *the exterior angle of a triangle*—and ideally state which triangle we are considering.

Similarly, using 'the exterior angle of a triangle' for triangle PRQ, we obtain the equation

$$2r = 80 + 2q. \tag{3.2}$$

We notice that to obtain these two equations we have made use of all the marked angles in figure 3.6. As you should be able to see, we do not need any more equations; these two are enough.

Can you see how to eliminate both r and q from equations (3.1) and (3.2) and so find the value of x, thus completing the solution to the problem?

Exercise 3.2

C **1.** The "star" octagon shown in the diagram is beautifully symmetrical and the centre of the star is at the centre of the circle.

If angle $NAE = 110°$, how big is angle ANB?

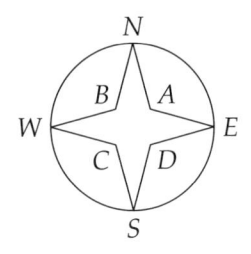

C **2.** The diagram shows a square $ABCD$ and an equilateral triangle ABE. The point F lies on BC so that $EC = EF$.

Calculate the angle FEB.

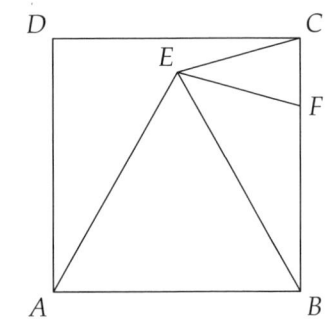

C **3.** The diagram shows a regular pentagon $CDEFG$ inside a trapezium $ABCD$.

Prove that $AB = 2 \times CD$.

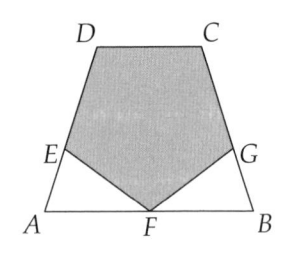

C **4.** In the diagram, PQ and TS are parallel.

Prove that $a + b + c = 360$.

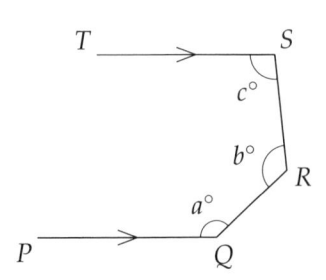

Chapter 3: Geometry

C 5. In the diagram, rectangles $ABCD$ and $AZYX$ are congruent, and angle $ADB = 70°$.

Find angle XMB.

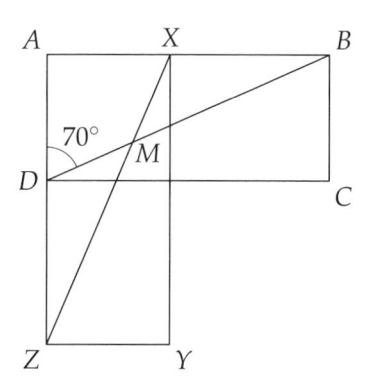

C 6. In the rectangle $ABCD$ the midpoint of AB is M and $AB : AD = 2 : 1$. The point X is such that triangle MDX is equilateral, with X and A on opposite sides of the line MD.

Find the value of $\angle XCD$.

H 7. Triangle ABG has a right angle at B.

Points C and E lie on side AG and points D and F lie on side BG so that the six line segments AB, BC, CD, DE, EF, FG are equal in length.

Calculate the angle AGB.

H 8. In triangle ABC, $\angle ABC$ is a right angle. Points P and Q lie on AC; BP is perpendicular to AC; BQ bisects $\angle ABP$.

Prove that $CB = CQ$.

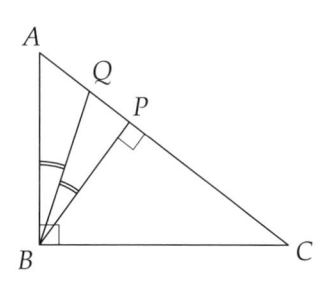

H 9. The diagram shows a triangle and two of its angle bisectors.

What is the value of x?

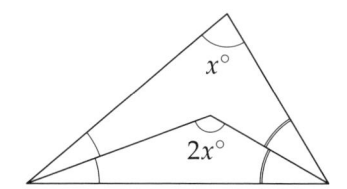

H **10.** The diagram shows two equilateral triangles. The angles marked $x°$ are equal.

Prove that $x > 30$.

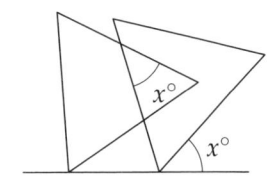

H **11.** The diagram shows an arc PQR of a circle, centre O. The lines PQ and OR meet at X, with $QR = RX$, and the lines OP and RQ meet at Y.

Prove that $OY = RY$.

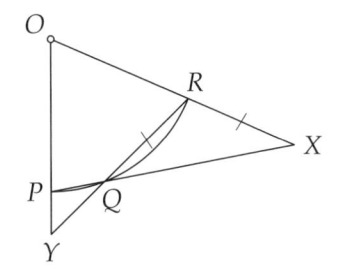

M **12.** The diagram shows a regular pentagon $ABCDE$. A circle is drawn such that AB is a tangent to the circle at A and CD is a tangent to the circle at D. The side DE of the pentagon is extended to meet the circumference of the circle at F.

Prove that $AE = AF$.

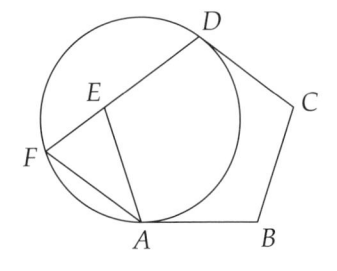

M **13.** The diagram shows a regular heptagon, a regular decagon and a regular 15-gon with an edge in common.

Find the size of angle XYZ.

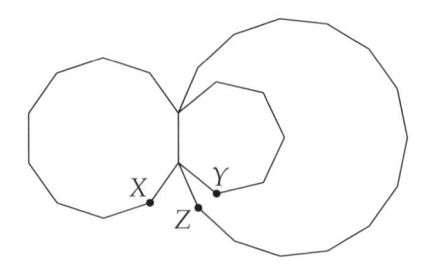

M **14.** Points T and U lie outside parallelogram $PQRS$, and are such that triangles RQT and SRU are equilateral and lie wholly outside the parallelogram.

Prove that triangle PTU is equilateral.

C 15. In the diagram, O is the centre of the circle and the straight lines $AOBP$ and RQP meet at P. The length of PQ is equal to the radius of the circle.

Prove that

$$\angle AOR = 3 \times \angle BOQ.$$

C 16. In a quadrilateral $ABCD$, $AB = BC$, $\angle BAC = 60°$, $\angle CAD = 40°$, AC and BD cross at X and $\angle BXC = 100°$.

Calculate $\angle BDC$.

3.3 Pythagoras

CAYLEY 345   HAMILTON 235   MACLAURIN –

Right-angled triangles occur in many geometric problems at this level, so that Pythagoras' theorem can often be applied.

Fact 3.3.A *In a right-angled triangle with hypotenuse h and 'legs' a and b (see figure 3.7)*
$$h^2 = a^2 + b^2.$$

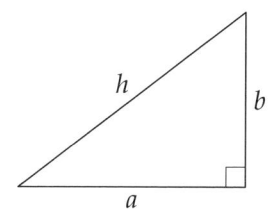

Figure 3.7: Pythagoras' theorem

There are several well-known right-angled triangles with integer side lengths—these correspond to so-called *Pythagorean triples*. There are infinitely many such triples, and the next fact only lists the simplest of them.

Fact 3.3.B *A triangle with sides in one of the following ratios is right-angled.*

(i) $3:4:5$
(ii) $5:12:13$
(iii) $7:24:25$
(iv) $8:15:17$

Dividing an isosceles triangle into two by drawing the median creates two right-angled triangles:

Fact 3.3.C *The line joining the apex to the midpoint of the base of an isosceles triangle is perpendicular to the base. So in figure 3.8, it follows that* $\angle XMZ = 90°$.

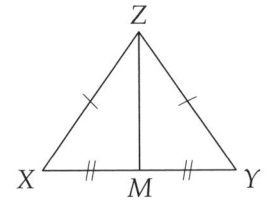

Figure 3.8: Median of an isosceles triangle

Techniques

Some problems clearly contain a right-angled triangle; in others, such a triangle has to be created.

- Identify any right angles in the figure.
- Consider creating a right-angled triangle, by using fact 3.3.C, or by constructing one or more perpendicular lines.

The latter method can be used, for example, with certain types of trapezium: drawing a perpendicular (shown dashed in figure 3.9) divides the trapezium into a rectangle and a right-angled triangle.

Chapter 3: Geometry   45

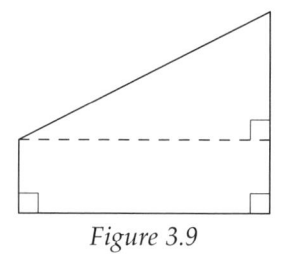

Figure 3.9

Example 3.3

A rectangular piece of paper $ABCD$, in which $AB = 6$ cm and $BC = 8$ cm, is folded once so that B folds exactly onto D and the folded paper is then laid flat on a table.

What area of the table is then covered by the paper?

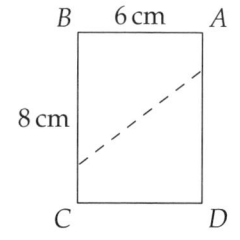

Discussion

Figure 3.10 shows the paper after it has been folded so that the new position of B is the point D. We have labelled the fold PQ, and the new position of A is labelled R.

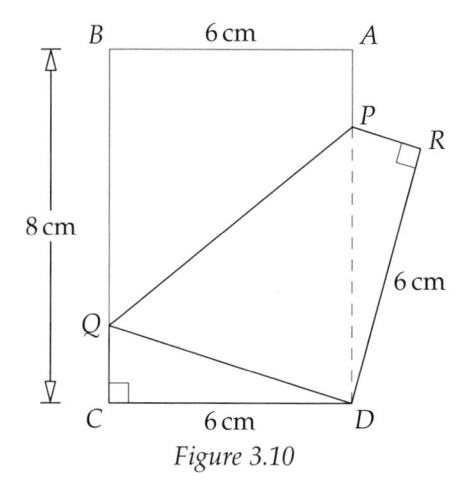

Figure 3.10

✧ Remember the advice in the section DIAGRAMS on page 33.

We know that $ABCD$ is a rectangle, so that $CD = 6$ cm, $BC = 8$ cm and the angles at A and C are right angles. Since AB is folded to RD we also know that the angle at R is a right angle and $RD = 6$ cm.

So the area we are asked to find—the area of the table covered by the folded paper—is the area of the pentagon $CDRPQ$. We clearly do not yet have enough information about this pentagon to find its area, so we need to find some other lengths.

There is one fact about the folding which we have not yet used: BQ folds to DQ. Since $BC = 8$ cm it follows that $DQ + QC = 8$ cm, so that if we let DQ be q cm then $QC = (8 - q)$ cm.

✧ Remember the advice in the section NOTATION on page 34. Here we let the length be q cm so that q is just a number.

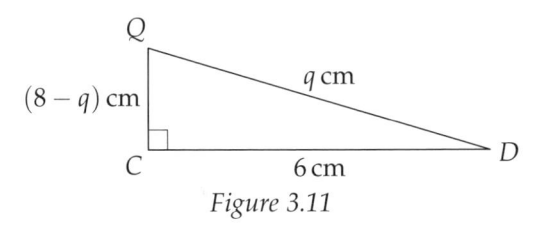

Figure 3.11

Figure 3.11 shows what we know about the right-angled triangle QDC. We can use Pythagoras' theorem in this triangle to obtain the equation

$$q^2 = (8 - q)^2 + 6^2. \tag{3.3}$$

✧ Remember the advice in the section USING STANDARD FACTS on page 35. In this case we explicitly refer to *Pythagoras' theorem*.

You should be able to solve equation (3.3) to find q. Of course, once we know q then we know $8 - q$ and hence we know the lengths of all the sides of triangle QDC. Since the triangle is right-angled it is then straightforward to find its area.

We now know more about the pentagon $CDRPQ$ but we still do not know enough to find its area. At this stage you may be tempted to state that the diagram is symmetrical, so that triangle PDR has the same dimensions as triangle QDC. However, unless you can *prove* that the figure is symmetrical then you should not make use of any apparent symmetry.

Chapter 3: Geometry

- ✧ You should not make use of the symmetry of a figure unless you can provide a convincing reason why the figure is symmetrical.

Though there are various ways to show that pentagon $CDRPQ$ has a line of symmetry, in this case it is not necessary to do so. Instead, we can just use the properties of folding and argue as follows, using an argument similar to the one above.

Because AP is folded to RP, triangle PDR has a base of length 6 cm and two other sides whose lengths add up to 8 cm. But that is exactly what we knew about triangle CDQ above, where we found there was only one possibility for the unknown lengths. Hence the sides of triangles PDR and QDC have the same lengths, and therefore the triangles have the same area.

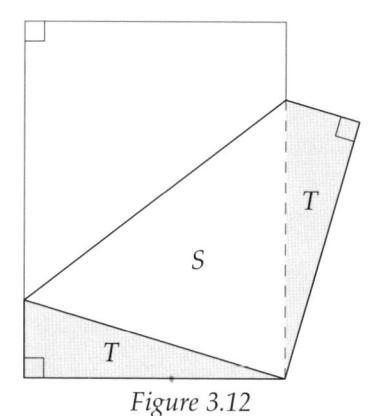

Figure 3.12

Suppose triangles PDR and QDC each have area T cm^2 and let the area of triangle PQD be S cm^2, as shown in figure 3.12, so that the area of the pentagon we require is $2T + S$ cm^2. Then, considering the area of the original rectangle, we obtain

$$2T + 2S = 6 \times 8.$$

In summary, since we know q we can find T. Once we know T, from the last equation we can find S and hence we can find the required area. Armed with this strategy, you should now be able to complete the question.

Exercise 3.3

C 1. A quadrilateral $ABCD$ has sides AB, BC, CD, DA of length x, y, z and t, respectively. The diagonals AC and BD cross at right angles.
Prove that
$$x^2 + z^2 = y^2 + t^2.$$

H 2. In quadrilateral $ABCD$, $AB = 1\,\text{cm}$, $CD = 2\,\text{cm}$, $AD = 3\,\text{cm}$ and $\angle BAD = \angle CDA = 60°$.
Calculate the length of side BC.

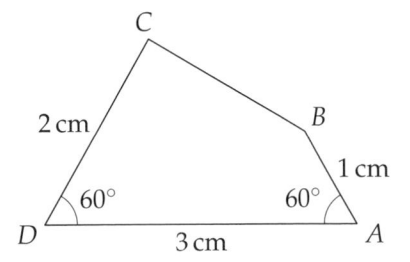

C 3. In the rectangle $ABCD$, the side AB has length $\sqrt{2}$ and the side AD has length 1. Let the circle with centre B and passing through C meet AB at X.
Find $\angle ADX$ (in degrees).

H 4. In the diagram, $ABCD$ is a rectangle with $AB = 16\,\text{cm}$ and $BC = 12\,\text{cm}$. Points E and F lie on sides AB and CD so that $AECF$ is a rhombus.
What is the length of EF?

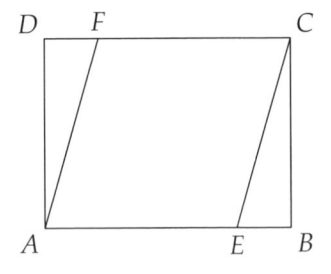

C 5. A square sheet of paper $ABCD$ is folded along FG, as shown, so that the corner B is folded onto the midpoint M of CD.
Prove that the sides of triangle GCM have lengths in the ratio $3:4:5$.

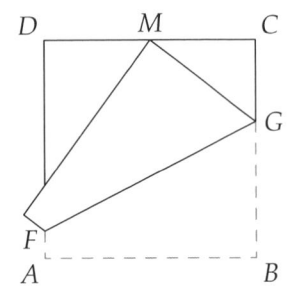

Chapter 3: Geometry

C **6.** A kite has sides AB and AD of length 25 cm and sides CB and CD of length 39 cm. The perpendicular distance from B to AD is 24 cm.

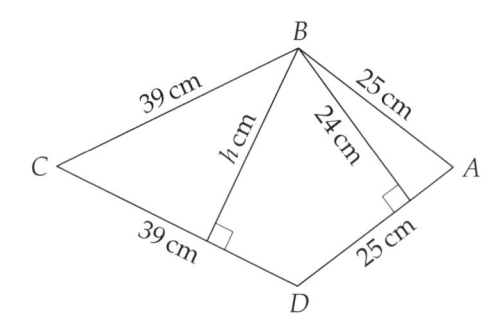

The perpendicular distance from B to CD is h cm. Find the value of h.

H **7.** The rectangle $PQRS$ represents a sheet of A4 paper, which means that $PQ : PS = \sqrt{2} : 1$.

The rectangle is folded, as shown, so that Q comes to a point X on SR and the fold line PY passes through the corner P.

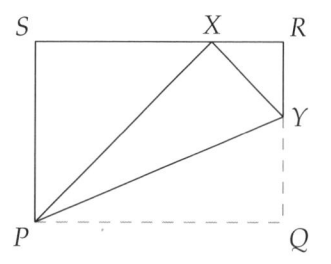

Taking the length of PS to be 1 unit, find the lengths of the three sides of the triangle RXY.

H **8.** Two congruent rectangles have a common vertex and overlap as shown in the diagram.

What is the total shaded area?

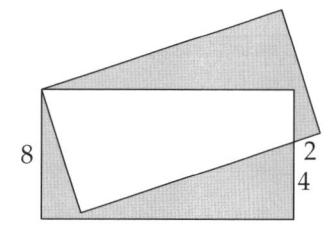

3.4 Area and perimeter

CAYLEY 1 2 3 4 6   HAMILTON 2 4 5   MACLAURIN 3 4 5

You should be familiar with the standard methods of finding the areas of simple shapes, such as a triangle, rectangle, parallelogram, or trapezium. You should also know the formulae for the area and circumference of a circle.

One other useful fact concerns the areas of similar triangles:

Fact 3.4.A *Two similar triangles with corresponding lengths in the ratio $k : l$ have areas in the ratio $k^2 : l^2$.*

Here we use the term 'corresponding lengths', rather than just sides, so that bases, heights and perimeters are included. For example, the ratio of the areas of the similar triangles in figure 3.13 is $h^2 : H^2$.

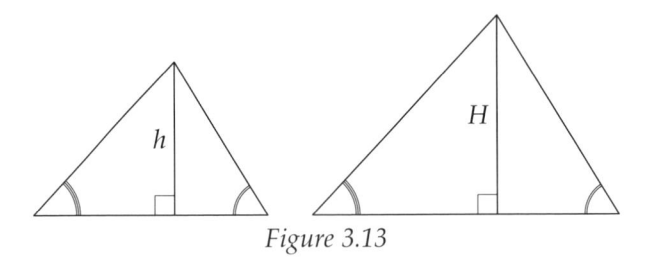

Figure 3.13

Techniques

In many cases it will be helpful to add something to the diagram:

- ✦ divide the diagram into convenient lengths or regions;
- ✦ draw a line to create a right-angled triangle or rectangle;
- ✦ consider a 'dissection' approach.

What we mean by a 'dissection' approach should be clear after reading our discussion of the following example.

◇ Remember the advice in the section DIAGRAMS on page 33.

Example 3.4

The diagram shows a rectangle $ABCD$ inscribed inside a triangle PQR.

The side, AB, of the rectangle is one third of the perpendicular height of the triangle from P to QR.

What is the ratio of the area of the rectangle to the area of the triangle?

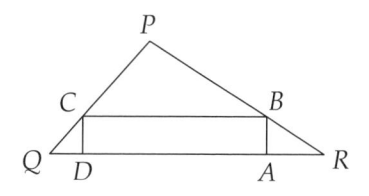

Discussion

We shall discuss two different approaches, similar triangles and dissection.

First approach—similar triangles Let $AB = h$, so that the height of the triangle PQR is $3h$, as shown in figure 3.14.

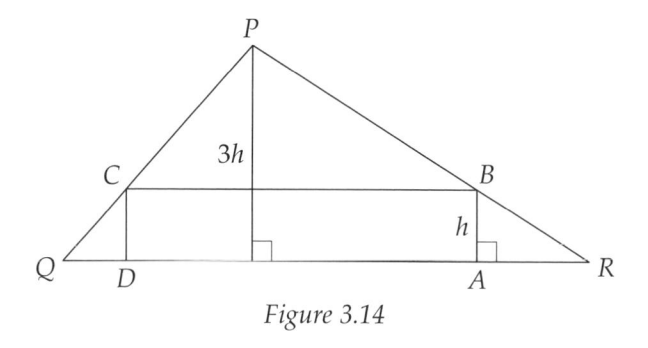

Figure 3.14

✧ Remember the advice in the section DIAGRAMS on page 33.

Can we relate the area of the rectangle to any other area in the figure? Notice that the rectangle and triangle PBC have the same base length BC, and the height of triangle PBC is $2h$. However, the rectangle has height h, so that the rectangle and triangle PBC both have area $BC \times h$.

We have thus reduced the problem to relating the areas of triangle PBC and triangle PRQ. But because BC and RQ are parallel—BC and AD are opposite sides of the rectangle—we deduce that $\angle BRA = \angle PBC$ and $\angle CQD = \angle PCB$, so that triangle PBC is similar to triangle PRQ.

✧ Remember the advice in the section USING STANDARD FACTS on page 35. In this case we explicitly refer to *similar triangles* and explain why the triangles are similar.

Now the similar triangles PBC and PRQ have heights $2h$ and $3h$, so that, using fact 3.4.A, we know that the ratio of their areas is

$$(2h)^2 : (3h)^2 = 4h^2 : 9h^2 = 4 : 9.$$

Since the rectangle and triangle PBC have equal areas it follows that the ratio of the area of the rectangle to the area of triangle PRQ is also $4 : 9$.

✧ Remember the advice in the section NAMING TRIANGLES on page 34. Though we did not need the sides here, we were still careful to name the triangles carefully.

Second approach—dissection One possible dissection is illustrated in figure 3.15. Firstly, divide the original triangle into two parts by the line forming the height. Then subdivide each of these parts into nine equal small triangles by drawing lines through the points of trisection* of the sides. Let these small triangles have areas t and T, as shown.

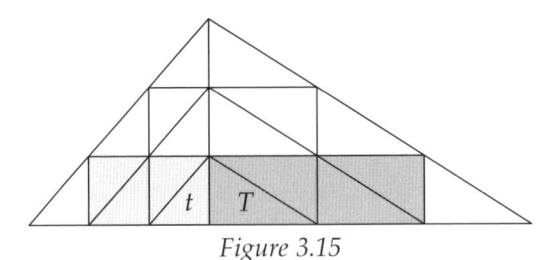

Figure 3.15

We see that the rectangle has area $4t + 4T$ and the original triangle has area $9t + 9T$, so that these areas are in the ratio $4 : 9$.

There is a difficulty with this approach. Starting with figure 3.15 the result is clear, but can we be sure that this diagram is the same as that given in the question?

✧ When using a dissection method, be sure to convince the reader that the dissection corresponds to the configuration given in the

---

*The points of trisection of a line segment divide it into three equal parts.

question. Adding dissecting lines to the given diagram is often not a good approach, because it may be far from easy to show that the resulting figure is a dissection with the required properties.

In figure 3.15 it follows from the dissection into equal parts that the height of the shaded rectangle is one third of the height of the whole triangle. In other words, the shaded rectangle is indeed the one referred to in the original problem.

In fact it is not necessary to divide the triangle into two: figure 3.16 shows another dissection, which subdivides the original triangle into nine equal parts by drawing lines through the points of trisection of the sides.

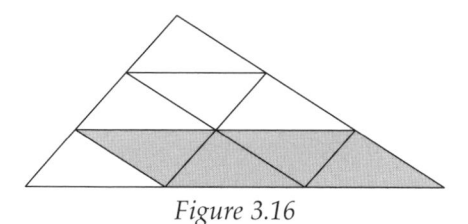

Figure 3.16

It is clear that the area of the shaded parallelogram is $\frac{4}{9}$ of the whole triangle. All that remains is to show that the parallelogram and an appropriate rectangle are equal in area. Can you see how to do that? And can you give a convincing reason why the resulting rectangle does indeed correspond to the one given in the question? (Hint: consider the base and height of the parallelogram.)

Exercise 3.4

C 1. A rectangular piece of paper is cut into two pieces by a straight line passing through one corner, as shown.

Given that area X : area $Y = 2 : 7$, what is the value of the ratio $a : b$?

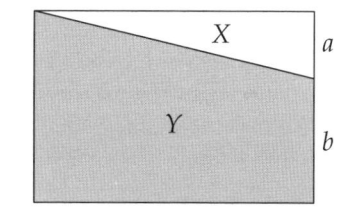

C 2. A hexagon is made by cutting a small equilateral triangle from each corner of a larger equilateral triangle. The sides of the smaller triangles have lengths 1, 2 and 3. The lengths of the perimeters of the hexagon and the original triangle are in the ratio 5 : 7.

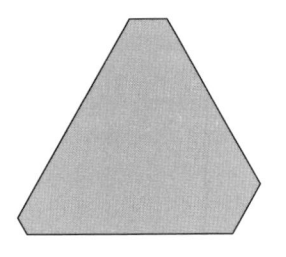

What fraction of the area of the original triangle remains?

C 3. The boundary of the shaded figure consists of four semicircular arcs whose radii are all different. The centre of each arc lies on the line AB, which is 10 cm long.

What is the length of the perimeter of the figure?

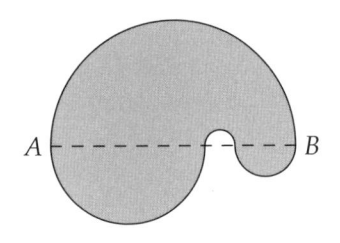

C 4. In triangle ABC, angle B is a right angle and X is the point on BC so that $BX : XC = 5 : 4$.

Also, the length of AB is three times the length of CX and the area of triangle CXA is 54 cm^2.

Calculate the length of the perimeter of triangle CXA.

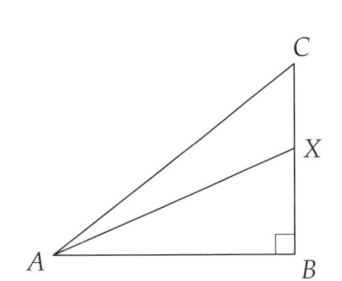

C 5. The diagram shows a square $ABCD$ of side 10 units. Line segments AP, AQ, AR and AS divide the square into five regions of equal area, as shown.

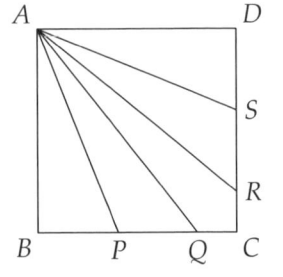

Calculate the length of QR.

Chapter 3: Geometry

H 6. A regular octagon with sides of length a is inscribed in a square with sides of length 1, as shown. Prove that $a^2 + 2a = 1$.

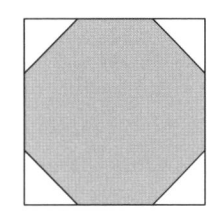

C 7. In the diagram, P, Q, R and S are four points on a line such that $PQ = RS$. Semicircles are drawn above the line with diameters PQ, RS and PS, and another semicircle with diameter QR is drawn below the line.

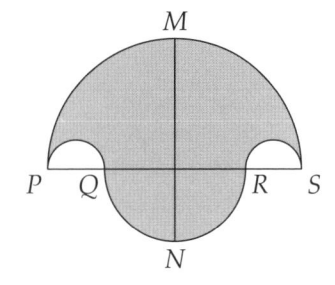

The line MN is the line of symmetry of the figure.

Prove that the shaded area is equal to the area of the circle with diameter MN.

C 8. The diagram shows nine $1\,\text{cm} \times 1\,\text{cm}$ squares and a circle. The circle passes through the centres of the four corner squares.

What is the area of the shaded region—inside two squares but outside the circle?

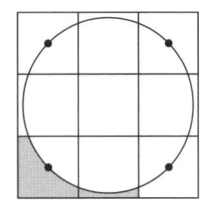

H 9. The diagram shows a quarter-circle with centre O and two semicircular arcs with diameters OA and OB.

Calculate the ratio of the area of the region shaded grey to the area of the region shaded black.

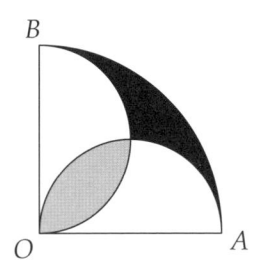

M **10.** The figure shows three touching semicircles whose centres lie in a straight line.

Two of the semicircles have radius 1 cm; these touch at T. The other semicircle has radius 2 cm.

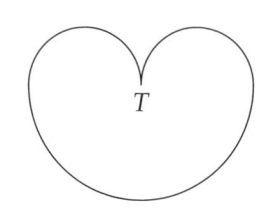

Prove that every straight line through T divides the perimeter of the figure into two parts of equal length.

C **11.** The diagram shows a symmetrical four-pointed star. Four vertices of the star form a square and the other four vertices lie on a circle. The square has sides of length $2a$ cm. The shaded area is one third of the area of the square.

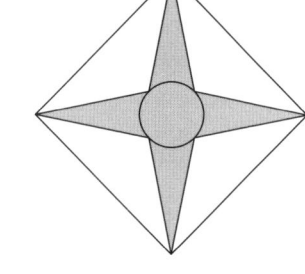

What is the radius of the circle?

H **12.** Squares S and T are each placed outside a square of side a and inside a square of side b, as shown. On the left, the *sides* of square S are parallel to the sides of the other two squares; on the right, the *diagonals* of square T are parallel to the sides of the other two squares.

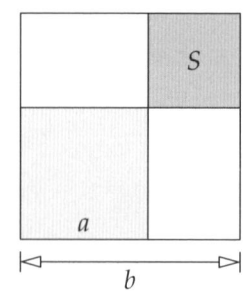

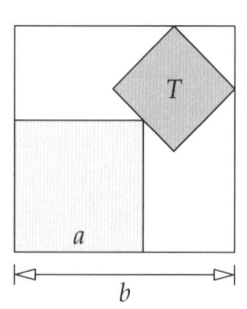

Find the ratio (area of S) : (area of T).

Chapter 3: Geometry

H **13.** The diagram shows a triangle PTU inscribed in a square $PQRS$. Each of the marked angles at P is equal to $30°$.

Prove that the area of the triangle PTU is one third of the area of the square $PQRS$.

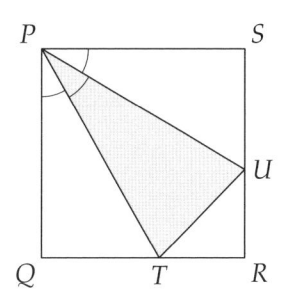

M **14.** The nonagon shown shaded in the diagram has been made by removing three pieces from an equilateral triangle of side 12.

All nine edges of the nonagon are parallel to sides of the triangle. Three edges have lengths 1, 2 and 3 as shown.

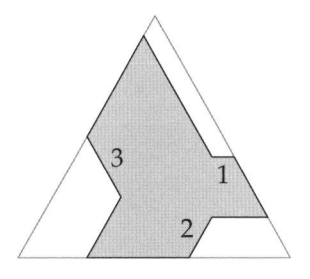

Calculate the length of the perimeter of the nonagon.

M **15.** The diagram shows a triangle in which the altitude from A divides the base BC in the ratio $18:7$.

Find the ratio in which the base is divided by a line parallel to the altitude which cuts the triangle into two equal areas.

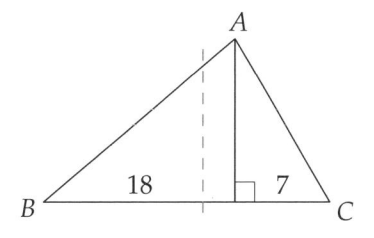

M **16.** The diagram shows a rectangle divided into eight regions by four straight lines. Three of the regions have areas 1, 2 and 3, as shown.

What is the area of the shaded quadrilateral?

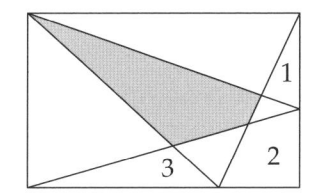

3.5 Touching circles

> CAYLEY –   HAMILTON 2 3 4 5   MACLAURIN 2 3 4 5

A *tangent* to a circle is a straight line (considered to extend indefinitely) which intersects the circle at a single point, called the *point of contact*. Equivalently, the line and circle are said to *touch*, or to be *touching*.

Fact 3.5.A *A tangent to a circle is at right angles to the radius through the point of contact (figure 3.17).*

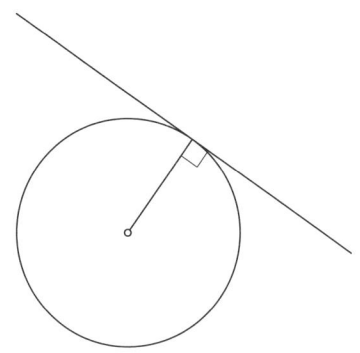

Figure 3.17: Tangent perpendicular to radius

Two circles are *touching* if they intersect in a single point, the *point of contact*.

Fact 3.5.B *Touching circles have a common tangent at their point of contact (figure 3.18). Hence*
  (i) *the line joining their centres passes through the point of contact;*
  (ii) *the distance between their centres is equal to the sum of their radii.*

Techniques

The key to solving problems involving touching circles, or a circle touching various lines, is to join up relevant points:

- ✦ join the centres of touching circles;
- ✦ join the centre of a circle to the point of contact of a tangent and mark a right angle.

Chapter 3: Geometry

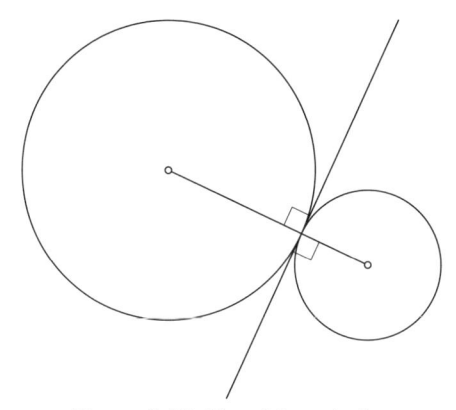

Figure 3.18: Touching circles

In addition, it may occasionally be helpful to draw the common tangent to two touching circles.

✧ Remember the advice in the section DIAGRAMS on page 33.

Example 3.5

The diagram shows two touching circles inside the rectangle $ABCD$, which has $AB = 6$ and $BC = 4$. The larger circle touches three sides of the rectangle, whilst the smaller circle touches two sides, as shown.

Calculate the radius of the smaller circle.

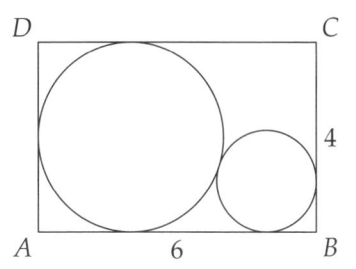

Discussion

Let us follow the advice given above and join appropriate points. Firstly, join the centres of the two circles, passing through the point of contact (touching circles). Also join the centre of each circle to its points of contact with the rectangle and mark in the right angles (tangent perpendicular to radius). We obtain figure 3.19.

✧ Remember the advice in the section USING STANDARD FACTS on page 35. In this case we explicitly refer to *touching circles* (to explain that the line of centres passes through the point of contact) and *tangent perpendicular to radius* (to explain the right angles).

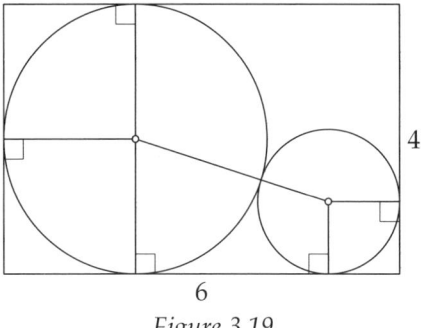

Figure 3.19

We see that the radius of the larger circle is 2. Let the radius of the smaller circle be r. After inserting the lengths of the radii we obtain figure 3.20. Now consider the shaded trapezium, three of whose sides are

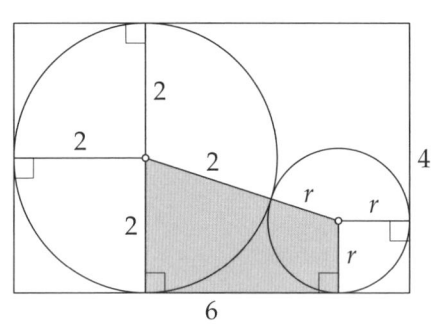

Figure 3.20

known. We see that the base has length $6 - 2 - r = 4 - r$.

Using the standard method of dealing with such a trapezium (see page 44) we divide it into a rectangle and a right-angled triangle, as shown in figure 3.21.

The right-angled triangle has sides of length $2 - r$, $4 - r$ and $r + 2$ and we can apply Pythagoras' theorem to obtain the equation

$$(2 - r)^2 + (4 - r)^2 = (r + 2)^2. \tag{3.4}$$

Chapter 3: Geometry

Figure 3.21

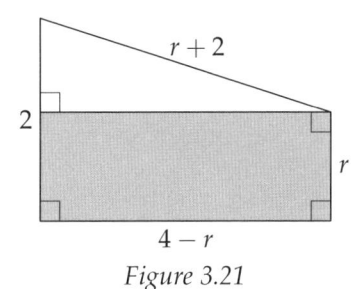

✧ Remember the advice in the section USING STANDARD FACTS on page 35. In this case we explicitly refer to *Pythagoras' theorem*.

We may simplify equation (3.4) by expanding the brackets and collecting like terms, to obtain

$$r^2 - 16r + 16 = 0,$$

a quadratic equation, which may be solved to find r.

All that remains is to decide which of the two solutions for r is relevant in this context.

✧ You should always give both solutions of a quadratic equation. Where necessary, you can then give an explanation of which of the two solutions are valid in the context of the problem: neither, just one, or both.

Exercise 3.5

H **1.** The region shown shaded in the diagram is bounded by three touching circles of radius 1 and the tangent to two of the circles.

Calculate the perimeter of the shaded region.

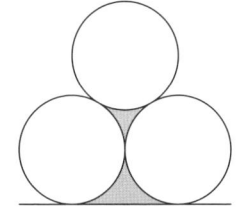

H **2.** The diagram shows four circles of radius 1 placed inside a square so that they are tangential to the sides of the square at the midpoints of the sides, and to each other. 1 Calculate the shaded area.

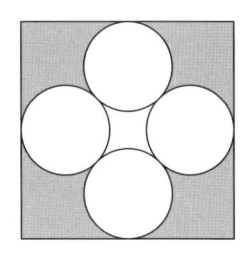

M **3.** The diagram shows a circle of radius 2 and a square. The circle touches two sides of the square and passes through one corner of the square. The area of the region shaded black (inside the square but outside the circle) is X and the area of the region shaded grey (inside the circle but outside the square) is Y.

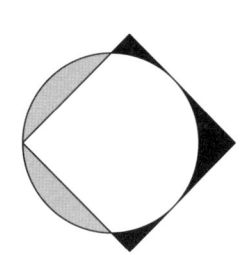

What is the value of $Y - X$?

H **4.** A circle is inscribed in a square and a rectangle is placed inside the square but outside the circle. Two sides of the rectangle lie along sides of the square and one vertex lies on the circle, as shown. The rectangle is twice as high as it is wide.

What is the ratio of the area of the square to the area of the rectangle?

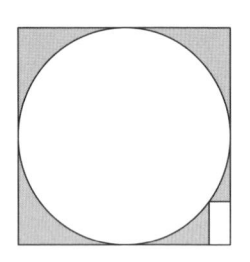

H **5.** A square just fits within a circle, which itself just fits within another square, as shown in the diagram.
Find the ratio of the two shaded areas.

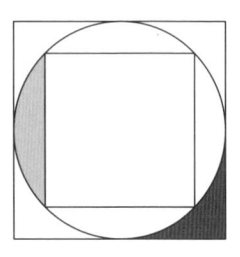

Chapter 3: Geometry

H 6. The diagram shows three touching circles, whose radii are a, b and c, and whose centres are at the vertices Q, R and S of a rectangle $QRST$. The fourth vertex T of the rectangle lies on the circle with centre S.

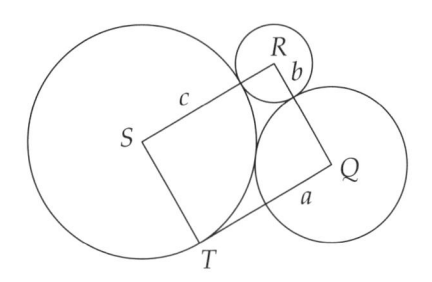

Find the ratio $a : b : c$.

M 7. A circle is inscribed in a right-angled triangle, as shown. The point of contact of the circle and the hypotenuse divides the hypotenuse into lengths x and y.

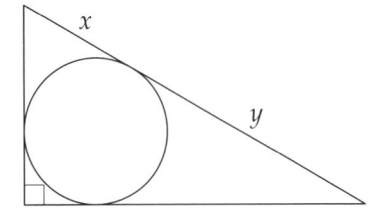

Prove that the area of the triangle is equal to xy.

M 8. Three circles touch the same straight line and touch each other, as shown.

Prove that the radii a, b and c, where c is smallest, satisfy the equation

$$\frac{1}{\sqrt{a}} + \frac{1}{\sqrt{b}} = \frac{1}{\sqrt{c}}.$$

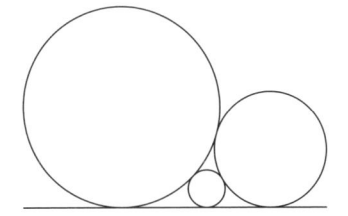

3.6 Coordinates

Cayley – Hamilton 4   Maclaurin 15

In some cases it is clear that an Olympiad problem involves coordinate geometry, because the statement of the problem refers to points or lines in coordinate form.

At first sight some other geometrical problems may appear to have nothing to do with coordinates, but they too may be amenable to such an approach; the example discussed below is a case in point.

However, we do not recommend the wholesale use of coordinate geometry as a means of solving Olympiad geometry problems. Our advice is to use coordinates only as a last resort, when all else fails. Coordinate methods can often become very messy, and in general it is better to use 'Euclidean' methods to solve geometrical problems.

You should be familiar with the basic coordinate methods of working with points and straight lines, such as finding distances, gradients and equations. You should also know how to find the point of intersection of two lines by solving their two equations simultaneously.

There are two results which are worth drawing attention to:

Fact 3.6.A *The gradients m_1 and m_2 of two perpendicular lines satisfy*

$$m_1 \times m_2 = -1.$$

Fact 3.6.B *The equation of the line which has x-intercept a and y-intercept b (see figure 3.22) is*

$$\frac{x}{a} + \frac{y}{b} = 1.$$

Techniques

If you do adopt a coordinate approach, unless the question itself refers to coordinates, you can choose the position of the axes yourself. Some positions may lead to a simpler solution than others, so it is worth thinking carefully about the best choice.

- ✦ When introducing coordinates, decide on the best position for the axes.

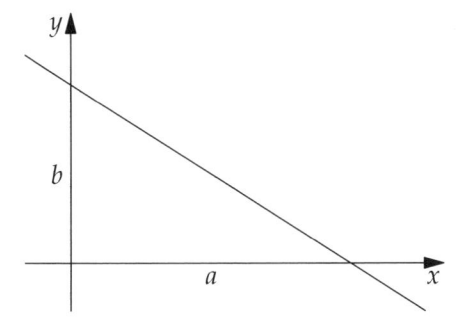

Figure 3.22: The line with intercepts a and b

✧ Remember the advice in the section NOTATION on page 34. Make your choice of axes clear, mark the axes on a diagram and label any key points.

Example 3.6

In the diagram, X is the point of intersection of lines drawn from the corners C and D of square $ABCD$ to the midpoints M and N of sides AB and BC.

Prove that the triangle MXD is right-angled with sides in the ratio $3 : 4 : 5$.

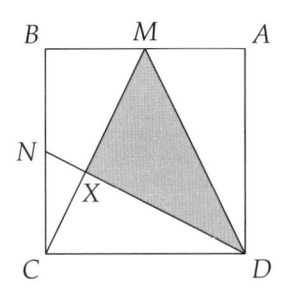

Discussion

There are several different approaches to this problem. Here we discuss a method using coordinates, in order to show that on occasion this can be an effective approach to a geometrical question, despite the reservations we have mentioned.

We choose C as origin and introduce coordinate axes along CD and CB, as shown in figure 3.23.

✧ Remember the advice in the section NOTATION on page 34. Here we are careful to describe our choice of coordinate axes and include them on a diagram.

Since no lengths are given in the question we may choose the scale on each axis so that the side of the square is 10 units. (We choose the value 10—rather than, say, 1 or 2—for reasons that will become clear later.)

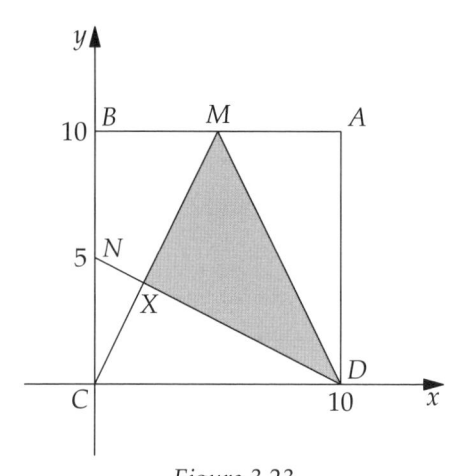

Figure 3.23

✧ Be very careful when assigning specific values to unknowns in a question. You need to convince yourself—and the marker—that the resulting method is still a general one, rather than applying only to the values you have chosen.

The coordinates of points M and N are $(5, 10)$ and $(0, 5)$, respectively. We see that the gradient of CM is 2 and the gradient of ND is $-\frac{1}{2}$. The product of these gradients is -1, so that the lines are perpendicular and hence $\angle MXD = 90°$.

✧ Remember the advice in the section USING STANDARD FACTS on page 35. In this case we explain how we know that the lines are perpendicular.

To find the lengths of the sides of triangle MXD we need to find the coordinates of X, which is the point of intersection of the lines CM and ND. Now CM has equation

$$y = 2x. \tag{3.5}$$

Chapter 3: Geometry

Also, ND has intercepts 5 and 10, so the equation of ND is

$$\frac{y}{5} + \frac{x}{10} = 1. \tag{3.6}$$

Substituting from equation (3.5) into equation (3.6), we obtain

$$\frac{2x}{5} + \frac{x}{10} = 1,$$

from which we find $x = 2$ and therefore, from equation (3.5), $y = 4$. In other words, the coordinates of X are $(2, 4)$. (One reason we chose the value 10 earlier was to avoid getting fractional coordinates for X.)

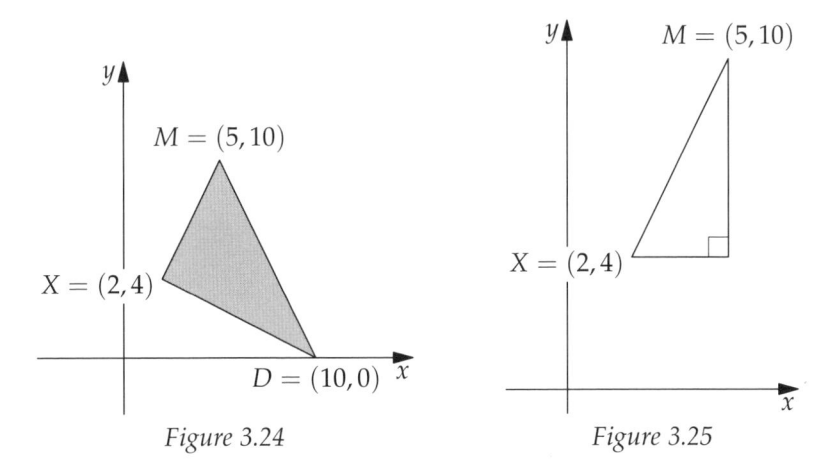

Figure 3.24

Figure 3.25

We now know the coordinates of all three points M, X and D, as shown in figure 3.24.

We can find the lengths of the sides MX and XD using a standard method. To find MX, we apply Pythagoras' theorem to a suitable right-angled triangle, such as that shown in figure 3.25, to obtain

$$MX = \sqrt{(5-2)^2 + (10-4)^2}$$

$$= \sqrt{3^2 + 6^2}$$

$$= \sqrt{9 + 36}$$

$$= \sqrt{45}$$

$$= 3\sqrt{5}.$$

Similarly,
$$XD = \sqrt{(10-2)^2 + (4-0)^2}$$
$$= 4\sqrt{5}.$$

Note that we have omitted some steps in the working here—can you fill them in?

✧ Remember the advice in the section WORKING TOWARDS A GIVEN RESULT on page 35.

We see that the lengths of the sides MX and XD are in the ratio 3 : 4. But we have already shown that the triangle MXD is right-angled, so that we conclude that it is a '3, 4, 5' triangle, as required.

Exercise 3.6

M 1. A quadrilateral is enclosed by four straight lines with equations
$$2y = x + 4$$
$$y = 2x - 4$$
$$2y = x - 2$$
$$y = 2x + 2.$$

Calculate the area of this quadrilateral.

H 2. A triangle is bounded by the lines whose equations are $y = -x - 1$, $y = 2x - 1$ and $y = k$, where k is a positive integer.

For what values of k is the area of the triangle less than 2008?

3.7 Three dimensions

Cayley 6   Hamilton 6   Maclaurin 256

The types of three-dimensional objects that might appear in intermediate Olympiad problems include cubes, cuboids, tetrahedra and cones.

Fact 3.7.A *A cuboid has six rectangular faces.*

Fact 3.7.B *A tetrahedron has four triangular faces.*

Fact 3.7.C *For a circular cone, with base radius r, height h and slant length ℓ,*
  (i) *the volume is $\frac{1}{3}\pi r^2 h$;*
  (ii) *the area of the curved surface is $\pi r \ell$.*

Techniques

The key to solving problems involving three-dimensional objects is usually to start by drawing more diagrams:

- draw appropriate two-dimensional diagrams, such as faces, cross-sections, or a net;
- reduce the given problem to one or more problems in two dimensions.

◇ Remember the advice in the section Diagrams on page 33.

Example 3.7

The diagram shows a tetrahedron $ABCD$, where A, B, C and D are vertices of a cuboid with sides of length x, y and z, as shown.

Let F_A, F_B, F_C and F_D represent the areas of the faces of the tetrahedron opposite A, B, C, and D respectively. Prove that $F_A^2 + F_C^2 = F_B^2 + F_D^2$.

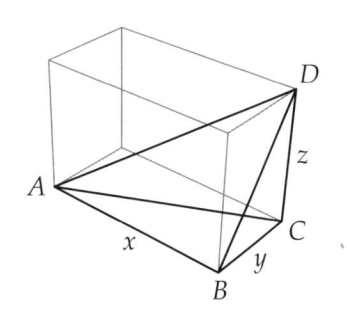

Discussion

Taking the advice given above, we draw the four triangular faces of the tetrahedron (figure 3.26).

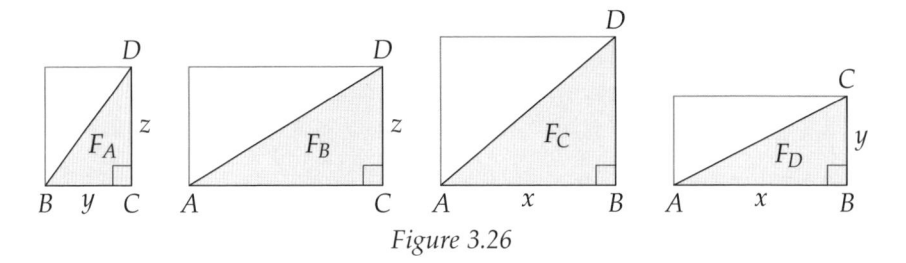

Figure 3.26

Since each face of the tetrahedron is part of a rectangular cross-section of the cuboid the triangles are all right-angled, as shown.

✧ Remember the advice in the section USING STANDARD FACTS on page 35. In this case we explicitly state the reason why the faces are right-angled.

In two cases the base and height of the triangular face are known, so we can find the areas:

$$F_A = \tfrac{1}{2}yz \quad \text{and} \quad F_D = \tfrac{1}{2}xz.$$

In the other two cases only one length is known, so we need to find the missing length in order to find the area. For example, in triangle ACD, in order to find F_B we first need to find AC. However, AC is also the hypotenuse of triangle ABC, so that we can use Pythagoras' theorem:

$$\begin{aligned}AC^2 &= AB^2 + BC^2 \\ &= x^2 + y^2.\end{aligned}$$

✧ Remember the advice in the section USING STANDARD FACTS on page 35. In this case we explicitly refer to *Pythagoras' theorem*.

Hence

$$\begin{aligned}F_B &= \tfrac{1}{2} \times AC \times z \\ &= \tfrac{1}{2} \times \sqrt{x^2 + y^2} \times z,\end{aligned}$$

Chapter 3: Geometry

so that
$$F_B^2 = \tfrac{1}{4}(x^2+y^2)z^2.$$

In a similar way we can find BD and hence F_C, giving
$$F_C^2 = \tfrac{1}{4}(y^2+z^2)x^2.$$

We now have all the ingredients we need to prove the result, but we do need to be careful to set out the final steps in a logical way. It would be quite wrong to substitute all our results into the equation $F_A^2 + F_C^2 = F_B^2 + F_D^2$ and "show that it works" by reducing the equation to, say, $0 = 0$.

⟡ Remember the advice in the section PROVING GIVEN EQUATIONS on page 9.

From the above results, we have
$$\begin{aligned}
F_A^2 + F_C^2 &= \tfrac{1}{4}y^2z^2 + \tfrac{1}{4}(y^2+z^2)x^2 \\
&= \tfrac{1}{4}(y^2z^2 + y^2x^2 + z^2x^2) \\
&= \tfrac{1}{4}(x^2y^2 + y^2z^2 + z^2x^2)
\end{aligned}$$

and
$$\begin{aligned}
F_B^2 + F_D^2 &= \tfrac{1}{4}(x^2+y^2)z^2 + \tfrac{1}{4}x^2y^2 \\
&= \tfrac{1}{4}(x^2z^2 + y^2z^2 + x^2y^2) \\
&= \tfrac{1}{4}(x^2y^2 + y^2z^2 + z^2x^2).
\end{aligned}$$

Therefore
$$F_A^2 + F_C^2 = F_B^2 + F_D^2,$$

as required.

Exercise 3.7

C 1. A regular tetrahedron *ABCD* has edges of length 2 units. The midpoint of the edge *AB* is *M* and the midpoint of the edge *CD* is *N*.
Find the exact length of the segment *MN*.

H 2. Two different cuboids are placed together, face-to-face, to form a large cuboid. The surface area of the large cuboid is $\frac{3}{4}$ of the total surface area of the original two cuboids.
Prove that the lengths of the edges of the large cuboid may be labelled x, y and z, where

$$\frac{2}{z} = \frac{1}{x} + \frac{1}{y}.$$

M 3. The coordinates of three vertices of a cube are (4, 0, 3), (6, 4, 1) and (2, 8, 5).
Find the coordinates of a fourth vertex.

M 4. An ant lives on the surface of a cuboid which has points *X*, *Y* and *Z* on three adjacent faces.
The ant travels between *X*, *Y* and *Z* along the shortest possible path between each pair of points. The angles $x°$, $y°$ and $z°$ are the angles between the parts of the ant's path, as shown.
Prove that $x + y + z = 270$.

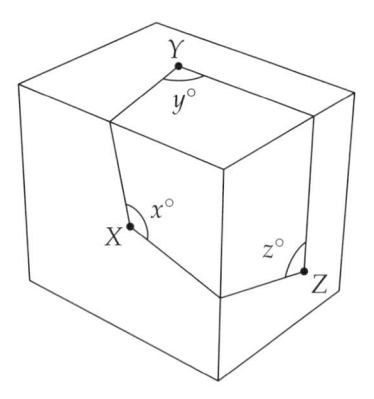

M 5. A sandcastle has a cylindrical base, on top of which is a second smaller cylinder, with a third even smaller cylinder on top. The three circular cylinders have the same height, and their radii are in the ratio 3 : 2 : 1. The height of each cylinder is equal to the radius of the smallest cylinder.

Exactly 24 full buckets of sand were used to construct the sandcastle. The bucket is in the form of a frustum (part of a cone, as shown), whose larger radius equals its perpendicular height, and is twice its smaller radius.

Find the ratio of the total height of the sandcastle to that of the bucket.

3.8   Miscellaneous problems

Cayley –   Hamilton 6   Maclaurin 3 4 5 6

We gather here some questions, usually harder ones, that do not fit naturally into the earlier sections of this chapter.

Exercise 3.8

M 1. A square is constructed inside a rectangle of length a and width b, with the square touching the diagonal of the rectangle as shown in the diagram.

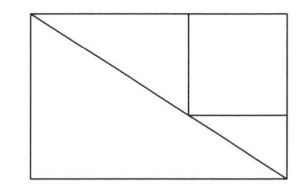

If the square has side h, prove that

$$\frac{1}{h} = \frac{1}{a} + \frac{1}{b}.$$

M 2. The diagrams show a rectangle that just fits inside right-angled triangle ABC in two different ways. One side of the triangle has length a.

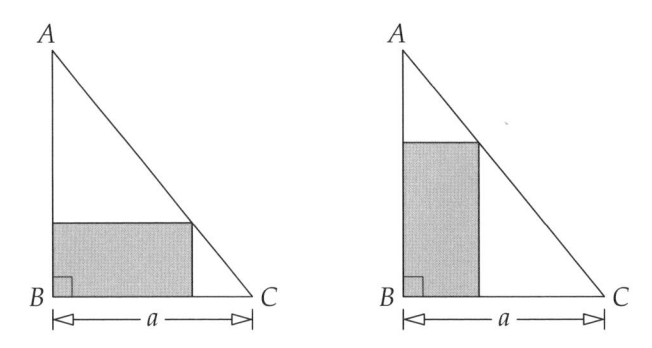

Prove that the perimeter of the rectangle is $2a$.

M 3. In trapezium $ABCD$ the sides AB and DC are parallel and $\angle BAD = \angle ABC < 90°$. Point P lies on AB with $\angle CPD = \angle DAB$.
Prove that $PC^2 + PD^2 = AB \times DC$.

M 4. The diameter AD of a circle has length 4. The points B and C lie on the circle, as shown, so that $AB = BC = 1$. Find the length of CD.

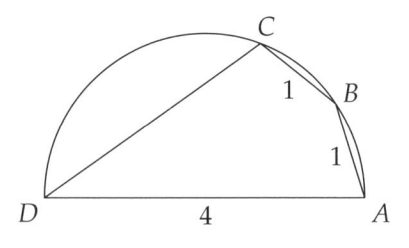

H 5. The triangle ABC is right-angled at A, with $AB = 6$ cm and $AC = 8$ cm.
Points X and Y are situated on BC such that $AB = AY$ and $AX = XC$. Two isosceles triangles ABY and AXC are thus created. These triangles overlap, forming the region AXY. Calculate the area of this region.

Chapter 3: Geometry

M **6.** A circle with centre O and radius 3 cm rolls without slipping around the inside of a regular hexagon $ABCDEF$.

The circle starts with a point P on its circumference in contact with the midpoint of the side AB, as shown.

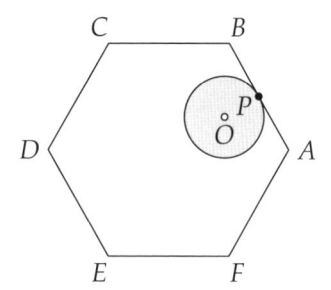

The circle then turns through one complete revolution anticlockwise, touching only sides AB and AF in the process. The circle ends in contact with the side AF, and O, P and A are in a straight line. Find the length of AB.

M **7.** In the figure, p, q, r and s are the lengths of four arcs which together form the circumference of the circle.

Find, in simplified form, an expression for s in terms of p, q and r.

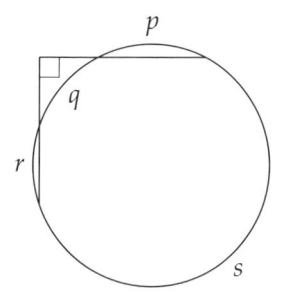

M **8.** The cross-section of a tunnel is a circular arc, as shown in the diagram. The maximum height of the tunnel is 10 feet. A vertical strut 9 feet high supports the roof of the tunnel from a point 27 feet along the ground from the side.

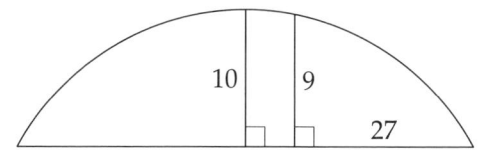

Calculate the width of the tunnel at ground level.

Chapter 4

Integers

Problems involving integers, that is, whole numbers, are quite common in Olympiads.

If a problem refers to digits, then the integer is assumed to be written in base 10, unless explicitly stated otherwise. The notation '*pqr...*' is used to represent the integer with digits (in order) $p, q, r, \ldots$.

Note that an integer may be zero or negative, whereas a digit cannot be negative (but may be zero).

4.1 General guidance

Calculators are not allowed in Olympiad papers, so it is well worth gaining some familiarity with the smaller values of special integers such as:

 squares and cubes;
 triangle numbers;
 prime numbers;
 Fibonacci numbers.

In any case, you should be able to work these out quickly and accurately.

At Intermediate level, problems about integers generally fall into one of two categories, those considering digits, and those treating integers as a whole. For example, solving a problem presented as a 'number sum' (sometimes called an *alphametic*) will usually involve individual digits, whereas for a problem presented in equation form it is not usually necessary, and often unhelpful, to work with digits.

✧ Where a problem gives no indication as to the appropriate approach it is normally best to start by working with the integers as a whole.

Valid arguments

In many problems of this sort it may be possible to find numerical answers, say by spotting numbers which work, or by trial and error. Though finding one or more answers may be relatively easy, what is difficult is to correctly exclude the possibility of further answers. How do you know you have found all the answers, and there are no more? To do this, some systematic approach or logical argument is needed.

 ✧ Finding individual answers, for example, by trial and error, may help you to understand a problem, but is not enough for a full solution. You also need to show that there are no further answers, by being systematic or using mathematical reasoning.

In a similar way, when you think that a result is true for a range of values—for example, for all odd integers greater than 3—you should provide a general proof. Looking at particular values—such as 5, 7, 9, 11, 13—may help you to understand the result, but is not sufficient to show that the result is true more generally.

 ✧ Always provide a proof of general results; it is not sufficient just to look at particular examples.

Notation

If you do introduce some symbols to stand for digits or integers, the advice given in the section Notation on page 7 applies:

 ✧ When introducing algebraic letters, you should consider carefully which quantities to represent. In particular, try to avoid introducing more symbols than necessary and always be careful to specify what your letters stand for.

Note that there may be more than one way to introduce symbols. For example, three unknown consecutive integers may be written as, say, n, $n+1$, $n+2$, but sometimes another choice, such as $n-1$, n, $n+1$, leads to simpler algebra.

Chapter 4: Integers

Checking

When an algebraic approach is used, the advice given in the sections CHECKING on page 11 and CHECKING SOLUTIONS TO EQUATIONS on page 28 also applies:

> ⟡ In all but the most straightforward cases, you should check that your answers do actually solve the given question.

This is good practice anyway, but see page 28 for a full discussion of why it is necessary.

4.2 Digits

CAYLEY 2 4 6   HAMILTON –   MACLAURIN 1

In this section we discuss problems which specifically refer to the digits of one or more integers.

Fact 4.2.A *There are precisely ten possible values for a digit (in base 10), namely 0, 1, 2, 3, 4, 5, 6, 7, 8 and 9.*

By its nature, a 'number sum', such as that in question 1 on page 82, automatically includes notation for the digits appearing in the problem. When solving such problems the hardest part is often explaining your method. Using appropriate terms, such as 'carry', or 'units column', will help you to make your strategy clear.

> ⟡ When writing out your solution of a 'number sum', aim to use standard terms to refer to steps in the process.

In other problems, it may be necessary to introduce notation for digits appearing in the problem. In this context, the following fact allows you to form equations from the information given in the question.

Fact 4.2.B *The two-digit integer 'ab' has value $10a + b$, the three-digit integer 'abc' has value $100a + 10b + c$, and so on.*

Techniques

> ✦ Consider converting a 'number sum' into a different, equivalent, form. For example, a subtraction may also be written as an addition.

✦ Use fact 4.2.B to convert the problem to an equation, introducing symbols for digits where necessary.
✦ Once you have an equation connecting digits, you may be able to make some deductions from the fact that the symbols are integers, or specifically digits, using fact 4.2.A.

For example, if we know that $a = 3b + 9c$, where a, b and c are digits, then we can deduce that a is a multiple of 3 since we are dealing with integers. Also, since a is a digit and therefore lies between 0 and 9 we may deduce that only certain values of b and c are possible, otherwise the expression $3b + 9c$ is too big.

Example 4.2

All the digits of a certain positive three-digit number are non-zero. When the digits are taken in reverse order a different number is formed. The difference between the two numbers is divisible by eight.

Given that the original number is a square number, find its possible values.

Discussion

The question refers to the digits of a number and to taking the digits in reverse order, so it will be useful to introduce symbols for the digits. Let the original integer be 'abc', where $a, b, c > 0$ since none of the digits is zero.

✧ Remember the advice in the section NOTATION on page 78. Here we are careful to specify that the letters are positive digits.

From fact 4.2.B, we know the original integer is $100a + 10b + c$. On reversing the digits, we get the integer 'cba', which is $100c + 10b + a$.

We are told two things about these numbers: they are different; and the difference between them is a multiple of eight. Let us deal with these in turn.

The integers 'abc' and 'cba' have the same middle digit. Since the numbers are different it follows that either their first digits are different, or their last digits are different (or both). In either case, this means that a and c are different.

Chapter 4: Integers 81

To find the difference between the numbers '*abc*' and '*cba*' we subtract the smaller from the larger; which is which depends on whether $a < c$ or $a > c$ (we know they are different).

In the first case, '*cba*' is larger, so the difference is

$$(100c + 10b + a) - (100a + 10b + c) = 99c - 99a$$
$$= 99(c - a).$$

Now this difference is a multiple of eight. But 99 is not divisible by two, so the only way for $99(c - a)$ to be a multiple of eight is for $c - a$ to be a multiple of eight.

We determined above that the digits a and c are different, and we are given that they are non-zero. Hence their difference lies between 1 and 8. Thus only one multiple of eight is possible: $c - a = 8$, when $c = 9$ and $a = 1$.

We now make use of the fact that the original integer is a square. What squares have the form '1*b*9'?

> ✧ Remember the advice in the section Valid arguments on page 78. Here, you may be able to *see* a possible square, but what is needed is an argument that shows that all such squares have been found.

Well '1*b*9' is greater than $100 = 10^2$, so we list the squares of integers larger than 10:

$$11^2 = 121;$$
$$12^2 = 144;$$
$$13^2 = 169;$$
$$14^2 = 196;$$
$$15^2 = 225.$$

We may stop here because the square is already above 199, which is the highest integer of the form '1*b*9'. Therefore there is only one number of the required form in the case $c > a$, namely 169.

We now need to deal with the second case, when $a > c$. The first steps in the argument are similar, leading to $a = 9$ and $c = 1$, so that the number has the form '9*b*1'. What squares have this form?

Well '9b1' is greater than $900 = 30^2$, so we look at the squares of integers larger than 30:

$$31^2 = 961;$$
$$32^2 = 1024.$$

We may stop here because the square is already above 991. Therefore there is only one number of the required form in the case $a > c$, namely 961.

Finally, we check the answers: $961 - 169 = 792 = 8 \times 99$ so both 169 and 961 are indeed solutions.

✧ Remember the advice in the section CHECKING on page 79.

Exercise 4.2

C 1. Show that there are no solutions to this "letter sum".

$$\begin{array}{r} S\ E\ V\ E\ N \\ +\quad\ \ O\ N\ E \\ \hline E\ I\ G\ H\ T \end{array}$$

[Each letter stands for one of the digits 0–9; different letters stand for different digits; no number begins with the digit 0.]

M 2. (a) Find a two-digit number which is four times the sum of its digits.

Now reverse the digits of your original number. This new number is k times the sum of its digits. What is the value of k?

(b) A two-digit number is n times the sum of its digits, where n is a positive integer.

Now when a new number is formed by reversing the digits of the original number, what is the corresponding value of k?

M 3. From a three-digit number (with no repeated digit and no non-zero digit) we can form six two-digit numbers by choosing all possible ordered pairs of digits. For example, the number 257 produces the six numbers 25, 52, 57, 75, 27, 72.

Find all such three-digit numbers with no repeated digit for which the sum of the six two-digit numbers is equal to the original three-digit number.

C 4. Find the positive integer whose value is increased by 518 059 when the digit 5 is placed at each end of the number.

C 5. How many different solutions are there to this word sum, where each letter stands for a different non-zero digit?

$$\begin{array}{r} M A T H S \\ + M A T H S \\ \hline C A Y L E Y \end{array}$$

4.3 Divisibility

CAYLEY 14   HAMILTON 12   MACLAURIN 12

In this section we look at problems concerning divisibility properties, that is, whether certain positive integers divide exactly into a given integer.

Note that there are several equivalent phrases that may be used:

n is divisible by m;

n is a multiple of m;

m is a divisor of n;

m is a factor of n.

The simplest case is divisibility by 2. An integer is either even or odd, and testing the last digit (the 'units' digit) determines which:

Fact 4.3.A

(i) *If an integer ends in an even digit—0, 2, 4, 6, or 8—then it is even. Conversely, if an integer is even, then it ends in an even digit.*

(ii) *If an integer ends in an odd digit—1, 3, 5, 7, or 9—then it is odd, and conversely.*

There are similar simple tests for divisibility by five, four or eight:

Fact 4.3.B *If an integer ends in 0 or 5, then it is a multiple of five, and conversely.*

Fact 4.3.C
  (i) *If the last two digits of an integer form a two-digit multiple of four, then it is a multiple of four, and conversely.*
  (ii) *If the last three digits of an integer form a three-digit multiple of eight, then it is a multiple of eight, and conversely.*

Thus we know that 31 928 is a multiple of four (because 28 is), whereas 70 154 is not (because 54 is not).

The tests for divisibility by three and nine make use of the sum of the digits:

Fact 4.3.D
  (i) *If the sum of the digits of an integer is a multiple of three, then it is a multiple of three, and conversely.*
  (ii) *If the sum of the digits of an integer is a multiple of nine, then it is a multiple of nine, and conversely.*

So 345 678 is a multiple of three, but not nine, since the sum of the digits is 33.

Finally, the test for divisibility by eleven uses the two sums of alternate digits:

Fact 4.3.E *If the difference between the sum of the digits in odd positions and the sum of the digits in even positions is a multiple of eleven, then an integer is a multiple of eleven, and conversely.*

For example, we may deduce that 81 719 is a multiple of 11 because $(8+7+9) - (1+1) = 22 = 2 \times 11$.

Note that no test for divisibility by seven is given here. Though some tests have been devised, they are usually at least as complicated as just doing the division, and none are really helpful in Olympiad problems.

The following result allows you to deal with more general multiples than just the special cases listed above.

Chapter 4: Integers

Fact 4.3.F *If an integer is a multiple of m × n for integers m and n, then it is a multiple of m (and of n).*

So if an integer is divisible by 12, for example, then it is also divisible by 2, 3, 4 and 6.

You need to be careful when trying to work the other way round since in general the converse of fact 4.3.F is false. For example, an integer which is divisible by 4 and 6 may not be divisible by 24.

Techniques

- ✦ Use the standard divisibility tests (fact 4.3.A to fact 4.3.E) to find relationships between the digits, introducing symbols for digits where necessary.
- ✦ Use fact 4.3.F to reduce a given statement to smaller cases; you can then apply the standard divisibility tests to these.

Example 4.3

The five-digit number '*a*679*b*', where *a* and *b* are digits, is divisible by 36. Find all possible such five-digit numbers.

Discussion

The problem helps us by providing symbols for the missing digits. First we make use of fact 4.3.F: we are told that the integer is divisible by 36, so it also divisible by 4 and by 9. Let us consider each of these in turn.

Since the integer is a multiple of 4 the last two digits form a multiple of 4 (fact 4.3.C), that is , the integer '9*b*' is a multiple of 4.

> ✧ When you make use of a standard result, you should make clear what you have done. Here we explain that we have used the test for divisibility by four.

Therefore *b* is an even digit: 0, 2, 4, 6 or 8. Testing each of these, we find that only 92 and 96 are multiples of 4. Hence $b = 2$ or $b = 6$.

Since the integer is a multiple of 9 the sum of the digits is also a multiple of 9 (fact 4.3.D), that is, $a + 6 + 7 + 9 + b = a + 22 + b$ is a multiple of 9. When $b = 2$ this means that $a + 24$ is a multiple of 9; when $b = 6$ it means that $a + 28$ is.

Now a is a digit, which we know is non-zero since we are told that '$a679b$' is a five-digit number. So a lies in the range 1 to 9; hence $a + 24$ lies in the range 25 to 33; and $a + 28$ lies in the range 29 to 37. The only multiples of 9 in the last two ranges are 27 and 36 (18 is too small and 45 too large).

Therefore when $b = 2$ we have $a + 24 = 27$, which means that $a = 3$; and when $b = 6$ we have $a + 28 = 36$, so $a = 8$.

We conclude that the possible five-digit numbers are 36 792 and 86 796.

It is easily checked that both these numbers satisfy all the conditions of the question.

✧ Remember the advice in the section CHECKING on page 79.

Exercise 4.3

C 1. How many four-digit multiples of 9 consist only of four different odd digits?

C 2. A palindromic number is one which reads the same when its digits are reversed, for example 23 832.

What is the largest six-digit palindromic number which is exactly divisible by 15?

C 3. The digits p, q, r, s and t are all different.

What is the smallest five-digit integer '$pqrst$' that is divisible by 1, 2, 3, 4 and 5?

H 4. Find the smallest positive integer which consists only of 0s and 1s when written in base 10, and which is divisible by 12.

H 5. (a) A positive integer N is written using only the digits 2 and 3, with each appearing at least once. If N is divisible by 2 and by 3, what is the smallest possible integer N?

(b) A positive integer M is written using only the digits 8 and 9, with each appearing at least once. If M is divisible by 8 and by 9, what is the smallest possible integer M?

H **6.** Find the possible values of the digits p and q, given that the five-digit number '$p543q$' is a multiple of 36.

M **7.** Find the smallest positive multiple of 35 whose digits are all the same as each other.

M **8.** Both the digits x and y are non-zero. The five-digit integer '$xyxyx$' is divisible by 3 and the seven-digit integer '$yxyxyxy$' is divisible by 18.
Find all possible values of x and y.

M **9.** Miko always remembers his four-digit PIN (personal identification number) because

(a) it is a perfect square, and

(b) it has the property that, when you divide it by 2, or 3, or 4, or 5, or 6, or 7, or 8, or 9, there is always a remainder of 1.

What is Miko's PIN?

4.4 Factors and equations

CAYLEY 15   HAMILTON 1 2 3   MACLAURIN 1 3 4 5

Some problems rely on factorisation properties of integers, others contain equations involving integers, and sometimes a problem involves both factors and equations.

Two prime factorisations which are occasionally useful are:

Fact 4.4.A
(i) $111 = 3 \times 37$;
(ii) $1001 = 7 \times 11 \times 13$.

You may come across the term *Diophantine equation* (named after the third century Greek mathematician Diophantus of Alexandria) for equations involving whole numbers. For example, $x^2 + y^3 = 81$, where x and y are integers, is a Diophantine equation.

Techniques

In general, equations involving integers are likely to have an infinite number of solutions, so in an Olympiad context you will need to find some means of restricting the number of possible solutions, thereby making the problem finite.

- ✦ You may be able to find bounds for any unknown integers, in which case you have reduced the problem to one of investigating a finite number of possibilities.
- ✦ An equation of the form $XY = k$, where k is a known integer, may be solved for integers X and Y by considering all possible ways to write k as a product of two factors. Remember to include negative factors in the enumeration.

There are many other special cases. For example, from the equation $X^2 + Y^2 = 5$, where X and Y are integers, we may deduce that either $X^2 = 1$ and $Y^2 = 4$, or $X^2 = 4$ and $Y^2 = 1$.

Example 4.4

A rectangular floor, which measures x feet by y feet, is covered in square tiles which are each 1 foot by 1 foot. All of the tiles on the perimeter of

Chapter 4: Integers

the rectangle are coloured blue, while all of the tiles in the interior of the rectangle are coloured yellow. There are three times as many yellow tiles on the floor as blue tiles.

Find all possible values for the area of the floor.

Discussion

The question helps us by providing symbols for the missing lengths. From the description, it is clear that x and y are integers.

A diagram, however rudimentary, will be helpful when making use of the information given in the question. In figure 4.1 the blue tiles are shaded dark grey and the yellow tiles are shaded light grey.

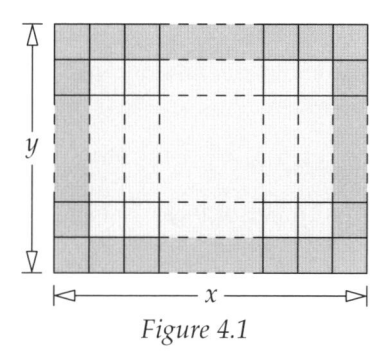

Figure 4.1

There are x blue tiles along two sides, and y along two others. Since this counts the corner tiles twice there are $2x + 2y - 4$ blue tiles altogether.

We could find the number of yellow tiles (they form a rectangle whose sides we can find), but it is simpler to work with the total number of both kinds of tiles, which is just xy.

Now there are three times as many yellow tiles as blue ones, so there are four times as many tiles altogether as blue ones, that is,

the total number of tiles = $4 \times$ (the number of blue tiles),

so that

$$xy = 4(2x + 2y - 4)$$
$$= 8x + 8y - 16.$$

This is a single equation with two integer unknowns, so we cannot solve it directly.

✧ Remember the advice in the section VALID ARGUMENTS on page 78. You may be able to *see* some values of x and y that work here, but what is needed is a method that finds them all, and shows there are no others.

We can make use of the fact that x and y are integers, using the "$XY = k$" technique mentioned above. First, we rewrite the equation so that all the variable terms are on the left:

$$xy - 8x - 8y = -16.$$

We want to form an expression on the left which is a product. Comparing the left-hand terms with $(x-8)(y-8) = xy - 8x - 8y + 64$, we see that we should add 64 to both sides, to obtain

$$xy - 8x - 8y + 64 = -16 + 64,$$

that is,

$$(x-8)(y-8) = 48.$$

Now there is a limited number of factorisations of 48. Also, x and y are positive, so that each of $x-8$ and $y-8$ is greater than -8, which rules out factorisations such as -3×-16. Indeed, all factorisations with negative factors are ruled out, because when both factors are negative one of them will be at most -8, that is, it will be -8 or less.

Furthermore, we are asked for the possible values for the area of the floor, in other words, we need to find xy, not x and y separately. Now we may interchange the values of x and y without changing the area, so we may assume that x is greater than (or equal to) y. In which case, $x-8$ will be greater than (or equal to) $y-8$.

On this basis, the possible factorisations of 48 are

$$48 \times 1, \quad 24 \times 2, \quad 16 \times 3, \quad 12 \times 4 \quad \text{and} \quad 8 \times 6.$$

These are values of $(x-8)(y-8)$, so adding 8 to each factor we obtain the values of xy as

$$56 \times 9, \quad 32 \times 10, \quad 24 \times 11, \quad 20 \times 12 \quad \text{and} \quad 16 \times 14.$$

We may check each of these in turn. For example, in the first case there are 504 tiles in all and $2 \times 56 + 2 \times 9 - 4 = 126$ blue tiles, so there are $504 - 126 = 378$ yellow tiles. And $378 = 3 \times 126$, as required.

Chapter 4: Integers 91

❖ Remember the advice in the section CHECKING on page 79.

You should confirm that each of the other possible values of xy does indeed work.

Hence the possible values for the area of the floor, in square feet, are 504, 320, 264, 240 and 224.

Exercise 4.4

C **1.** In this multiplication sum, p, q, r and s stand for different digits.

$$\begin{array}{r} p\ q \\ \times\ r\ q \\ \hline s\ s\ s \end{array}$$

Find the digit which each letter represents, explaining how you know that you have found all possible solutions.

C **2.** Four copies of the polygon shown are fitted together (without gaps or overlaps) to form a rectangle.

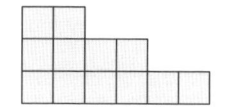

How many different rectangles are possible?

H **3.** Numbers are placed in the blocks shown alongside according to the following two rules:

  A. For two adjacent blocks in the bottom row, the number in the block to the right is twice the number in the block to the left.

  B. The number in a block above the bottom row is the sum of the numbers in the two adjacent blocks on the row below.

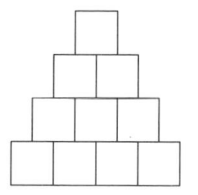

What is the smallest positive integer that can be placed in the bottom left-hand block so that the sum of all ten numbers is a cube?

H 4. Find the number of different ways that 75 can be expressed as the sum of two or more consecutive positive integers. (Writing the same numbers in a different order does not constitute a 'different way'.)

H 5. Prove that there is exactly one sequence of five consecutive positive integers in which the sum of the squares of the first three integers is equal to the sum of the squares of the other two integers.

M 6. How many different ways are there to express $\frac{2}{15}$ in the form $\frac{1}{a} + \frac{1}{b}$, where a, b are positive integers with $a \leq b$?

H 7. A particular four-digit number N is such that:
   (a) the sum of N and 74 is a square; and
   (b) the difference between N and 15 is also a square.
   What is the number N?

M 8. Show that the equation
$$\frac{1}{x} + \frac{1}{y} = \frac{5}{11}$$
has no solutions for positive integers x, y.

C 9. Solve the equation $5a - ab = 9b^2$, where a and b are positive integers.

M 10. (a) Given that
$$(x-y)(y-z)(z+x) = -90$$
$$\text{and} \quad (x-y)(y+z)(z-x) = 42$$
show that $z(x-y)^2 = 24$.

(b) Given that x, y and z are positive integers, solve the system of simultaneous equations:

$$(x-y)(y-z)(z+x) = -90$$
$$(x-y)(y+z)(z-x) = 42$$
$$(x+y)(y-z)(z-x) = -60.$$

M **11.** The magician Mij has 140 green balls and 140 red balls. To perform a trick, Mij places all the balls in two bags. In the black bag there are twice as many green balls as red balls. In the white bag the number of red balls is a multiple of the number of green balls.

Determine all the ways in which Mij can place the balls in the two bags in order to perform the trick.

4.5 Miscellaneous problems

Cayley 1 3 4 5 6   Hamilton 1 4 6   Maclaurin 1 4 5 6

We gather here some questions, many of them harder ones, that do not fit naturally into the earlier sections of this chapter.

Example 4.5

An 'unfortunate' number is a positive integer which is equal to 13 times the sum of its digits.

Find all 'unfortunate' numbers.

Discussion

We do not know how many digits an 'unfortunate' number can have.

However, we can quickly see that such an integer has more than one digit: if an integer has only one digit, then the sum of the digits is the integer itself, and an integer cannot be equal to 13 times itself.

We may also suspect that an 'unfortunate' number cannot be too large. Suppose an 'unfortunate' number has N digits. Then the sum of its digits is at most $N \times 9 = 9N$, the value when all the digits are 9, as large as possible. But the integer itself is at least 10^{N-1}, the smallest N-digit integer. Now if N is sufficiently large, then 10^{N-1} will be greater than $13 \times 9N = 117N$, so that the integer cannot be equal to 13 times the sum of its digits and there can therefore be no 'unfortunate' numbers with N digits. For example, when $N = 7$ we have $10^{N-1} = 1\,000\,000$ and $117N = 819$, in other words, the smallest value of a 7-digit integer is $1\,000\,000$ and the largest possible value of 13 times the sum of its digits is 819, so that the number cannot be 'unfortunate'.

Indeed, even when $N = 4$ there can be no 'unfortunate' numbers, because then $10^{N-1} = 10^3 = 1000$ which is greater than $117N = 117 \times 4 = 468$. But when $N = 3$ we have $10^{N-1} = 100$ and $117N = 117 \times 3 = 351$, so that there may be some 'unfortunate' numbers in this case (we do not know, all we can say is that this method of proving there are none fails).

How can we prove that there are no 'unfortunate' numbers for *all* N higher than 3?

> ✧ Remember the advice in the section VALID ARGUMENTS on page 78. Here we cannot just continue by looking at individual values of N, we need a general result.

Well, we found above that $10^{N-1} > 117N$ when $N = 4$. For higher values of N the situation gets worse: each time we increase N by 1, the value of 10^{N-1} is multiplied by 10 and the value of $117N$ is multiplied by $\frac{N+1}{N}$. But $\frac{N+1}{N} = 1 + \frac{1}{N}$ is less than 2 and is therefore certainly less than 10, so 10^{N-1} is multiplied by more than $117N$. It follows that $10^{N-1} > 117N$ for all N greater than 3.

We conclude that there are no 'unfortunate' numbers with four or more digits. We already determined that there are no 'unfortunate' numbers with one digit, so we are left with only two cases to consider: two-digit and three-digit integers.

Chapter 4: Integers

Suppose an 'unfortunate' number has two digits. Now an 'unfortunate' number is a multiple of 13 and there are only seven two-digit multiples of 13 (from $13 = 1 \times 13$ to $91 = 7 \times 13$), so it is not too difficult to check which of them satisfies the 'unfortunate' number property. However, looking at all the possibilities in this way is not really feasible for three-digit integers because there are rather more to check, so let us find another way to deal with the two-digit case.

Let the two-digit integer be '*ab*', that is, $10a + b$, where a is positive. Then the sum of the digits is $a + b$ and therefore we have

$$10a + b = 13(a + b),$$

which may be rearranged to

$$0 = 3a + 12b.$$

Since $a > 0$ and $b \geq 0$ the right-hand side is positive, so the equation has no solutions. We conclude that there are no two-digit 'unfortunate' numbers.

Now suppose an 'unfortunate' number has three digits and let the number be '*abc*', that is, $100a + 10b + c$, where a is positive. Then the sum of the digits is $a + b + c$ and therefore we have

$$100a + 10b + c = 13(a + b + c),$$

which may be rearranged to

$$87a = 3b + 12c,$$

that is,

$$29a = b + 4c.$$

But $b + 4c$ is at most $9 + 4 \times 9 = 45$, so that $29a$ is at most 45 and hence a can only be 1. As a result, we have

$$29 = b + 4c. \qquad (4.1)$$

We now need to determine which values of b and c satisfy this equation.

◇ Remember the advice in the section VALID ARGUMENTS on page 78. You may be able to *see* some solutions here, but what is needed is an argument that shows that all solutions have been found.

One way to do this, though not a very satisfactory one, is to let b, say, be 0, 1, 2, ..., 9 in turn and calculate the corresponding value of c, discarding those which are not integers between 0 and 9.

A better way is to rewrite equation (4.1) in the form

$$b - 1 = 4(7 - c).$$

Since the right-hand side is 4 times an integer we see that $b - 1$ is a multiple of 4. The values of b (as a single digit) for which this is true are 1, 5 and 9. The corresponding values of c are 7, 6 and 5, and the resulting three-digit integers are 117, 156 and 195. Checking confirms that each of these is 'unfortunate':

$$117 = 13 \times (1 + 1 + 7);$$
$$156 = 13 \times (1 + 5 + 6);$$
$$195 = 13 \times (1 + 9 + 5).$$

✦ Remember the advice in the section CHECKING on page 79.

Therefore the only 'unfortunate' numbers are 117, 156 and 195.

Exercise 4.5

C **1.** The sum of three positive integers is 11 and the sum of the cubes of these numbers is 251.
Find all such numbers.

M **2.** How many positive integers leave a remainder of 31 when divided into 2011?

C **3.** Find all possible solutions to the 'word sum' on the right.

$$\begin{array}{r} O\,D\,D \\ +\,O\,D\,D \\ \hline E\,V\,E\,N \end{array}$$

Chapter 4: Integers

Each letter stands for one of the digits 0–9 and has the same meaning each time it occurs. Different letters stand for different digits. No number starts with a zero.

C 4. The number N is the product of the first 99 positive integers. The number M is the product of the first 99 positive integers after each has been reversed. That is, for example, the reverse of 8 is 8; of 17 is 71; and of 20 is 02.

Find the exact value of $N \div M$.

C 5. Every cell of the following crossnumber is to contain a single digit. No clue has an answer starting with zero.

Prove that there is exactly one solution to the crossnumber.

ACROSS
   2. Sum of the digits of 2 Down.
   4. Prime.
   5. 1 Down + 2 Across + 3 Down.

DOWN
   1. Product of two primes.
   2. Multiple of 99.
   3. Square of 4 Across.

M 6. Consider the following three equations:

$$11 - 2 = 3^2$$
$$1111 - 22 = 33^2$$
$$111111 - 222 = 333^2$$

Prove that the pattern suggested by these three equations continues for ever.

M 7. How many solutions are there to the equation $x^2 + y^2 = x^3$, where x and y are positive integers and x is less than 2011?

C 8. If you have an endless supply of 3×2 rectangular tiles, you can place 100 tiles end to end to tile a 300×2 rectangle. Similarly, you can put k tiles side by side to tile a $3k \times 2$ rectangle.

Find the values of the integers k and m for which it is possible to tile a $6k \times m$ rectangle with 3×2 tiles.

C 9. (a) You are told that one of the integers in a list of distinct positive integers is 97 and that their average value is 47. If the sum of all the integers in the list is 329, what is the largest possible value for a number in the list?

   (b) Suppose the sum of all the numbers in the list can take any value. What would the largest possible number in the list be then?

C 10. A *qprime* number is a positive integer which is the product of exactly two different primes, that is, one of the form $q \times p$, where q and p are prime and $q \neq p$.

What is the length of the longest possible sequence of *consecutive* integers all of which are qprime numbers?

Chapter 4: Integers

H **11.** Every cell of the following crossnumber is to contain a single digit. All the digits from 1 to 9 are used.

Prove that there is exactly one solution to the crossnumber.

ACROSS
1. A multiple of 21.
4. A multiple of 21.
5. A multiple of 21.

DOWN
1. A multiple of 12.
2. A multiple of 12.
3. A multiple of 12.

1	2	3
4		
5		

M **12.** The sum of all the factors of the positive integer n, including 1 but excluding n, is written as $S(n)$. For example, $S(9) = 1 + 3 = 4$, $S(10) = 1 + 2 + 5 = 8$, $S(20) = 1 + 2 + 4 + 5 + 10 = 22$. If $S(n) > n$ then n is said to be *abundant*. So, for example, 20 is abundant but 9 and 10 are not.

(a) Find the smallest abundant positive integer.

(b) Prove that if $n = pq$, where p and q are unequal prime numbers, then n is not abundant.

(c) Prove that if m is abundant and p is a prime number which is not a factor of m then $S(pm) > (2 + p)m$.

M **13.** An artist is preparing to draw on a sheet of A4 paper (a rectangle with sides in the ratio $1 : \sqrt{2}$). The artist wishes to place a rectangular grid of squares in the centre of the paper, leaving a margin of equal width on all four sides.

Show that such an arrangement is possible for a 1×2 or a 2×3 grid but impossible for any other $g \times (g + 1)$ grid.

M **14.** Three different positive integers have the property that each of them divides the sum of the other two.

Find all such sets of three numbers.

Chapter 5

Combinatorics

Loosely speaking, combinatorics is the branch of mathematics dealing with collections of a finite number of objects determined by certain constraints, for example, the ways to write 5 as a sum of two or more positive integers, ignoring the order, such as:

$$1+1+1+1+1, \quad 1+1+1+2, \quad 1+2+2, \quad 2+3.$$

We have divided combinatorics problems into two categories: counting (or enumeration) problems; and placement problems.

5.1 General guidance

Patterns and proof

A common procedure when trying to solve a combinatorics problem is to look at some simple cases, in order to get a feel for the problem. Indeed, you may be able to "spot" a pattern in the results you obtain. Though this can help you to understand the problem, it does not constitute a proof that the pattern is always there—what you need to do is find a proof which shows that your suspected result is always true.

- ✧ always provide a proof of general results—it is not sufficient just to show the first part of a pattern and assume that it continues for ever in the same form.

Special cases

Even when you can prove a general result, there may be some special cases where either the result fails, or your proof fails. Be on the alert for these.

> ⋄ When you have derived a general result, you should check whether there are any particular cases for which your reasoning does not apply. For such cases you may be able to find another line of reasoning, or you may be able to show that the result does not hold.

Given conditions

Some special conditions, such as whether order matters, may be given explicitly in the statement of the problem. You should show why these conditions are needed when writing out your argument.

> ⋄ In a full written solution you should make clear where you make use of any specific conditions given in the question.

Working with cases

A common technique is to break a combinatorics problem down into different cases. Should you do so, you need to explain this to the reader.

> ⋄ When you are dealing with different cases, make it clear that you are doing so, In particular make clear which case you are considering.

Also, you need to be careful that you do not omit any cases, and that you do not consider a case more than once.

> ⋄ When working with cases, you should ensure that you include every case, and that you do not include any case twice. In addition, you should explain how you know that you have done so.

This particularly applies when you are simply counting, where there is a real risk of either omitting something, or of 'double counting', or both.

Diagrams

Not all combinatorics problems involve a figure, but some do, even though it may not be given in the question. In any case, some sort of diagram may help you to explain your reasoning. It is rare for anyone to criticise a solution for having too many diagrams!

- ⬥ The purpose of your diagrams is to convey information, so be sure to draw diagrams clearly and label them carefully.

- ⬥ Be prepared to draw more diagrams as your understanding of the problem develops. For example, draw separate diagrams to show the steps in your argument, especially when you are dealing with different cases.

Checking

Just as when solving any mathematical problem, it is a good idea to check that any solutions that you have obtained do actually work. Apart from confirming that you have solved the given problem, a check may reveal some special cases which need separate consideration (see above).

- ⬥ Check that any solution you obtain fits the criteria given in the original question.

5.2 Counting

CAYLEY 4   HAMILTON 4   MACLAURIN 36

Counting problems ask questions such as "How many ways ...?". This is a rather broad category, so the methods used can be very different and may sometimes even be particular to a given problem. Nevertheless, there are two helpful facts which are widely applicable.

Fact 5.2.A *Suppose that outcome A can be achieved in m ways and outcome B, unrelated to A, can be achieved in n ways. Then the number of ways that both A and B can be achieved is $m \times n$.*

For example, suppose we wish to find the number of two-digit positive integers. The first digit may be 1, 2, ..., 9 so there are 9 ways to select the first digit; the last digit may be 0, 1, ..., 9 so there are 10 ways to select the last digit. Hence there are 9×10 two-digit positive integers. (You may think of a quicker way to establish this!)

Fact 5.2.A helps to find the number of ways of ordering N different objects, because there are N ways to select the first, $N-1$ ways to select the second, and so on. This leads to the next fact.

Fact 5.2.B *The number of ways of arranging N different objects* in order *is*

$$N \times (N-1) \times (N-2) \times \cdots \times 3 \times 2 \times 1.$$

The expression $N \times (N-1) \times \cdots \times 2 \times 1$ is referred to as the *factorial* of N and is denoted $N!$. So $5!$ means $5 \times 4 \times 3 \times 2 \times 1$, which equals 120.

To see how fact 5.2.B may be used, suppose we wish to find how many four-digit numbers there are whose digits are different primes. The prime digits are 2, 3, 5 and 7, so the number of four-digit numbers of the required type is equal to the number of ways of placing these four digits in order, that is, $4 \times 3 \times 2 \times 1 = 4!$, or 24.

Techniques

✦ Consider breaking the problem into parts by looking at outcomes of different types.

For example, you may break a problem about two-digit integers into two parts by considering separately those with two digits the same, and those with unequal digits.

Example 5.2

Two points X and Y lie in a plane. Two straight lines are drawn in the plane, passing through X but not through Y. A further n straight lines are drawn in the plane, passing through Y but not through X. No line is parallel to any other line.

Find, in terms of n, the number of regions into which all $n+2$ lines divide the plane.

Discussion

Since they are not parallel the original two lines through X divide the plane into four regions, as shown in figure 5.1.

When one new line is drawn through Y, but not through X, it passes through three of these four regions, as shown in figure 5.2. The new line divides each region into two and thus the total number of regions is

Chapter 5: Combinatorics

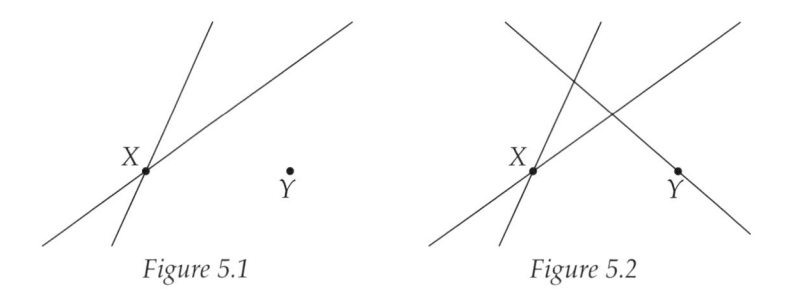

Figure 5.1   *Figure 5.2*

increased by three. Note that this statement relies on the conditions given in the question—that the lines through Y do not pass through X and that no line is parallel to any other—and without the conditions the statement would not always be true.

> ✧ Remember the advice in the section GIVEN CONDITIONS on page 102.

We could proceed to count the number of regions when the number of lines passing through Y is 2, 3, ... and so on. However, we cannot derive a general result for n by continuing to look at examples in this way; what is needed is a general argument.

> ✧ Remember the advice in the section PATTERNS AND PROOF on page 101.

We observe that every line, apart from the first, that is drawn through Y passes through four regions: it passes through one region on each side of Y and it enters one more region each time it crosses one of the two lines through X, as shown in figure 5.3. (Once again this statement relies on the conditions given in the question—that the lines through Y do not pass through X and that no line is parallel to any other.) So when such a line is drawn these four regions are each divided into two, and the total number of regions is increased by four.

To summarise:

> the original two lines through X create four regions,
>
> the first line through Y increases the total number of regions by three, and
>
> after the first, each other line through Y increases the total number of regions by four.

Figure 5.3

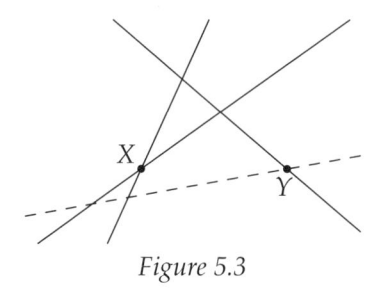

Because there are n lines altogether, the total number of regions is therefore

$$4 + 3 + (n-1) \times 4 = 4n + 3.$$

There may be a concern that this result might not hold for all values of n, in particular for $n = 0$ and 1, since these cases were treated specially in our argument (clearly $n \geq 0$ from the context of the question). It is worth checking that the result does indeed hold for $n = 0$ and 1.

✧ Remember the advice in the section SPECIAL CASES on page 102.

Exercise 5.2

C **1.** How many right-angled triangles can be made by joining three vertices of a cube?

H **2.** The eight points A, B, C, D, E, F, G and H are equally spaced on the perimeter of a circle, so that the arcs $AB, BC, CD, DE, EF, FG, GH$ and HA are all equal.

Joining any three of these points forms a triangle. How many of these triangles are right-angled?

M 3. For Erewhon's rail network, it is possible to buy only single tickets from any station on the network to any other station on the network. Each ticket shows the name of the station at which a journey starts and, below this, the name of the destination station

It is proposed to add several new stations to the network. For how many different combinations of the number of existing stations and the number of new stations will exactly 200 new types of tickets be required?

M 4. I have a large supply of 1 p, 2 p, and 3 p stamps.

(a) Explain why there are at least as many ways to make up $(N+1)$ p as there are to make up N p, for any positive integer N.

(b) Explain why the number of ways to make up $(N+1)$ p is always greater than the number of ways to make up N p.

[We consider 2 p, 1 p, 1 p to be the same way of making up 4 p as 1 p, 2 p, 1 p.]

5.3 Placement

Cayley 45   Hamilton 6   Maclaurin 6

By a placement problem we mean one which involves placing numbers into "boxes" of some sort—a Sudoku puzzle, for example. This is a broad category, including many possible types of question.

One common type of problem involves placing the numbers from 1 to n under some condition, for which the following fact may be helpful (we met this earlier, as fact 2.4.B):

Fact 5.3.A *The sum of the integers from 1 to n is equal to $\frac{1}{2}n(n+1)$.*

Techniques

This topic gives setters a lot of scope to devise original questions that require the solver to use their initiative. There may well be more than one valid approach to such problems, so it is difficult to give general advice about methods of solution, but two relevant techniques are:

- ✦ Find the total of all the numbers which have to be placed.
- ✦ Consider using algebra, but think carefully before you introduce a lot of symbols.

A good supply of diagrams or tables, where appropriate, can help you to explain your method carefully, particularly when you devise an original method of solution.

It is rarely a good idea to start solving such a problem by considering cases in turn, though you may find that towards the end of a solution you are forced to use a 'case by case' approach. However, if you find yourself considering more than a handful of cases, then you have probably missed a better method.

Example 5.3

Three chords are drawn in a circle to create seven regions, as shown.

The numbers from 1 to 7 are to be placed, one in each region, so that, for each chord, the total of the numbers in the circle on one side of the chord is equal to the total of the numbers on the other side.

How many possible values are there for the number x in the central region?

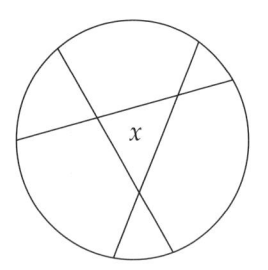

Discussion

Firstly, following the advice given above, let us find the total of all the numbers placed in the circle: $1 + 2 + \cdots + 7 = \frac{1}{2} \times 7 \times 8 = 28$. Hence the total of the numbers on each side of *every* chord is 14. (You may notice that the following argument does not make use of the actual value, 14, of this total; it merely uses the fact that all the totals are the same.)

Figure 5.4

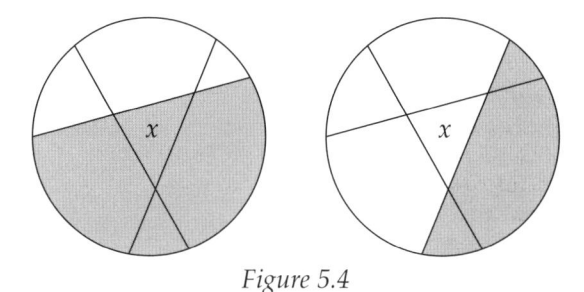

So the numbers in each of the two shaded regions shown in figure 5.4 have the same total; these two regions have the darker region shown in figure 5.5 in common.

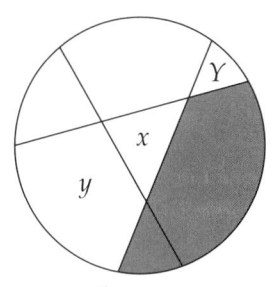

Figure 5.5

The numbers which are not in common also have equal totals, that is,

$$x + y = Y, \qquad (5.1)$$

where y and Y are the numbers indicated in figure 5.5.

There is nothing special about our choice of chords: we get a similar result to equation (5.1), that is, an equation connecting x and the two numbers on either side of x, for each of the three possible configurations shown in figure 5.6.

From these three equations we see that Y is bigger than x in each configuration, so there are at least three numbers greater than x. In other words, x is at most 4, so the possible cases are $x = 1, 2, 3$ or 4.

We need to consider each case in turn, but first notice that the largest number 7 can only be placed in one of the positions corresponding to Y. Thus in each case we can start by entering x, 7 and y, where $x + y = 7$; we have done this in figure 5.7 for the two cases $x = 3$ and $x = 1$.

Figure 5.6

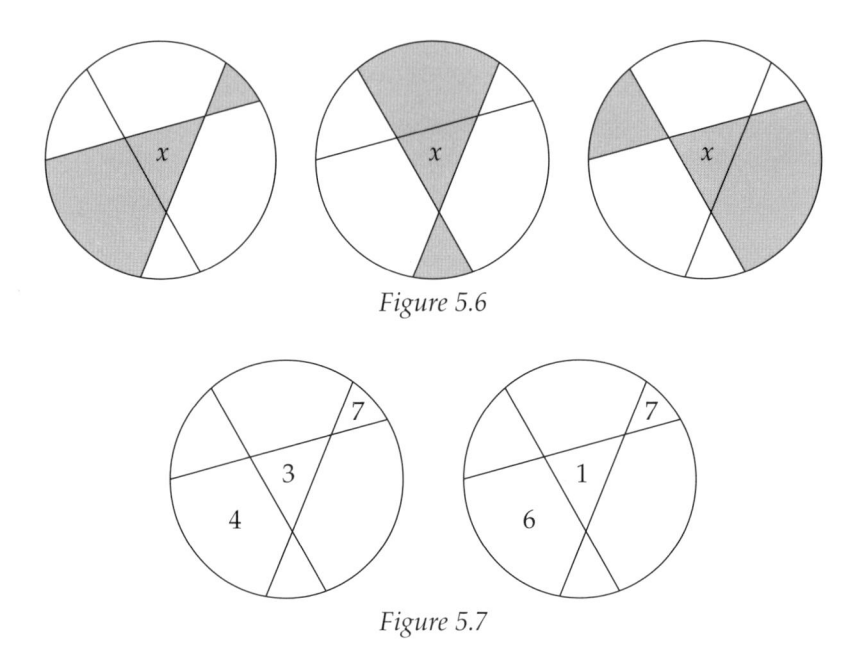

Figure 5.7

✧ Remember the advice in the section DIAGRAMS on page 102.

When $x = 3$ we see immediately that there is a difficulty: there is nowhere to place 6, because $6 = 3 + 3$ and we would have to use 3 again, which is not allowed. Therefore the case $x = 3$ is impossible.

When $x = 1$ the unused numbers are 2, 3, 4 and 5. From equation (5.1) we know we need to pair these up, as pairs (y, Y) with $1 + y = Y$. This can be achieved with the pairings $(2, 3)$ and $(4, 5)$, giving the solution shown in figure 5.8.

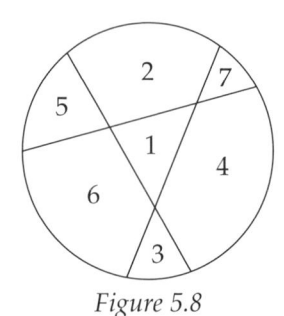

Figure 5.8

Now we have done a lot of work since using the condition given in the question—about the totals of the numbers on either side of each chord—so there may be some concern as to whether this solution really does comply with that condition. However, a simple check verifies that all the totals in figure 5.8 are indeed the same, so that 1 is a possible value for x.

✧ Remember the advice in the section CHECKING on page 103.

You should now be able to complete the solution to the problem by dealing with the two remaining cases, $x = 2$ and $x = 4$.

Exercise 5.3

C **1.** The diagram shows seven circles. Each of the three arrows indicates a 'line of three circles'.

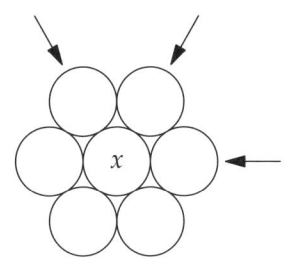

The digits from 1 to 7 inclusive are to be placed in the circles, one per circle, so that the sum of the digits in each of the three indicated 'lines of three circles' is the same.

Find all possible values of x.

C 2. The numbers 1 to 9 are to be placed in the circles in such a way that the sum of the four numbers along each side of the triangle has the same value, T, say.

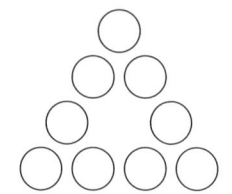

   (a) Prove that $17 \leq T \leq 23$.
   (b) Find a suitable arrangement of the numbers when $T = 23$.
   (c) Show that when $T = 20$ then there are at most 8 *different* choices for the collection of three numbers which should be placed at the vertices of the triangle.

H 3. The numbers 1 to 10 are to be placed in the unshaded boxes, so that the two rows of four boxes and the two columns of three boxes all have the same total T.

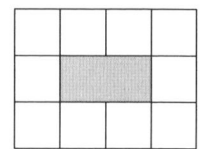

   (a) Find a solution when $T = 20$.
   (b) Find the minimum possible value of T.

H 4. Sam wishes to place all the numbers from 1 to 10 in the circles, one to each circle, so that each line of three circles has the same total.
   Prove that Sam's task is impossible.

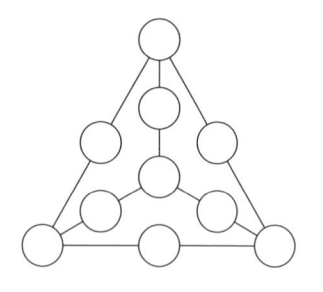

M 5. The numbers 1 to 9 are placed in the cells of a 3×3 square grid, one to each cell. In each of the four 2×2 blocks of adjacent cells, such as the one shaded, the four numbers have the same total T.
   What is the maximum possible value of T?

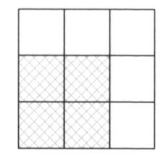

5.4 Miscellaneous problems

Cayley 356   Hamilton 56   Maclaurin 56

We gather here some questions, often harder ones, that do not fit naturally into the earlier sections of this chapter.

Fact 5.4.A *In a results table:*
   (i) the sum of the entries in the column 'Won' is equal to the sum of the entries in the column 'Lost';
   (ii) the sum of the entries in the column 'Goals for' is equal to the sum of the entries in the column 'Goals against'.

Exercise 5.4

C 1. At McBride Academy there are 300 pupils who represent the school in both summer and winter sports. In summer, 60% of these play tennis and the other 40% play badminton. In winter they play hockey or swim but not both. 56% of the hockey players play tennis in summer and 30% of the tennis players swim.

   How many pupils both swim and play badminton?

C 2. Four football teams—the Apes, the Baboons, the Chimps and the Gorillas—play each other once in a season.

   After some of the matches have been played the table of results, with some entries missing, looks like this:

Team	Played	Won	Lost	Drawn	Goals for	Goals against
A	·	0	·	0	2	3
B	·	·	·	0	·	1
C	2	·	·	·	4	·
G	·	0	·	1	·	5

   Complete the table, explaining how each entry is worked out, and find the score in each match played so far.

C 3. Teams A, B, C and D competed against each other once. The results table was as follows:

Team	Win	Draw	Loss	Goals for	Goals against
A	3	0	0	5	1
B	1	1	1	2	2
C	0	2	1	5	6
D	0	1	2	3	6

(a) Find (with proof) which team won in each of the six matches.

(b) Find (with proof) the scores in each of the six matches.

C 4. A bug starts in the small triangle T at the top of the diagram. She is allowed to eat through a neighbouring edge to get to a neighbouring small triangle. So at first there is only one possible move (downwards), and only one way to reach this new triangle.

(a) How many triangles, including T and B, must the bug visit if she is to reach the small triangle B at the bottom using a route that is as short as possible?

(b) How many different ways are there for the bug to reach B from T by a route of this shortest possible length?

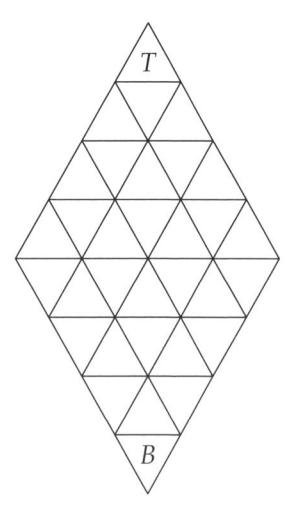

H 5. In how many distinct ways can a cubical die be numbered from 1 to 6 so that consecutive numbers are on adjacent faces? Numberings that are obtained from each other by rotation or reflection are considered indistinguishable.

Chapter 5: Combinatorics

H **6.** In the diagram, the number in each cell shows the number of adjacent (touching) cells which are shaded. The total of all the numbers for this shading pattern is 16. Any shading pattern obtained by rotating or reflecting this one also has a total of 16.

2	1	2
3	2	2
1	2	1

Prove that there are exactly two shading patterns (not counting rotations or reflections) which have a total of 17.

M **7.** A lottery involves five balls being selected from a drum. Each ball has a different positive integer printed on it.

Show that, whichever five balls are selected, it is always possible to choose three of them so that the sum of the numbers on these three balls is a multiple of 3.

M **8.** Every day for the next eleven days I shall eat exactly one sandwich for lunch, either a ham sandwich or a cheese sandwich.

However, during that period I shall never eat a ham sandwich on two consecutive days.

In how many ways can I plan my sandwiches for the next eleven days?

Appendix A

Cayley, Hamilton and Maclaurin

The three IMOK Olympiad papers are named after the notable British mathematicians Cayley, Hamilton and Maclaurin. Each year the IMOK booklet includes one of the following biographies.

Arthur Cayley

16 August 1821–26 January 1895

From a young age, Arthur Cayley showed great numerical flair and his mathematics teacher advised Cayley to continue his studies in this area, going against his father's wishes that he enter the family business.

Cayley did continue to study mathematics, at Trinity College, Cambridge, graduating in 1842. For four years he then taught at Cambridge and had 28 papers published in the *Cambridge Mathematical Journal* during this period. He then spent 14 years as a lawyer, choosing law as a profession in order to make money so he could pursue mathematics, publishing about 250 mathematical papers during this time.

In 1863, Cayley was appointed Sadleirian Professor of Pure Mathematics at Cambridge. He published over 900 papers and notes during his lifetime, covering many aspects of modern mathematics. He is remembered mainly for his work in developing the algebra of matrices and for his studies in geometry.

Around 1849 Cayley wrote a paper linking his ideas on permutations with Cauchy's. Five years later, he wrote two papers about abstract groups. At that time the only known groups were permutation groups and even these formed a radically new area, yet Cayley defined an abstract group and gave a table to display the group multiplication. He gave the 'Cayley tables' of some special permutation groups, but, much more significantly for the introduction of the abstract group concept, he realised that invertible matrices and quaternions form groups (with the usual operation of multiplication).

Cayley also developed the theory of algebraic invariance, and his development of n-dimensional geometry has been applied in physics to the study of the space-time continuum. His work on matrices served as the foundation for quantum mechanics, which was developed by Werner Heisenberg in 1925. Cayley also suggested that Euclidean and non-Euclidean geometry are special types of geometry. He united projective geometry and metrical geometry, which is dependent on sizes of angles and lengths of lines.

Sir William Rowan Hamilton

4 August 1805–2 September 1865

Hamilton was a distinguished Irish mathematician and astronomer, born and educated in Dublin. He studied classics and science at Trinity College, where he became Professor of Astronomy aged only 21. He was self-taught in mathematics, reading a Latin copy of Euclid, followed by works of Newton and then Laplace (in French).

Studying Laplace's *Mécanique Céleste* seems to have persuaded Hamilton to devote his energies to mathematics and he became one of the most original and creative mathematicians of his time, developing major ideas in optics, dynamics, algebra and graph theory. In his *Theory of Systems of Rays* (1828) he predicted the existence of conical refraction in biaxial crystals (later confirmed experimentally) and unified the field of optics under the principle of varying action. His work in dynamics has become of fundamental importance in modern physics, particularly quantum theory.

Hamilton's later years, clouded by personal problems, were largely devoted to the invention and development of his theory of quaternions. Although he thought this work would revolutionise physics, quaternions have been supplanted by the methods of vector and tensor analysis. How-

Appendix A: Cayley, Hamilton and Maclaurin

ever, Hamilton's insight opened the way for the discoveries and developments in abstract algebra that were made by later mathematicians.

The idea for quaternions occurred to Hamilton whilst he was walking with his wife along the Royal Canal in Dublin. He was so pleased with his discovery that he scratched the fundamental formula of quaternion algebra into the stone of Brougham Bridge:

$$i^2 = j^2 = k^2 = ijk = -1.$$

Hamilton's name also lives on in the field of graph theory. Given a connected network, is it possible to find a tour of the vertices which visits each vertex once and only once and returns to the starting point? For example, it can be shown that the network shown on the left of figure A.1 does not have such a *Hamiltonian circuit*. Hamilton considered the question of whether there is a tour of this kind for the network formed by the vertices and edges of a dodecahedron, the polyhedron shown on the right of figure A.1.

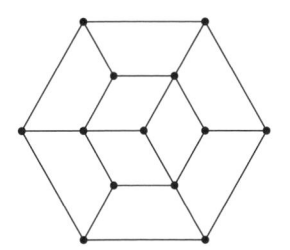

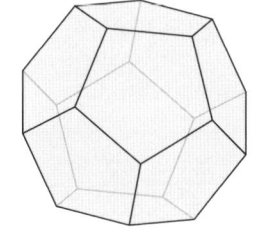

Figure A.1

Professor Colin Maclaurin

February 1698–June 1746

The most significant Scottish mathematician and physicist of the eighteenth century, Colin Maclaurin was only 11 years old when he first attended the University of Glasgow. There he came into contact with the Professor of Mathematics, Robert Simson, whose enthusiasm and interest in geometry was to influence the young boy. After graduating in 1713, Maclaurin remained in Glasgow for a further year to read divinity (it had originally been his intention to enter the Presbyterian Church). He then continued to study mathematics and divinity whilst staying with his uncle, the minister at Kilfinnan on Loch Fyne.

Maclaurin was appointed professor of mathematics at Marischal College in the University of Aberdeen in 1717. At this time his main interest was in the mathematical and physical ideas of Sir Isaac Newton; he met Newton during a visit to London in 1719, the same year that he was elected a fellow of the Royal Society. Maclaurin also did notable work in geometry, particularly higher plane curves, and his first published work was *Geometrica organica, sive descriptio linearum curvarum universalis*, published in 1720. One curve still bears his name, the *Trisectrix of Maclaurin*.

After two years spent travelling in Europe, during which he was awarded a Grand Prize by the Académie des Sciences in Paris, for his work on the impact of bodies, Maclaurin took up the post of Professor of Mathematics at the University of Edinburgh in 1725, and remained there for the rest of his career. In 1740, he again received a prize from the Académie des Sciences, this time for a study of the tides. The prize was jointly awarded to Maclaurin and two other famous mathematicians, Leonhard Euler and Daniel Bernoulli.

In 1742, Maclaurin published the *Treatise of fluxions*, in which he uses the special case of Taylor's series now named after him and for which he is best remembered today:

$$f(x) = f(0) + \frac{f'(0)}{1!}x + \frac{f''(0)}{2!}x^2 + \frac{f'''(0)}{3!}x^3 + \ldots$$

He also wrote a book of problems for students, *Ane Introduction to the Mathematicks*, one of which was used as the basis for question 2 of the 2004 Hamilton Olympiad Paper:

> Maritus, uxor, et filius habent annos 96, ita ut anni Mariti et filii, simul faciant annos uxoris + 15. Sed uxoris cum filii faciant mariti + 2.

Maclaurin defended mathematical education at universities because of its practical applications, and his own work included gravitation, astronomy, cartography, the structure of honeycombs and the measurement of the volumes of barrels. The field of actuarial science dates back to the calculations he helped to supply when one of the first pension funds was founded in 1743, the Scottish Ministers' Widows' Fund.

Appendix B

Answers to questions in the examples

Example 2.4 The conditions are $a, b \neq 0, -1$ and $a + b \neq -1$.

Example 3.2 $x = 40$ and $\angle RAQ = 40°$.

Example 3.3 $q = \dfrac{25}{4}$, $T = \dfrac{21}{2}$, $S = \dfrac{27}{2}$ and the area is $\dfrac{69}{2}$ cm^2.

Example 3.5 $r = 8 \pm 4\sqrt{3}$; only the positive value is relevant.

Example 5.3 Both $x = 2$ and $x = 4$ are possible, as shown.

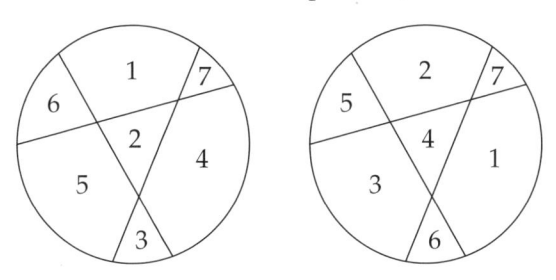

Hence there are three possible values for x.

Appendix C

Solutions to the exercises

Solutions are given for all the problems in the exercises.

The solutions are based on those given in the IMOK booklets, but may differ from them. For example, some alternative methods have been omitted, and occasionally a different approach is given. Not all the solutions given here are complete; in some cases the reader is expected to fill in the missing details.

Exercise 2.2

1. The interior small cubes of each face of the original cube, shown grey in the diagram, are those with exactly one blue face; the interior small cubes along each edge, shown white in the diagram, are those with exactly two blue faces.

Exercise 2.2 question 1

If the original cube has sides of length $(n + 2)$ cm, then there are n^2 small cubes in each face with exactly one blue face, and n small cubes along each edge with exactly two blue faces.

Since the original cube has 6 faces and 12 edges, from the information given about the numbers of each type of cube, we have $6n^2 = 10 \times 12n$, that is $n^2 - 20n = 0$, or $n(n - 20) = 0$. Hence $n = 0$ or $n = 20$.

The case $n = 0$ is not possible since the original cube has edges greater than 2 cm in length.

Therefore $n = 20$ and the edge length of the original cube is 22 cm.

2. Let there be x clownfish in the aquarium.

If 60 clownfish are added there are $x + 60$ clownfish and 340 tropical fish in total.

Since the proportion of clownfish is then doubled, we have

$$2 \times \frac{x}{280} = \frac{x + 60}{340}.$$

Multiplying both sides by 20 we get

$$\frac{x}{7} = \frac{x + 60}{17}$$

and hence

$$17x = 7(x + 60).$$

It follows that $x = 42$ and thus there are 42 clownfish in the aquarium.

3. Let the sides of the isosceles triangle have lengths s cm, t cm and t cm. Then the perimeter lengths of the triangle, parallelogram and rhombus are $(s + 2t)$ cm, $(2s + 2t)$ cm and $4t$ cm, respectively.

From the information given about the perimeters, we get the equations $2s + 2t = s + 2t + 3$ and $4t = s + 2t + 7$. The first equation shows that $s = 3$; and then the second shows that $t = 5$.

Hence the perimeter of the triangle is 13 cm.

4. FIRST SOLUTION

Since the smaller rectangles are placed together edge-to-edge, they have a side length in common. Let this side have length y and let the other sides have lengths x_1 and x_2 as shown.

Appendix C: Solutions to the exercises

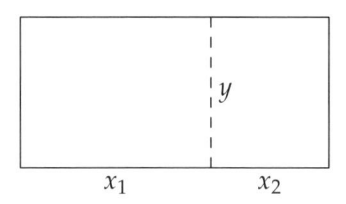

Exercise 2.2 question 4 (first solution)

The perimeters of the smaller rectangles are $2x_1 + 2y$ and $2x_2 + 2y$, so the total perimeter of the two smaller rectangles is $2x_1 + 2x_2 + 4y$. The perimeter of the large rectangle is

$$2(x_1 + x_2) + 2y = 2x_1 + 2x_2 + 2y.$$

We are given that the length of the perimeter of the large rectangle is $\frac{2}{3}$ of the total perimeter of the two original rectangles. Hence we may form the equation

$$2x_1 + 2x_2 + 2y = \tfrac{2}{3}(2x_1 + 2x_2 + 4y).$$

We may simplify this equation by multiplying both sides by 3 and expanding the brackets, to obtain

$$6x_1 + 6x_2 + 6y = 4x_1 + 4x_2 + 8y,$$

which simplifies to

$$x_1 + x_2 = y.$$

This means that the length and width of the large rectangle are the same. In other words, the rectangle is actually a square.

SECOND SOLUTION

The total perimeter length P of the original two rectangles is equal to the perimeter length of the large rectangle added to the lengths of the two edges which are joined together.

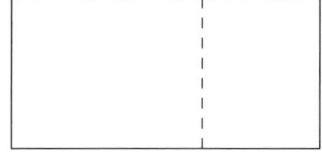

Exercise 2.2 question 4 (second solution)

But the perimeter length of the large rectangle is $\frac{2}{3}P$ and hence the two edges which are joined together have total length $\frac{1}{3}P$.

However, the two edges which are joined together are parallel to two sides of the large rectangle and have the same length as them. Hence these two sides of the large rectangle have total length $\frac{1}{3}P$.

Since the perimeter length of the large rectangle is $\frac{2}{3}P$, the other two sides of the large rectangle also have total length $\frac{1}{3}P$.

It follows that all the sides of the rectangle are equal in length, in other words, the rectangle is a square.

5. Each camper eats half a tin of soup, one third of a tin of meatballs, and a quarter of a tin of chocolate pudding. This is a total of
$$\frac{1}{2} + \frac{1}{3} + \frac{1}{4} = \frac{13}{12}$$
tins of food per person.

If there are N people, they thus use $\frac{13}{12}N$ tins of food in total. This gives us the equation
$$\frac{13N}{12} = 156,$$
or
$$N = \frac{12}{13} \times 156$$
$$= 144.$$

6. Let a be the smallest number and d be the difference between the first and second numbers. Then the other differences are $2d$, $4d$ and $8d$, so the five numbers are a, $a+d$, $a+3d$, $a+7d$ and $a+15d$.

The condition that 'the average of the five numbers is 11 more than the middle number' gives
$$\frac{5a + 26d}{5} = a + 3d + 11,$$
which means that $d = 5$.

The condition that 'the sum of the second and fourth numbers is equal to the largest number' now gives
$$2a + 8d = a + 15d$$
and hence $a = 35$.

Appendix C: Solutions to the exercises

So the five numbers are 35, 40, 50, 70 and 110.

REMARK
Slightly neater algebra is obtained if instead we define a and d so that the numbers are represented as $a - 3d$, $a - 2d$, a, $a + 4d$ and $a + 12d$.

7. Let the distance from home to town be D km. Now in every minute Eoin travels one-fortieth of the way to town: that is, a distance of $\frac{1}{40}D$ km. So after t minutes, he has travelled a distance
$$\frac{tD}{40} \text{ km.}$$
Similarly, in every minute Angharad travels one-sixtieth of the way to town: that is, a distance of $\frac{1}{60}D$ km. But she has had 12 minutes extra walking time. So after Eoin has been walking for t minutes, she has been walking for $t + 12$ minutes and so has travelled a distance
$$\frac{(t+12)D}{60} \text{ km.}$$
We are asked how long Eoin has been walking when they meet. They meet when they have travelled equal distances, which is when
$$\frac{tD}{40} = \frac{(t+12)D}{60}.$$
We cancel the Ds from each side (note that $D \neq 0$) and multiply both sides by 120 to obtain
$$120 \times \frac{t}{40} = 120 \times \frac{t+12}{60}.$$
Simplifying, we get
$$3t = 2(t+12),$$
which we solve to give $t = 24$.

Thus Eoin catches Angharad after he has walked for 24 minutes.

8. Because s is odd, the middle unit square lies on both diagonals. So the number of discarded squares which lie on a diagonal is $s + (s-1) = 2s - 1$.

The number of squares left on each edge is now $s - 2$ so the total number of discarded squares is
$$2s - 1 + 4(s-2) = 6s - 9.$$

Therefore the number of unit squares remaining is
$$s^2 - (6s - 9) = s^2 - 6s + 9 = (s-3)^2.$$

9. FIRST SOLUTION

Let there be R red balls and G green balls in the bag. Then the volunteers remove $\frac{2}{5}R$ red balls and $\frac{3}{7}G$ green balls.

Since the same number of balls of each colour are removed, $\frac{2}{5}R = \frac{3}{7}G$. Rearranging, we get $G = \frac{14}{15}R$.

The fraction of balls contained in the bucket is
$$\frac{\frac{3}{5}R + \frac{4}{7}G}{R + G}$$
and substituting for G gives
$$\frac{\frac{3}{5}R + \frac{8}{15}R}{R + \frac{14}{15}R}$$

Cancelling R and simplifying, we find that $\frac{17}{29}$ is the fraction of balls contained in the bucket.

SECOND SOLUTION

Let n be the number of volunteers, so that n red balls and n green balls are removed. Hence the total number of red balls is $\frac{5}{2}n$ and the total number of green balls is $\frac{7}{3}n$, a total of $\frac{29}{6}n$.

Therefore the number of balls contained in the bucket is $\frac{29}{6}n - 2n = \frac{17}{6}n$, that is, $\frac{17}{29}$ of all the balls.

THIRD SOLUTION

If $\frac{2}{5}$ of the red balls are removed then this is equivalent to removing $\frac{6}{15}$ of the red balls.

Similarly, if $\frac{3}{7}$ of the green balls are removed then this is equivalent to removing $\frac{6}{14}$ of the green balls.

Now consider the schematic diagram, showing the proportions of the balls.

Since the same numbers of red and green balls are removed, the units of proportion are equal. Hence the fraction of all the balls contained in the bucket is
$$\frac{9+8}{15+14} = \frac{17}{29}.$$

Appendix C: Solutions to the exercises

	Removed	Remaining	Total
Red	6	9	15
Green	6	8	14

Exercise 2.2 question 9 (third solution)

10. Let n be the number of times the mathematician has filled the bottle from the tap.

    Consider the final mixture in the container. There is 1 litre of orange squash plus $\frac{1}{2}n$ litres of water so the final mixture contains $1 + \frac{1}{2}n$ litres.

    Since 10% of the final mixture is 1 litre of orange squash, we have
    $$\tfrac{1}{10}\left(1 + \tfrac{1}{2}n\right) = 1.$$
    Hence $n = 18$, so the mathematician has filled the bottle 18 times.

11. (a) The angle between the hands of the clock at two o'clock is $60°$.

    (b) FIRST SOLUTION

    The next time after two o'clock that the angles between the hands is $60°$ is when the minute hand has rotated $120°$ more than the minute hand. Let this be at a time x minutes after two o'clock.

    Now the minute hand rotates $360°$ in 60 minutes, that is, $6°$ per minute. So in x minutes it rotates $6x°$.

    The hour hand rotates $30°$ in 60 minutes, that is, $\frac{1}{2}°$ per minute. So in x minutes it rotates $\frac{1}{2}x°$.

    Therefore
    $$6x - \tfrac{1}{2}x = 120$$
    and so
    $$\frac{11x}{2} = 120,$$
    that is,
    $$x = \frac{240}{11}$$
    $$= 21\tfrac{9}{11}.$$
    So the required time is $21\frac{9}{11}$ minutes after 2 o'clock.

SECOND SOLUTION

The difference between the angles turned through by the two hands of the clock in one hour is 330°. So the time taken for the minute hand to rotate 120° more than the hour hand is

$$\frac{120}{330} \text{ hour} = \frac{4}{11} \text{ hour} = 21 \text{ minutes.}$$

So the required time is $21\frac{9}{11}$ minutes after 2 o'clock.

12. After the spider begins the second stage of its journey, 20 minutes pass before the end. In that time the minute hand moves through 120°. The spider thus moves through 480°. This implies that the spider is moving four times as fast as the minute hand.

After the spider begins the second stage of its journey, let the minute hand move through $x°$. The spider thus moves through $(180 - x)°$ in the same time.

Because the spider is four times as quick as the minute hand, we have $180 - x = 4x$ and so $x = 36$. Hence the total angle that the minute hand sweeps out is $36° + 120° = 156°$, which corresponds to 26 minutes.

Therefore at the end of the spider's journey the clock reads 6:26.

Appendix C: Solutions to the exercises 131

Exercise 2.3

1. Let Mars, Venus and Pluto have ages m, v and p respectively. Then we have the three equations
$$m + v + p = 192,$$
$$m + p = 30 + v \quad \text{and}$$
$$v + p = 4 + m.$$
After subtraction, the first and second equations give $v = 162 - v$, so that $v = 81$.

Similarly, the first and third equations give $m = 188 - m$, so that $m = 94$.

Substituting these values into the first equation, we obtain $p = 17$.

Hence Mars, Venus and Pluto are 94, 81 and 17 years old, respectively.

2. Let Julie and Garron have £J and £G respectively.

From the information in the question we may form the equations
$$J - 12 = 2(G + 12) \tag{1}$$
$$J + 12 = 3(G - 12). \tag{2}$$
Subtracting equation (1) from equation (2) gives $24 = 3G - 36 - 2G - 24$, thus $G = 84$.

Substituting into equation (1) then gives $J - 12 = 2(84 + 12) = 192$, therefore $J = 204$.

Hence Julie has £204 and Garron has £84.

3. We write B for the price of a loaf of bread in pence, M for the price of a carton of milk in pence, and J for the price of a jar of jam in pence.

Then we can interpret the given information as saying
$$3B + 5M + 4J = 1010$$
$$\text{and} \quad 5B + 9M + 7J = 1820.$$
If we double the first equation we get
$$6B + 10M + 8J = 2020,$$

and if we then subtract the second equation from this we get
$$B + M + J = 200,$$
or, in words, that the total cost of a loaf of bread, a carton of milk and a jar of jam is £2.

4. Let the cost of a Fudge Bar be F pence, the cost of a Sparkle be S pence and the cost of a Chomper be C pence.
Then,
$$4F + S + C = 100 \tag{1}$$
$$2F + S + 3C = 70 \tag{2}$$
$$F + 2S = 50. \tag{3}$$

Subtracting equation (2) from three times equation (1) we get
$$10F + 2S = 230. \tag{4}$$

Now subtracting equation (4) from ten times equation (3) we obtain $18S = 270$, and hence $S = 15$.

Thus a Sparkle costs 15 p. (A Fudge Bar costs 20 p and a Chomper costs 5 p.)

5. Let x p, y p and z p be the costs on Monday of a banana, lemon and orange respectively. Let the common reduced amount on Tuesday be r p.
From the given information, we have
$$3x = y + z, \tag{1}$$
$$2(z - r) = 3(x - r) + y - r \tag{2}$$
$$\text{and} \quad \tfrac{1}{2}(y - r) = 5 \tag{3}$$

Expanding equation (2), we get $2z - 2r = 3x - 3r + y - r$, so that $2z = 3x - 2r + y$.

Substituting for $3x$ from equation (1), we obtain $2z = y + z - 2r + y$, and hence $z = 2y - 2r = 2(y - r)$.

But $y - r = 10$ from equation (3), thus $z = 2 \times 10 = 20$.

Hence the cost of an orange on Monday was 20 p.

6. Adding the two equations yields the equation $2x^2 = 2x$, which we may rearrange to give $x(x - 1) = 0$ and so either $x = 0$ or $x = 1$.

Substituting $x = 0$ into the first equation we get $y^2 = y$ and so $y = 0$ or $y = 1$.

Substituting $x = 1$ into the first equation we get $y^2 = -y$ and so $y = 0$ or $y = -1$.

The four possible solutions are therefore $(0,0)$, $(0,1)$, $(1,0)$ and $(1,-1)$, all of which satisfy both equations.

7. There are three equations here but four unknown values, a, b, c and d. Thus it is not possible just to solve the equations to find the values of a, b, c and d. What we can do is to find relationships between them and then deduce possible values of a, b, c and d.

From the given information,

$$a + b = \tfrac{1}{2}(c + d) \tag{1}$$
$$a + c = 2(b + d) \tag{2}$$
$$a + d = \tfrac{3}{2}(b + c). \tag{3}$$

We may proceed in various ways; we show two methods, substitution and elimination.

FIRST METHOD: SUBSTITUTION

From (1), we have

$$a = -b + \tfrac{1}{2}(c + d). \tag{4}$$

Substituting in (2), we get

$$-b + \tfrac{1}{2}(c + d) + c = 2(b + d)$$

and hence

$$\tfrac{3}{2}c - \tfrac{3}{2}d = 3b,$$

that is,

$$c - d = 2b. \tag{5}$$

Substituting from (4) in (3), we get

$$-b + \tfrac{1}{2}(c + d) + d = \tfrac{3}{2}(b + c)$$

so that

$$-c + \tfrac{3}{2}d = \tfrac{5}{2}b. \tag{6}$$

Now adding (5) and (6) we obtain

$$\tfrac{1}{2}d = \tfrac{9}{2}b$$

and hence
$$d = 9b.$$

Once we have minimised $b + d$, then we automatically minimise $a + c$, because of equation (2), and hence minimise the sum we are interested in.

Since b and d are positive integers, $b = 1$ and $d = 9$ are the smallest possible values with $d = 9b$. From (5) and (4), we see that the corresponding values of c and a are $c = 11$ and $a = 9$, both of which are also positive integers, as required.

Checking these values in (1) to (3), we confirm that they are valid solutions of the given equations.

Hence the smallest possible value of $a + b + c + d$ is 30.

SECOND METHOD: ELIMINATION

We may rearrange the three equations (1), (2) and (3) to give

$$2a + 2b = c + d \tag{7}$$
$$a + c = 2b + 2d \tag{8}$$
$$2a + 2d = 3b + 3c. \tag{9}$$

Adding (7) and (8), we get
$$3a + 2b + c = 2b + c + 3d$$
and hence
$$a = d.$$

Then (7) and (9) may be rewritten
$$2b - c + d = 0 \tag{10}$$
and
$$3b + 3c - 4d = 0. \tag{11}$$

Now adding $3 \times$ (10) and (11), we obtain
$$9b - d = 0$$
and hence
$$d = 9b.$$

The solution now proceeds in the same way as the first method.

Appendix C: Solutions to the exercises

8. It is worth beginning with the observation that none of x, y or z can be zero, since that would immediately invalidate the equations. This allows us, in subsequent work, to cancel a factor of x, y or z from both sides of an equation. Note also that we may not assume that x, y or z are whole numbers.

FIRST SOLUTION

Label the equations as follows:

$$\frac{5xy}{x+y} = 6 \tag{1}$$

$$\frac{4xz}{x+z} = 3 \tag{2}$$

$$\frac{3yz}{y+z} = 2. \tag{3}$$

From (1),
$$5xy = 6x + 6y$$
and from (2),
$$8xz = 6x + 6z,$$
so
$$5xy - 8xz = 6y - 6z. \tag{4}$$

We can, however, also deduce from (1) and (2) that
$$\frac{5xy}{x+y} = \frac{8xz}{x+z},$$
so, cancelling x,
$$5y(x+z) = 8z(x+y)$$
and therefore
$$5xy - 8xz = 3yz. \tag{5}$$

But, from (3),
$$3yz = 2y + 2z. \tag{6}$$

Putting (4), (5) and (6) together, we have
$$6y - 6z = 2y + 2z$$

and so
$$y = 2z.$$
Now, substituting $y = 2z$ in (3) and cancelling z, we have
$$\frac{6z}{3} = 2,$$
so $z = 1$ and $y = 2$. Then $x = 3$, using (5), for example.

Note that it is now necessary to check that this triple of values works for all the equations. All we have shown so far is that, if the equations are true, then the only possible values of x, y and z are 3, 2 and 1; this does not mean that, if x, y and z are 3, 2 and 1, then the equations are true—for example, the equations may have *no* solutions.

SECOND SOLUTION

Since none of x, y or z is zero, we can define
$$a = \frac{1}{x}, \; b = \frac{1}{y} \text{ and } c = \frac{1}{z}.$$
By taking the reciprocals of the three equations, we obtain
$$b + a = \tfrac{5}{6}$$
$$a + c = \tfrac{4}{3}$$
$$c + b = \tfrac{3}{2}.$$
Hence, by adding, we deduce that
$$a + b + c = \frac{11}{6},$$
so $c = 1$, $b = \tfrac{1}{2}$ and $a = \tfrac{1}{3}$. Therefore $x = 3$, $y = 2$ and $z = 1$.

Again we should check these values satisfy the original equations, or show that our logic is reversible.

9. 'Substitution' is one of the standard methods of solving simultaneous equations: use one equation to find an expression for one unknown, then substitute this expression into the other equation, thereby forming a single equation in just one of the unknowns. Though it is possible to use a substitution method straight away here, the algebra is rather unpleasant, so we demonstrate two other approaches.

Appendix C: Solutions to the exercises

In passing, we note that the question places no restrictions on x and y. In particular, we cannot assume that they are integers.

METHOD 1

Adding the two given equations, we get
$$x + y + x^2 + 2xy + y^2 = 6$$
so that
$$(x+y)^2 + (x+y) - 6 = 0,$$
which factorises to give
$$(x+y-2)(x+y+3) = 0.$$
Hence
$$x+y = 2 \quad \text{or} \quad x+y = -3. \qquad (1)$$

Also, subtracting the two given equations, we get
$$x - y + x^2 - y^2 = 12$$
which factorises to give
$$(x-y) + (x-y)(x+y) = 12$$
so that
$$(x-y)(1+x+y) = 12.$$
Hence, using (1),
$$x - y = 4 \quad \text{or} \quad x - y = -6, \qquad (2)$$
which occur when $x+y = 2$ and $x+y = -3$ respectively.

We can now solve equations (1) and (2) by, for example, adding and subtracting, to obtain
$$(x,y) = (3,-1) \text{ or } \left(-\tfrac{9}{2}, \tfrac{3}{2}\right).$$
We now need to check whether these two pairs of values really do satisfy the equations given in the question. Each of them does, so the required solutions are $x = 3, y = -1$ and $x = -\tfrac{9}{2}, y = \tfrac{3}{2}$.

METHOD 2

Factorise each of the given equations to give
$$x(1+y+x) = 9 \qquad (3)$$
$$\text{and} \quad y(1+x+y) = -3. \qquad (4)$$

Since no side of either equation is zero, we may divide equation (3) by (4) to obtain $\frac{x}{y} = -3$, so that $x = -3y$. Now substitute this expression for x into equation (4) to get
$$y(1 - 2y) = -3,$$
which may be rearranged to give
$$2y^2 - y - 3 = 0,$$
or
$$(y + 1)(2y - 3) = 0.$$
Therefore $y = -1$ or $y = \frac{3}{2}$ and, since $x = -3y$, we have solutions
$$(x, y) = (3, -1) \text{ or } \left(-\frac{9}{2}, \frac{3}{2}\right).$$
We now need to check whether these two pairs of values really do satisfy the equations given in the question. Each of them does, so the required solutions are $x = 3$, $y = -1$ and $x = -\frac{9}{2}$, $y = \frac{3}{2}$.

10. **FIRST SOLUTION**

We may rewrite the given equations by factorising the left-hand sides:
$$(x - y)(x + y) = -5 \qquad (1)$$
$$(2x - y)(x + y) = 5. \qquad (2)$$
Since -5 is non-zero, we may divide equation (2) by equation (1) to get
$$\frac{2x - y}{x - y} = -1,$$
which may be rearranged to give
$$2x - y = y - x$$
and hence
$$x = \tfrac{2}{3}y.$$
Now substitute $x = \tfrac{2}{3}y$ in $x^2 - y^2 = -5$ to obtain
$$\tfrac{4}{9}y^2 - y^2 = -5,$$
so that
$$y^2 = 9$$

Appendix C: Solutions to the exercises

and hence
$$y = \pm 3.$$
Since $x = \frac{2}{3}y$ we deduce that $x = 2, y = 3$ or $x = -2, y = -3$. We confirm that both of these are indeed solutions by checking in the original equations.

SECOND SOLUTION

The given equations are
$$x^2 - y^2 = -5 \tag{3}$$
$$2x^2 + xy - y^2 = 5. \tag{4}$$

Adding (3) and (4) we get
$$3x^2 + xy - 2y^2 = 0$$
which may be factorised to give
$$(3x - 2y)(x + y) = 0.$$
Hence $x = \frac{2}{3}y$ or $x = -y$. But, from equation (3), we know that $x \neq -y$ so we have $x = \frac{2}{3}y$.

Substitute $x = \frac{2}{3}y$ in (3) to obtain
$$\tfrac{4}{9}y^2 - y^2 = -5,$$
so that
$$y^2 = 9$$
and hence
$$y = \pm 3.$$
Since $x = \frac{2}{3}y$ we deduce that $x = 2, y = 3$ or $x = -2, y = -3$. We confirm that both of these are indeed solutions by checking in the original equations.

11. The cubic equation factorises as $(x + y)(x^2 - xy + y^2) = 9$. Replacing $x + y$ by 3 we get $3(x^2 - xy + y^2) = 9$ and so $x^2 - xy + y^2 = 3$.

Now, substitute $y = 3 - x$ into this quadratic and simplify to obtain $x^2 - 3x + 2 = 0$, from which $(x - 1)(x - 2) - 0$.

Therefore, x can either equal 1 or 2, in which case y will equal 2 or 1 respectively. Checking in the given equations, we confirm that both of these are indeed solutions.

The full solution is therefore $(x, y) = (1, 2)$ or $(2, 1)$.

12. FIRST SOLUTION

Let the heights in cm of Anne, Bob, Claire and Duncan be a, b, c, d respectively.

Then $a = c + 8$ and $b = d - 4$. We know that neither Anne nor Duncan is the shortest of the four and also that neither Claire nor Bob is the tallest. So the possible pairings of the tallest and shortest of the friends are Anne and Bob, Anne and Claire, Duncan and Bob, Duncan and Claire.

    Case (i) Anne is the tallest and Bob is the shortest.
        This gives the equation $a + b = c + d + 2$. Substituting for a and b we get $c + 8 + d - 4 = c + d + 2$, which is not possible.

    Case (ii) Anne is the tallest and Claire is the shortest.
        This gives the equation $a + c = b + d + 2$. Also, $a + b + c + d = 672$, so we may deduce that $b + d = 335$ and that $a + c = 337$. Hence $a = 172\frac{1}{2}$, $b = 165\frac{1}{2}$, $c = 164\frac{1}{2}$, $d = 169\frac{1}{2}$. These values are consistent with all the information given.

    Case (iii) Duncan is the tallest and Bob is the shortest.
        This gives the equation $d + b = a + c + 2$. Also, $a + b + c + d = 672$, so we may deduce that $b + d = 337$ and that $a + c = 335$. Hence $a = 171\frac{1}{2}$, $b = 166\frac{1}{2}$, $c = 163\frac{1}{2}$, $d = 170\frac{1}{2}$. However, these values are not consistent with Duncan being the tallest and Bob the shortest, so a contradiction exists and this case is not possible.

    Case (iv) Duncan is the tallest and Claire is the shortest.
        This gives the equation $c + d = a + b + 2$. Substituting for a and b we get $c + d = c + 8 + d - 4 + 2$, which is not possible.

So only one of the four cases leads to values of a, b, c, d which are consistent with the information given and we conclude that the heights of Anne, Bob, Claire and Duncan are 1 m $72\frac{1}{2}$ cm, 1 m $65\frac{1}{2}$ cm, 1 m $64\frac{1}{2}$ cm and 1 m $69\frac{1}{2}$ cm respectively.

Appendix C: Solutions to the exercises

SECOND SOLUTION

Let the heights in cm of Anne, Bob, Claire and Duncan be a, b, c, d respectively. From the information in the question,

$$a + b + c + d = 672$$
$$a - c = 8$$
$$d - b = 4,$$

and adding these equations gives

$$2(a + d) = 684.$$

Hence $a + d = 342$ and $b + c = 330$. Now let the heights of the tallest and shortest be t cm and s cm, respectively. Then, from the given information, $(t + s) + (t + s - 2) = 672$, so that $t + s = 337$. One of Anne and Duncan is the tallest, so that a, d are $t, 342 - t$ in either order. Similarly, b, c are $s, 330 - s$ in either order, that is, $337 - t$ and $t - 7$.

Noting that $t - (t - 7) = 7$, which therefore cannot be $a - c$ or $d - b$, we deduce that $t - (337 - t)$ is either $a - c$ or $d - b$, that is 8 or 4. Hence $2t - 337 = 8$ or $2t - 337 = 4$ and so $t = \frac{341}{2}$ or $\frac{345}{2}$.

But in the first case t is less than $342 - t$, which is not possible.

In the second case, the heights of Anne, Bob, Claire and Duncan are $172\frac{1}{2}$ cm, $165\frac{1}{2}$ cm, $164\frac{1}{2}$ cm and $169\frac{1}{2}$ cm, respectively.

13. We may write the first equation as

$$(x - y)(x + y)(x^2 + y^2) = 5$$

which may be simplified to give

$$(x - y)(x^2 + y^2) = 5 \qquad (1)$$

since $x + y = 1$ from the second equation.

We now substitute $y = 1 - x$ from the second equation into equation (1) to get

$$(2x - 1)(x^2 + 1 - 2x + x^2) = 5.$$

Expanding and simplifying, we obtain

$$2x^3 - 3x^2 + 2x - 3 = 0,$$

the left-hand side of which may be factorised to give
$$(2x - 3)(x^2 + 1) = 0.$$
Therefore the only real solution is $x = \frac{3}{2}$, since $x^2 + 1 > 0$ for all real x, and the corresponding value of y is $-\frac{1}{2}$.

On checking, we see that these values satisfy the given equations. We conclude that $(\frac{3}{2}, -\frac{1}{2})$ is the only real solution of the given equations.

Exercise 2.4

1. (a) $1, 2, 2, 1, \frac{1}{2}$.
    (b) The sequence is $1, 2, 2, 1, \frac{1}{2}, \frac{1}{2}, 1, 2, \ldots$ and so repeats every six terms. Hence the fiftieth term equals the second, which is 2.
    (c) If the first two terms are a and b (neither of them zero), then the sequence is
    $$a, b, \frac{b}{a}, \frac{1}{a}, \frac{1}{b}, \frac{a}{b}, a, b, \ldots,$$
    which also repeats every six terms. If $a = b = 1$ then the sequence is constant.
    Note that if either of the first two terms is zero then the sequence is undefined.

2. Let a be the first term of the sequence and b the second term.
    Thus the first eight terms of the sequence are:
    $$a, b, a+b, 2a+b, 2a+2b, 3a+3b, 5a+4b, 7a+6b.$$
    The seventh term equals the eighth term, hence $5a + 4b = 7a + 6b$.
    Therefore $2a + 2b = 0$ and so $a = -b$.
    Hence the value of the sixth term is $3a + 3b = -3b + 3b = 0$.

3. (a) Let t_n denote the nth term of the sequence. Then $t_1 = 3$; $t_2 = 1 - \frac{1}{3} = \frac{2}{3}$; $t_3 = 1 - \frac{3}{2} = -\frac{1}{2}$; $t_4 = 1 - \left(-\frac{2}{1}\right) = 3$. Thus the sequence repeats itself every three terms and $t_5 = t_2 = \frac{2}{3}$; $t_6 = t_3 = -\frac{1}{2}$.
    (b) When $t_1 = x$, we have
    $$t_2 = 1 - \frac{1}{x} = \frac{x-1}{x}$$
    $$t_3 = 1 - \frac{x}{x-1} = \frac{-1}{x-1}$$
    $$t_4 = 1 - \frac{x-1}{-1} = x.$$
    Thus every such sequence repeats itself every three terms and
    $$t_5 = \frac{x-1}{x};$$

$$t_6 = \frac{-1}{x-1}.$$

(c) The product of the first three terms is

$$x \times \frac{x-1}{x} \times \frac{-1}{x-1} = -1.$$

Similarly, the product of the next three terms is -1, and so on. Thus the product of the first 100 terms is $(-1)^{33} \times x = -x$.

4. (a) If the first term in the sequence is c, then the second term is

$$\frac{c+3}{c-1}.$$

If we let these two terms be equal, then

$$c = \frac{c+3}{c-1},$$

which can be rearranged to give

$$c^2 - 2c - 3 = 0,$$

that is,

$$(c-3)(c+1) = 0.$$

Hence $c = -1$ or $c = 3$.

(b) The question states that the first term of the sequence is not 1. For some later term of the sequence to equal 1 there would have to exist a value of x for which

$$\frac{x+3}{x-1} = 1,$$

that is,

$$x + 3 = x - 1.$$

It is clear that this equation has no solutions, so it is not possible for any term in the sequence to be equal to 1.

Appendix C: Solutions to the exercises

Exercise 2.5

1. Divide the region into three rectangles, as shown. Let the central shaded rectangle have height h cm, so that its dimensions are h cm × 1 cm.

   Then from the perimeter of the figure, we have $8a + 2h - 6 = 72$. Hence
   $$h = 39 - 4a. \qquad (1)$$

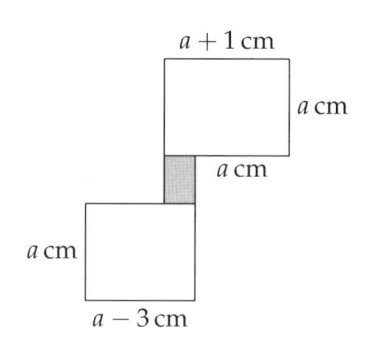

   From the area of the figure, we have
   $$(a+1) \times a + 1 \times h + (a-3) \times a = 147.$$
   Substituting for h from equation (1), we get
   $$a^2 + a + 39 - 4a + a^2 - 3a = 147,$$
   which may be simplified to give
   $$2a^2 - 6a - 108 = 0,$$
   that is,
   $$a^2 - 3a - 54 = 0,$$
   so that
   $$(a-9)(a+6) = 0.$$
   Hence $a = 9$ or $a = -6$, but the latter is not possible because a is positive. So $a = 9$.

2. FIRST SOLUTION

   Let the distance cycled to the house be d km; let the time taken on the journey there be t_1 hours and let the time taken on the way back be t_2 hours.

   From the given information about average speeds,
   $$12 = \frac{d}{t_1}$$
   and
   $$15 = \frac{2d}{t_1 + t_2}.$$

These equations may be rearranged to give
$$12t_1 = d \qquad (1)$$
and
$$15t_1 + 15t_2 = 2d. \qquad (2)$$
Substituting from equation (1) into equation (2), we get
$$15t_1 + 15t_2 = 24t_1$$
so that
$$t_1 = \tfrac{5}{3}t_2.$$
Then equation (1) gives
$$12 \times \tfrac{5}{3}t_2 = d,$$
and hence
$$20 = \frac{d}{t_2}.$$
Thus the average speed cycling home is 20 km/h.

SECOND SOLUTION

Let the distance cycled to the house be d km; let the average speed for the journey home be v km/h.
Then from the information given
$$\text{the time for the outward journey} = \frac{d}{12} \text{ hours,}$$
$$\text{the time for the homeward journey} = \frac{d}{v} \text{ hours,}$$
$$\text{and the time for the whole journey} = \frac{2d}{15} \text{ hours.}$$
Therefore we have
$$\frac{d}{12} + \frac{d}{v} = \frac{2d}{15},$$
which may be rearranged to give
$$\frac{1}{v} = \frac{2}{15} - \frac{1}{12}$$
$$= \frac{8-5}{60}$$

Appendix C: Solutions to the exercises

$$= \frac{1}{20}.$$

Hence $v = 20$ and the average speed cycling home is 20 km/h.

3. Let the shortest side of the right-angled triangle be a and let the difference between successively increasing sides be d. The remaining two sides will therefore have lengths $a + d$ and $a + 2d$.

   Using Pythagoras' theorem, we have
   $$(a + 2d)^2 = (a + d)^2 + a^2.$$

   Expanding the brackets, we get
   $$a^2 + 4ad + 4d^2 = a^2 + 2ad + d^2 + a^2,$$

   which, after simplification, becomes
   $$a^2 - 2ad - 3d^2 = 0.$$

   The left-hand side may be factorised to obtain
   $$(a - 3d)(a + d) = 0$$

   and so either $a = 3d$ or $a = -d$.

   All lengths are positive and hence $a = 3d$.

   The three sides of the triangle are therefore $3d$, $4d$ and $5d$, which are in the ratio $3 : 4 : 5$, as required.

   REMARK

   Slightly simpler equations result if the original sides are taken to be $a - d$, a and $a + d$.

4. Let there be r red socks and $44 - r$ black socks.

   To pick a non-matching pair, I would either have to choose a red followed by a black or *vice-versa*. The probability of choosing a red and then a black is
   $$\frac{r}{44} \times \frac{44 - r}{43}$$
   and the probability of choosing a black and then a red is
   $$\frac{44 - r}{44} \times \frac{r}{43}.$$

These two probabilities are identical, and hence the probability of picking a non-matching pair is
$$\frac{2r(44-r)}{44 \times 43} = \frac{192}{473}.$$
This equation may be simplified to give
$$r(44-r) = 384,$$
that is,
$$r^2 - 44r + 384 = 0.$$
After factorising, we obtain
$$(r-12)(r-32) = 0$$
and so $r = 12$ or $r = 32$.

In other words, there are either 12 or 32 red socks.

Notice that these two solutions are symmetrical; I must have 12 socks of one colour and 32 of the other.

5. Let the height of each candle be h cm. In one hour the first candle will burn $\frac{1}{10}h$ cm and the second candle will burn $\frac{1}{8}h$ cm. Thus in t hours, the candles will burn
$$\frac{ht}{10} \text{ cm} \quad \text{and} \quad \frac{ht}{8} \text{ cm,}$$
respectively.

If both candles are lit at midday, then t hours after midday the heights of the first and second candles will be
$$\left(h - \frac{ht}{10}\right) \text{ cm} \quad \text{and} \quad \left(h - \frac{ht}{8}\right) \text{ cm,}$$
respectively.

We are asked to find the time at which the height of the first candle is twice the height of the second candle. We therefore need to find the value of t such that
$$h - \frac{ht}{10} = 2\left(h - \frac{ht}{8}\right).$$

We may divide every term by h, since we know that h is not zero, and expand the brackets to obtain the equation
$$1 - \frac{t}{10} = 2 - \frac{t}{4}.$$
Multiplying both sides by 20, we get
$$20 - 2t = 40 - 5t,$$
and so
$$t = \frac{20}{3}$$
$$= 6\tfrac{2}{3}.$$

Hence the height of the first candle is twice that of the second after 6 hours and 40 minutes, in other words, this happens at 18:40.

6. Let there be x dogs and y cats in the town.

   Then the number of dogs who think they are cats is $\tfrac{1}{10}x$, and the number of cats who think they are cats is $\tfrac{9}{10}y$.

   Therefore, from the information given,
   $$\frac{x}{10} + \frac{9y}{10} = \frac{x+y}{5},$$
   that is,
   $$x + 9y = 2x + 2y,$$
   that is,
   $$x = 7y.$$
   So $\tfrac{1}{8}$ of the cats and dogs in the town are cats and the required percentage is $12\tfrac{1}{2}\%$.

7. Let the speed at which Inzamam walks be v miles per minute. Hence Inzamam runs at a speed of $2v$ miles per minute.

   Let the time taken on Monday be t minutes, so that the time taken on Tuesday is $t - 6$ minutes.

   Let the distance to school be s miles.

   Hence on Monday
   $$s = \tfrac{2}{3}t \times v + \tfrac{1}{3}t \times 2v$$
   $$= \tfrac{4}{3}tv$$

and on Tuesday
$$s = \tfrac{2}{3}(t-6) \times 2v + \tfrac{1}{3}(t-6) \times v$$
$$= \tfrac{5}{3}v(t-6)$$

Hence
$$\tfrac{4}{3}tv = \tfrac{5}{3}v(t-6).$$

Now $v \neq 0$, so this equation may be rearranged to give
$$4t = 5(t-6)$$
and therefore
$$t = 30.$$

Thus Inzamam walks for twenty minutes and runs for ten minutes on Monday.

Since Inzamam runs twice as fast as he walks, the time taken to walk to school on Wednesday is therefore $20 + 2 \times 10 = 40$ minutes.

8. Let F be the amount of grass in the field initially, C the amount a cow eats in one day and A the increase of grass in one day.

Then from the given information we have
$$F + 3A = 6 \times 3 \times C \qquad (1)$$
$$\text{and} \quad F + 7A = 3 \times 7 \times C. \qquad (2)$$

Subtracting equation (1) from equation (2), we obtain $4A = 3C$ and hence $F = 21A$.

Now let n be the number of days it takes one cow to eat all of the grass. Then we have $F + nA = nC$, and, using the values above, we obtain $n = 63$.

Thus it would take 63 days for one cow to eat all the grass.

9. Let $a = 1+x$ and $b = 1-x$. Then $ab = 1 - x^2$ and the given equation becomes $a^4 - 2b^4 = a^2b^2$, so that
$$a^4 - a^2b^2 - 2b^4 = 0,$$
that is,
$$\left(a^2 + b^2\right)\left(a^2 - 2b^2\right) = 0.$$

Hence either $a^2 + b^2 = 0$ or $a^2 - 2b^2 = 0$.

Appendix C: Solutions to the exercises

In the first case $a = b = 0$, which is impossible; in the second case
$$a = \pm\sqrt{2}b.$$
In terms of x, this means that
$$1 + x = \pm\sqrt{2}(1 - x),$$
so that either
$$\begin{aligned}x &= \frac{\sqrt{2}-1}{\sqrt{2}+1}\\&= \frac{\sqrt{2}-1}{\sqrt{2}+1} \times \frac{\sqrt{2}-1}{\sqrt{2}-1}\\&= 3 - 2\sqrt{2},\end{aligned}$$
or
$$\begin{aligned}x &= \frac{\sqrt{2}+1}{\sqrt{2}-1}\\&= \frac{\sqrt{2}+1}{\sqrt{2}-1} \times \frac{\sqrt{2}+1}{\sqrt{2}+1}\\&= 3 + 2\sqrt{2}.\end{aligned}$$

Exercise 3.2

1. FIRST SOLUTION

   From the symmetry, $NWSE$ is a square and angles ENA, AEN and BNW are equal. Considering triangle AEN, these angles are each $35°$.

   Since $\angle ENW = 90°$, we deduce that $\angle ANB = 20°$.

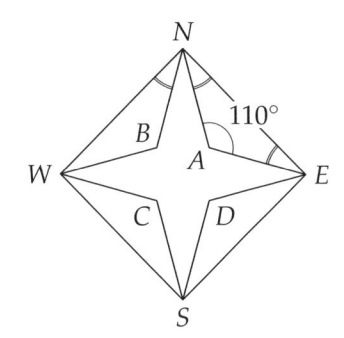

   SECOND SOLUTION

   Let O be the centre of the star and join O to N and to A, extending this line to M. Then OM and ON are lines of symmetry, so that OM bisects both $\angle NAE$ and $\angle NOE$. Hence $\angle NAM = 55°$ and $\angle NOM = 45°$.

   Now $\angle NAM$ is exterior to triangle NOA, so that $\angle ANO = 10°$ and therefore, from the symmetry, $\angle ANB = 20°$.

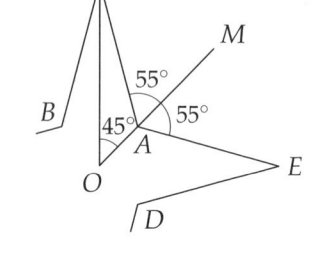

   THIRD SOLUTION

   From the symmetry, $ABCD$ is a square and $\angle BAN$ and $\angle EAD$ are equal.

   By considering angles at A, $\angle BAN = 80°$ and hence, from angles in a triangle, $\angle ANB = 20°$.

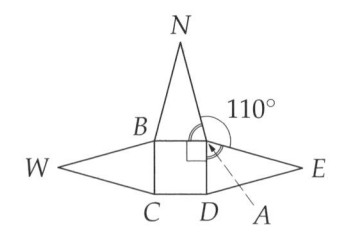

   FOURTH SOLUTION

   Extend EA to meet NB at M. Now $\angle NMA = 90°$ from the rotational symmetry (rotating $90°$ anticlockwise about the centre moves AE to BN).

   Then, since $\angle NAE$ is an exterior angle of triangle NMA, $\angle ANB = 20°$.

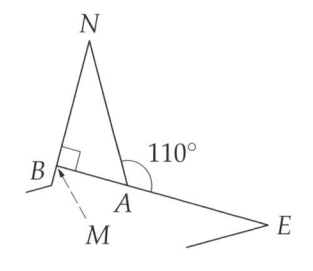

FIFTH SOLUTION

Join A and B to O, the centre of the star. From the symmetry, $\angle BOA = 90°$ and angles OAN, EAO and NBO are equal. These angles are each $125°$, by considering angles at A.

Now the sum of the angles in quadrilateral $NBOA$ is $360°$, so $\angle ANB = 20°$.

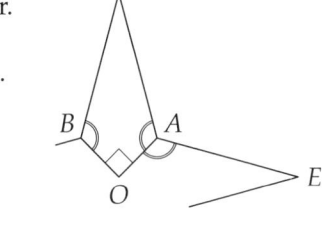

SIXTH SOLUTION

Let $\angle ANB$ equal $x°$. Then, by symmetry, the star octagon has four interior angles equal to x and four equal to $250°$ (using angles at a point).

Now the sum of the interior angles of an octagon is $12 \times 90°$, so that $4x + 4 \times 250 = 1080$, giving $x = 20$ and so $\angle ANB = 20°$.

2. The diagram seems to include several isosceles triangles, and we solve the problem by proving this is the case.

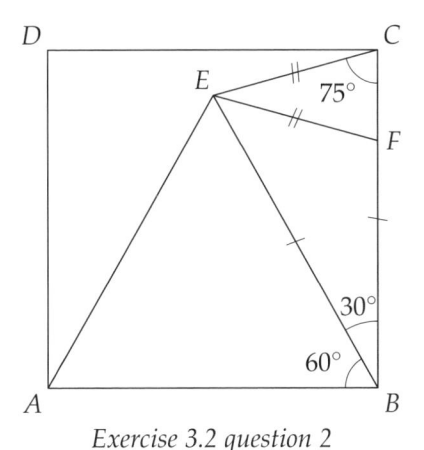

Exercise 3.2 question 2

For example, since the square $ABCD$ and the equilateral triangle ABE share the side AB, all their sides are the same length. That means the triangle BCE is isosceles.

Now, angle EBC is $90° - 60° = 30°$ (since it is the difference between the interior angle of a square and the interior angle of an equilateral triangle). Hence angles BCE and CEB are each $\frac{1}{2}(180° - 30°) = 75°$, because they are the base angles of an isosceles triangle.

We are also given that triangle CEF is isosceles. Since we have worked out that angle $FCE = 75°$, we deduce that angle $CEF = 180° - (2 \times 75°) = 30°$.

Finally, we find that angle $FEB = \angle CEB - \angle CEF = 75° - 30° = 45°$.

3. First of all, we amass some basic facts.

   Since the exterior angles of any polygon add up to $360°$, the exterior angles of a regular pentagon are each $360° \div 5 = 72°$. Thus the interior angles are each $180° - 72° = 108°$.

   Now, we claim that triangle AEF is isosceles. Indeed, $\angle AEF = 72°$ since it is an exterior angle of the pentagon. Also, since AB and DC are parallel, $\angle EAF$ is supplementary to angle EDC (they are allied angles). So $\angle EAF = 180° - 108° = 72°$ too.

   This gives us that $AF = EF$.

   Similarly, triangle BGF is isosceles, and $BF = GF$.

   But now $AB = AF + FB = EF + FG = CD + CD$ because the sides of a regular pentagon are equal, so $AB = 2 \times CD$ as required.

4. FIRST SOLUTION

   Draw a line parallel to PQ and TS passing through R. This line divides the angle $b°$ into two parts; suppose these parts have sizes $b_1°$ and $b_2°$, as shown.

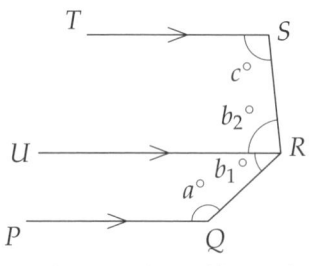

   Exercise 3.2 question 4 (first solution)

   Then angles $a°$ and $b_1°$ are supplementary (because PQ and UR are parallel), as are angles $b_2°$ and $c°$. Therefore

   $$a + b_1 = 180$$

Appendix C: Solutions to the exercises

$$\text{and} \quad b_2 + c = 180.$$

By adding these two equations, we obtain the desired result since $b_1 + b_2 = b$.

SECOND SOLUTION

Extend QR and TS until they meet at a new point U.

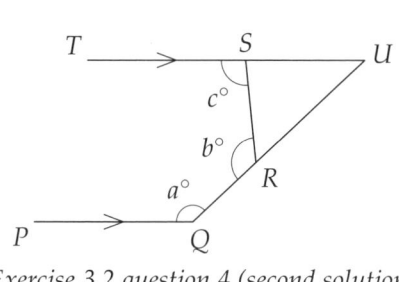

Exercise 3.2 question 4 (second solution)

Then angles $a°$ and $\angle SUR$ are supplementary (because PQ and TU are parallel), that is, $a° + \angle SUR = 180°$.

However, we have

$$\angle SUR + \angle URS + \angle RSU = 180°$$

by properties of angles in a triangle. This means that

$$a° = \angle URS + \angle RSU.$$

We also have $b° + \angle URS = 180° = c° + \angle RSU$ since they are angles on a straight line.

Putting all this together we get

$$a° + b° + c° = \angle URS + \angle RSU + (180° - \angle URS) + (180° - \angle RSU)$$
$$= 360°,$$

as needed.

5. FIRST SOLUTION

   Since rectangles $ABCD$ and $AZYX$ are congruent,

   $$\angle ZXA = \angle ADB = 70°,$$

   and from right-angled triangle BAD, we have $\angle DBA = 20°$.

Now angle ZXA is an exterior angle of triangle XMB, so that $\angle ZXA = \angle DBA + \angle XMB$. Hence $70° = 20° + \angle XMB$ and therefore $\angle XMB = 50°$.

SECOND SOLUTION

Since rectangles $ABCD$ and $AZYX$ are congruent,
$$\angle ZXA = \angle ADB = 70°.$$
Using angles on a straight line, we may deduce three exterior angles of quadrilateral $ADMX$, as shown.

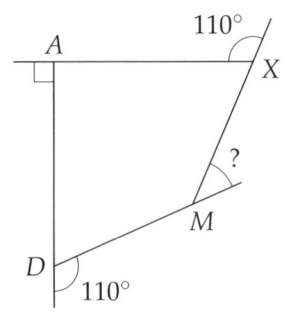

Exercise 3.2 question 5 (second solution)

But the sum of the exterior angles of a polygon is $360°$, so that $\angle XMB = 50°$.

6. The key to this solution is to join MC and consider triangle MCX.

    We are given that $ABCD$ is a rectangle, so that $BC = AD$ and $\angle DAM = 90° = \angle MBC$.

    We are also given that $AB = 2 \times AD$ and that M is the midpoint of AB. Therefore $DA = AM = MB = BC$.

    It follows that triangles DAM and MBC are congruent (SAS) and we deduce that $DM = MC$.

    But triangle MDX is equilateral, so that $MX = DM$ and hence $MX = MC$. In other words, triangle MCX is isosceles.

Appendix C: Solutions to the exercises

Exercise 3.2 question 6

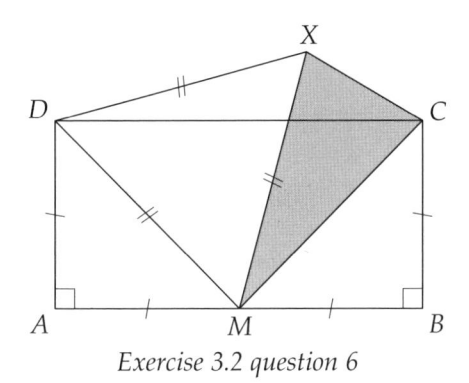

Now consider the angles at M.

(i) Triangle DAM is right-angled with $\angle DAM = 90°$. It is also isosceles, so $\angle AMD = \angle ADM = 45°$, since the angle sum is $180°$.

(ii) Similarly, from triangle MBC, $\angle CMB = 45°$.

(iii) Finally, because triangle MDX is equilateral, $DMX = 60°$.

Hence $\angle CMX = 180° - 45° - 45° - 60° = 30°$, since angles on a straight line add up to $180°$.

Lastly, we consider the angles at point C.

We know that triangle XCM is isosceles with $\angle CMX = 30°$. Hence each base angle is
$$\frac{180° - 30°}{2} = 75°;$$
in particular, $\angle XCM = 75°$.

Also, $ABCD$ is a rectangle, so that $\angle DCB = 90°$, and triangle MBC is right-angled and isosceles, so that $\angle MCB = 45°$. Therefore
$$\angle DCM = \angle DCB - \angle MCB$$
$$= 90° - 45°$$
$$= 45°.$$

We can now calculate the value of $\angle XCD$. We have
$$\angle XCD = \angle XCM - \angle DCM$$
$$= 75° - 45°$$
$$= 30°.$$

7. Let $\angle BGA = \alpha$.

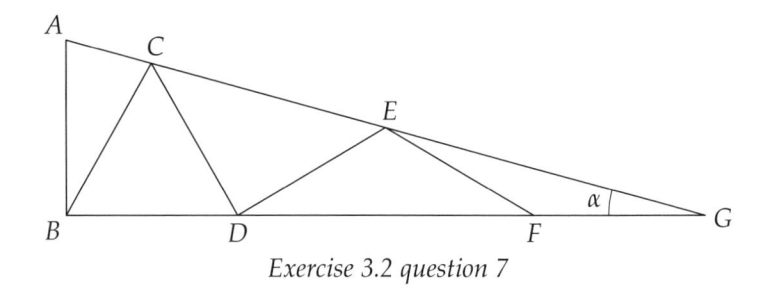

Exercise 3.2 question 7

Triangle EFG is isosceles because $EF = FG$. So $\angle GEF = \angle FGE = \alpha$. Using the exterior angle theorem in triangle EFG, we get $\angle DFE = \angle GEF + \angle FGE = 2\alpha$.

Triangle DFE is isosceles since $DE = EF$. So $\angle EDF = \angle DFE = 2\alpha$. Using the exterior angle theorem in triangle EDG, we get $\angle DEC = \angle EDG + \angle DGE = 2\alpha + \alpha = 3\alpha$.

Triangle CDE is isosceles since $CD = DE$. So $\angle ECD = \angle DEC = 3\alpha$. Using the exterior angle theorem in triangle CDG, we get $\angle BDC = \angle GCD + \angle DGC = 3\alpha + \alpha = 4\alpha$.

Triangle BDC is isosceles since $BC = CD$. So $\angle CBD = \angle BDC = 4\alpha$. Using the exterior angle theorem in triangle CBG, we get $\angle BCA = \angle CBG + \angle BGC = 4\alpha + \alpha = 5\alpha$.

Finally, triangle ABC is isosceles because $AB = BC$. So $\angle CAB = \angle BCA = 5\alpha$.

Now consider triangle ABG. Its interior angles are $90°$, α and 5α. So $6\alpha = 90°$, that is, $\alpha = 15°$.

8. We know that $\angle ABC = 90°$ and the sum of the angles in triangle ABC is $180°$.

Therefore
$$\angle QBC = 90° - \angle ABQ. \qquad (1)$$

Similarly, in triangle BPQ, $\angle BPQ = 90°$ so that
$$\angle BQC = 90° - \angle QBP. \qquad (2)$$

But $\angle ABQ = \angle QBP$ and hence, from equations (1) and (2), we have $\angle QBC = \angle BQC$.

Thus $CB = CQ$ from 'sides opposite equal angles'.

Appendix C: Solutions to the exercises 159

9. Let the sum of the two unlabelled angles in the smaller triangle be y. Then the sum of the two unlabelled angles in the whole triangle is equal to $2y$.

   The sum of the angles in a triangle is 180°, hence in the small triangle
   $$2x + y = 180 \tag{1}$$
   and in the whole triangle
   $$x + 2y = 180. \tag{2}$$
   Doubling equation (1) and subtracting equation (2), we get $3x = 180$ and thus $x = 60$.

10. Each of the angles in an equilateral triangle is equal to 60°. We add two 60° angles to the figure, label three other angles $a°$, $b°$ and $c°$, and label some points, as shown.

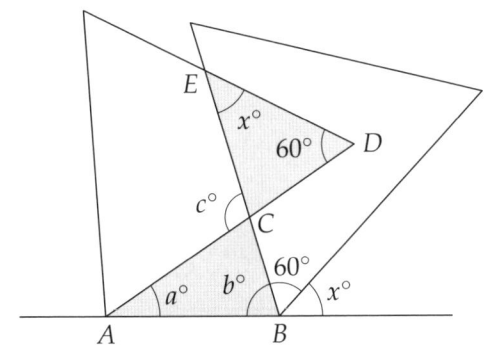

    Exercise 3.2 question 10

    At B, since angles on the straight line add up to 180° we have $b + 60 + x = 180$, that is,
    $$b = 120 - x. \tag{1}$$
    Now the angle labelled $c°$ is an exterior angle of triangle CDE, so that $c = x + 60$; it is also an exterior angle of triangle ABC, so that $c = a + b$. Hence $a + b = x + 60$ and therefore, using equation (1), we have $a = x + 60 - (120 - x) = 2x - 60$.

    But $a > 0$ for the given configuration to occur, hence $2x - 60 > 0$, that is, $x > 30$, as required.

11. Let $\angle RXQ = \alpha$. Then because $QR = RX$ we have $\angle RQX = \angle RXQ = \alpha$.

Using 'the exterior angle of a triangle' for triangle RXQ, we obtain $\angle QRO = \angle RXQ + \angle RQX = \alpha + \alpha = 2\alpha$.

We now proceed in one of two ways: the first method uses circle theorems; the second method uses nothing more than facts about triangles.

FIRST METHOD

Let Z be any point on the circle which is not on arc PQR.

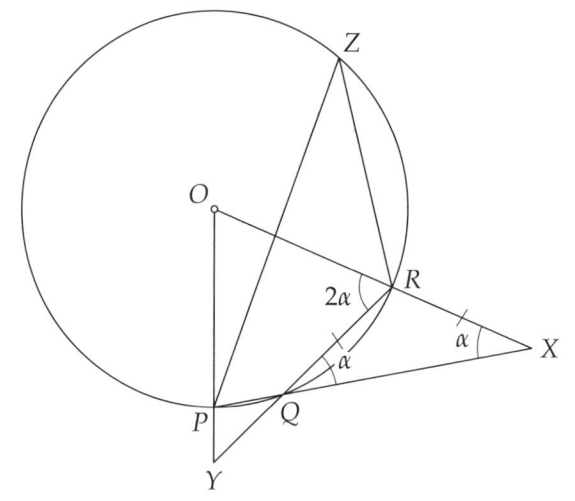

Exercise 3.2 question 11 (first method)

Then $\angle RQX$ is an exterior angle of the cyclic quadrilateral $PQRZ$ and therefore $\angle RQX = \angle PZR$. Hence $\angle PZR = \alpha$.

Since 'the angle at the centre is twice the angle at the circumference' we deduce that $\angle POR = 2\alpha$.

We therefore have $\angle YOR = \angle POR = 2\alpha = \angle QRO = \angle YRO$, so that $OY = RY$ from 'sides opposite equal angles'.

SECOND METHOD

Since PQR is the arc of a circle, centre O, we have $OP = OQ = OR$ (radii).

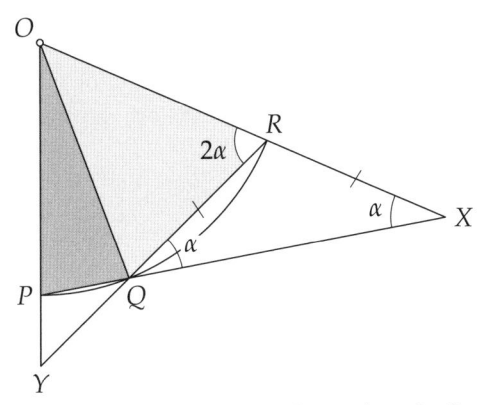

Exercise 3.2 question 11 (second method)

In particular, $OQ = OR$, so that triangle OQR is isosceles and $\angle RQO = \angle QRO = 2\alpha$.

The sum of the angles on a straight line equals 180°, hence

$$\angle OQP = 180° - \angle RQX - \angle RQO$$
$$= 180° - \alpha - 2\alpha$$
$$= 180° - 3\alpha.$$

Now $OP = OQ$, so that triangle OQP is also isosceles and $\angle OPQ = \angle OQP = 180° - 3\alpha$.

The sum of the angles in a triangle equals 180°, hence, in triangle OPX,

$$\angle POX = 180° - \angle OPX - \angle OXP$$
$$= 180° - \angle OPQ - \angle RXQ$$
$$= 180° - (180° - 3\alpha) - \alpha$$
$$= 2\alpha$$

Thus $\angle YOR = \angle POX = 2\alpha = \angle QRO = \angle YRO$, so that $OY = RY$ from 'sides opposite equal angles'.

12. FIRST SOLUTION

Since $ABCDE$ is a regular pentagon

$$\angle AEF = \frac{360°}{5}$$

$$= 72°. \tag{1}$$

We also deduce that each interior angle of the regular pentagon is 108°, since angles on a straight line are supplementary.

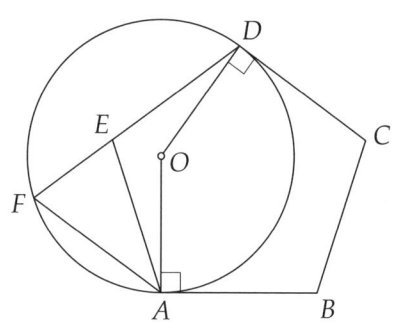

Exercise 3.2 question 12 (first solution)

Let O be the centre of the circle. The angle between a tangent and the radius drawn to the point of contact is 90°, hence

$$\angle OAB = \angle ODC = 90°.$$

The sum of the interior angles of the pentagon $OABCD$ is 540°. Hence $\angle AOD = 540° - 90° - 90° - 108° - 108° = 144°$. Now the angle subtended at the centre of a circle is twice the angle subtended at the circumference, so

$$\angle EFA = \frac{\angle AOD}{2}$$
$$= 72°. \tag{2}$$

From equations (1) and (2) we deduce that $\angle EFA = \angle AEF$, that is, triangle AEF has equal base angles. Therefore $AE = AF$, as required, using 'sides opposite equal angles'.

SECOND SOLUTION

Make use of the 'alternate segment theorem', from which $\angle CDA = \angle DFA$, as shown.

Can you see how to complete the argument?

13. Recall that each exterior angle of a regular polygon with n sides is equal to $360° \div n$.

Appendix C: Solutions to the exercises

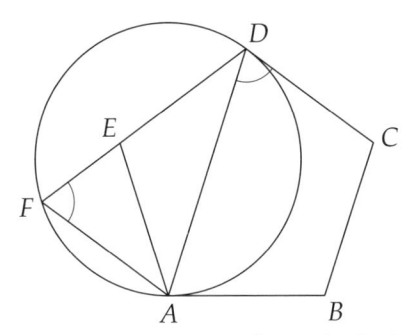

Exercise 3.2 question 12 (second solution)

FIRST SOLUTION

Extend the common edge PO to point T, as shown. The angles labelled $x°$, $y°$ and $z°$ are exterior angles of the regular decagon, regular heptagon and regular 15-gon respectively.

Hence we can use the above result, as follows,

$$x = \frac{360}{10} = 36,$$

$$y = \frac{360}{7} = 51\tfrac{3}{7}$$

and $$z = \frac{360}{15} = 24.$$

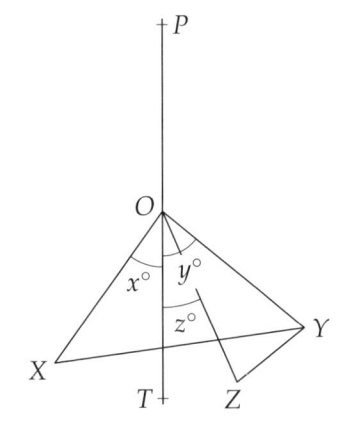

It follows that $\angle XOY = x° + y° = 87\tfrac{3}{7}°$ and $\angle ZOY = y° - z° = 27\tfrac{3}{7}°$.
Now the sides of the three polygons are all equal, so the triangles XOY and ZOY are isosceles. We can therefore find their base angles:

$$\angle XYO = \frac{180° - 87\tfrac{3}{7}°}{2} = 46\tfrac{2}{7}°$$

and $$\angle ZYO = \frac{180° - 27\tfrac{3}{7}°}{2} = 76\tfrac{2}{7}°.$$

Thus $\angle XYZ = \angle ZYO - \angle XYO = 76\tfrac{2}{7}° - 46\tfrac{2}{7}° = 30°.$

SECOND SOLUTION

Let PO be the common edge, as shown. Since $OX = OY = OZ = OP$ the points X, Y, Z and P lie on a circle centre O.

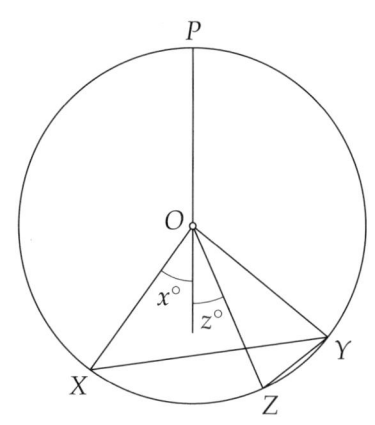

Exercise 3.2 question 13 (second solution)

Now 'the angle at the circumference is half the angle at the centre', so

$$\angle XYZ = \tfrac{1}{2}\angle XOZ$$
$$= \tfrac{1}{2}(x+z)°.$$

But, from the above result,

$$x = \frac{360}{10} = 36$$

$$\text{and} \quad z = \frac{360}{15} = 24,$$

so that $\angle XYZ = \tfrac{1}{2}(36+24)° = 30°$.

14. From the properties of a parallelogram and an equilateral triangle we have $PQ = SR = US = UR$ and $SP = RQ = QT = RT$.

Also

$$\angle USP = 60° + \angle RSP$$
$$= 60° + \angle PQR$$
$$= \angle PQT,$$

Appendix C: Solutions to the exercises

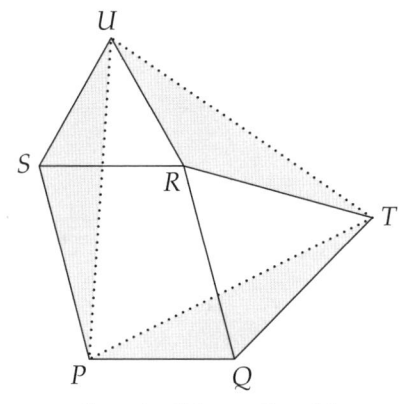

Exercise 3.2 question 14

and, from 'angles at a point',

$$\angle URT = 360° - 60° - 60° - \angle QRS$$
$$= 240° - (180° - \angle PQR)$$
$$= 60° + \angle PQR$$
$$= \angle PQT.$$

Therefore triangles USP, PQT and URT are congruent (SAS) and it follows that $UP = PT = TU$.

15. Let $\angle OPQ = \alpha$. Since the length of PQ is equal to the radius of the circle and hence triangle OPQ is isosceles, it follows that $\angle QOP = \alpha$.

    Applying the exterior angle theorem to triangle OPQ, we obtain $\angle RQO = \angle QOP + \angle OPQ = 2\alpha$. Since OQ and OR are both radii of the circle and hence triangle OQR is isosceles, it follows that $\angle ORQ = 2\alpha$.

    Now applying the exterior angle theorem to triangle OPR, we get $\angle AOR = \angle OPR + \angle ORP = \alpha + 2\alpha = 3\alpha$.

    Therefore $\angle AOR = 3 \times \angle BOQ$, as required.

16. We are given that $\angle BXC = 100°$, so that $\angle AXD$ is also $100°$ since it is vertically opposite.

    Considering the sum of the angles in triangle ADX, we deduce that $\angle BDA = 40°$; considering the sum of the angles of triangle ABD, we deduce that $\angle DBA = 40°$.

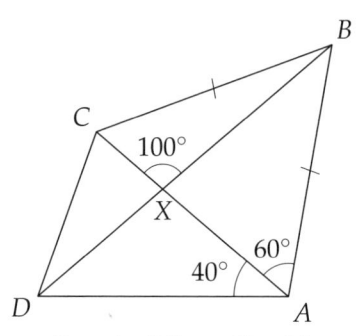

Exercise 3.2 question 16

Hence $\angle BDA = \angle DBA$, so that $AD = AB$.

Now in triangle ABC we have $AB = BC$ and $\angle BAC = 60°$; therefore triangle ABC is equilateral and $AC = AB$.

It follows that $AC = AD$, so that triangle ACD is isosceles and hence $\angle ADC = \angle ACD = 70°$, since $\angle CAD = 40°$.

Therefore $\angle BDC = \angle ADC - \angle BDA = 70° - 40° = 30°$.

Exercise 3.3

1. Let O be the point of intersection of the diagonals and let the lengths of OA, OB, OC and OD be a, b, c and d, respectively, as shown.

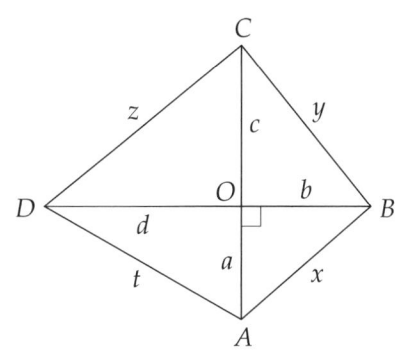

   Exercise 3.3 question 1

   Using Pythagoras' theorem in each of the right-angled triangles OAB, OBC, OCD and ODA we obtain

   $$x^2 = a^2 + b^2,$$
   $$y^2 = b^2 + c^2,$$
   $$z^2 = c^2 + d^2,$$
   $$\text{and}\quad t^2 = d^2 + a^2,$$

   from which $x^2 + z^2 = a^2 + b^2 + c^2 + d^2 = y^2 + t^2$, as required.

   REMARK

   Note that the result remains true even if the quadrilateral $ABCD$ is not convex.

2. Let E be the point on AB produced such that triangle ADE is equilateral. Hence $BE = 2\,\text{cm}$ and $CE = 1\,\text{cm}$.

   Let F be the midpoint of CD.

   Triangle EBF has $EB = EF = 2\,\text{cm}$ and $\angle BEF = 60°$, so it is equilateral.

   Now BC is the median from B to EF in this equilateral triangle, so $\angle BCE = 90°$.

Exercise 3.3 question 2

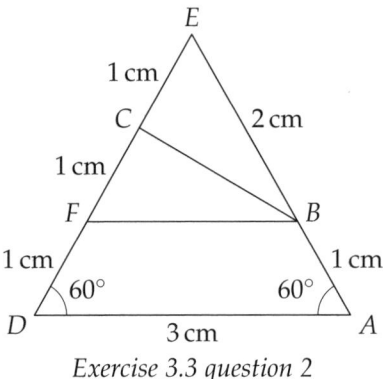

Applying Pythagoras' theorem in triangle BCE, we get $BC^2 + 1^2 = 2^2$ so the length of BC is $\sqrt{3}$ cm.

REMARK

An alternative method is to mark the point G on AD such that $AG = 1$ cm. Then triangles ABG and GCD are equilateral and it can be shown that angle CBG is a right angle.

3. We begin with a diagram showing the information given in the question. We have used the fact that $ABCD$ is a rectangle, so that $BC = AD = 1$ and $DC = AB = \sqrt{2}$, and angles ABC, BCD and CDA are right angles.

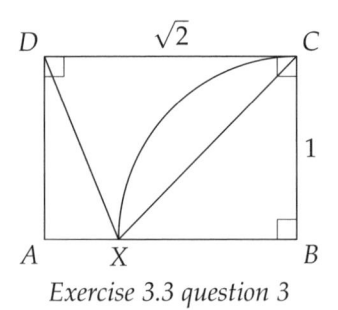

Exercise 3.3 question 3

Since BX and BC are both radii of the circle, BX also has length 1. This means that triangle XBC is isosceles and so $\angle BXC = \angle BCX$.

Furthermore, since $\angle ABC$ is a right angle, $\angle BXC$ and $\angle BCX$ are both equal to $45°$.

From the fact that ∠BCD is a right angle, it follows that ∠XCD = 90° − 45° = 45°.

We may use Pythagoras' theorem in triangle XBC to obtain
$$XC^2 = BX^2 + BC^2$$
$$= 1^2 + 1^2$$
$$= 2$$
and so $XC = \sqrt{2}$.

We are given that DC also has length $\sqrt{2}$ and so triangle XCD is isosceles. This means that ∠CXD and ∠CDX are equal, and so each is equal to $\frac{1}{2}(180° - 45°) = 67\frac{1}{2}°$.

Lastly, we use the fact that ∠CDA is a right angle to conclude that ∠ADX = $90° - 67\frac{1}{2}° = 22\frac{1}{2}°$.

4. Let the sides of the rhombus AECF have length x cm. Hence $AE = x$ and $EB = 16 - x$.

Since ABCD is a rectangle, angle EBC is a right angle.

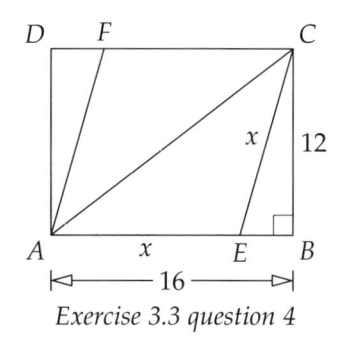

Exercise 3.3 question 4

Using Pythagoras' theorem in triangle ABC, we have $AC^2 = 16^2 + 12^2 = 400$, so that $AC = 20$.

Using Pythagoras' theorem in triangle EBC, we have
$$EC^2 = CB^2 + EB^2$$
and hence
$$x^2 = 12^2 + (16 - x)^2,$$
which may be rearranged to give
$$x^2 = 144 + 256 - 32x + x^2.$$

It follows that
$$32x = 400$$
and so
$$x = \frac{25}{2}.$$

We may now proceed in various ways; we show two different methods.

FIRST METHOD

Let M be the point of intersection of the diagonals AC and EF of $AECF$. Since $AECF$ is a rhombus, angle FMC is a right angle and M is the mid-point of AC and EF.

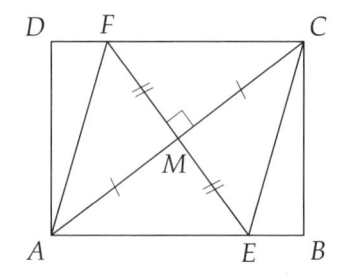

Exercise 3.3 question 4 (first method)

Using Pythagoras' theorem in triangle FMC, we have
$$CF^2 = \left(\tfrac{1}{2}AC\right)^2 + \left(\tfrac{1}{2}EF\right)^2$$
and hence
$$\left(\frac{25}{2}\right)^2 = 10^2 + \left(\tfrac{1}{2}EF\right)^2.$$
It follows that
$$625 = 400 + EF^2$$
and so
$$EF = 15.$$

Therefore the length of EF is 15 cm.

SECOND METHOD

We make use of the fact that

Appendix C: Solutions to the exercises 171

area of rhombus $AECF =$

area of rectangle $ABCD - 2 \times$ (area of triangle EBC).

Now the area of a rhombus is half the product of its diagonals. Also, the area of triangle EBC is $\frac{1}{2} EB \times BC$ and $EB = 16 - \frac{25}{2} = \frac{7}{2}$. We therefore have

$$\tfrac{1}{2} AC \times EF = 16 \times 12 - \tfrac{7}{2} \times 12.$$

Hence

$$10 \times EF = 192 - 42 = 150$$

and so

$$EF = 15.$$

Therefore the length of EF is 15 cm.

REMARK

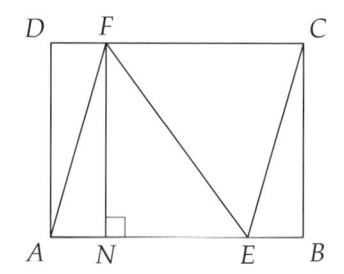

Exercise 3.3 question 4 (second method)

Another method uses Pythagoras' theorem in the right-angled triangle ENF.

5. This problem does not give us units, and so we choose them so that the side length of the square is $2s$. Since M is the midpoint of CD, we have $CM = s$. Then we define $x = CG$. Since $BC = 2s$ it follows that $GB = 2s - x$. But, as GM is the image of GB after folding, $GM = 2s - x$ too.

Now Pythagoras' theorem for triangle MCG gives us

$$s^2 + x^2 = (2s - x)^2.$$

We multiply out to get

$$s^2 + x^2 = 4s^2 - 4sx + x^2.$$

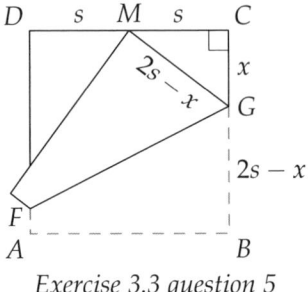

Exercise 3.3 question 5

Eliminating the x^2 terms and dividing by s (which is not zero), we obtain
$$s = 4s - 4x,$$
which has the solution $x = \frac{3}{4}s$.

Thus the triangle GCM has sides of length $x = \frac{3}{4}s$, s and $2s - x = \frac{5}{4}s$. Multiplying all the sides by 4, we get $3s$, $4s$ and $5s$, so the side lengths are in the ratio $3 : 4 : 5$, as required.

6. FIRST SOLUTION

    As shown in the figure, let the perpendicular from B to the line AD meet the line AD at the point X; let the perpendicular from B to the line CD meet the line CD at the point Y and let the distance DY be y cm.

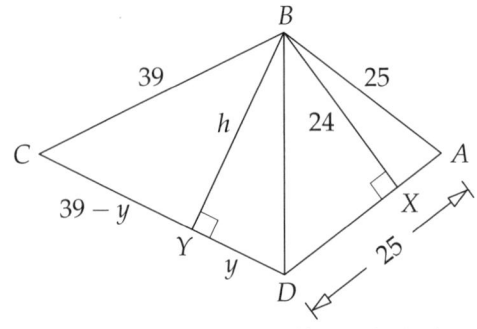

Exercise 3.3 question 6 (first solution)

Considering triangle ABX and using Pythagoras' theorem we obtain
$$AX = \sqrt{25^2 - 24^2} = 7.$$

Appendix C: Solutions to the exercises

Similarly, from triangle BDX we have
$$BD = \sqrt{24^2 + (25-7)^2} = 30. \tag{1}$$
Now from triangles BDY and BCY, again by Pythagoras' theorem, we deduce that
$$h^2 + (39-y)^2 = 39^2$$
$$\text{and} \quad h^2 + y^2 = 30^2. \tag{2}$$
Subtract to get
$$(39-y)^2 - y^2 = 39^2 - 30^2,$$
which may be simplified to give
$$78y = 900,$$
so that
$$y = \frac{150}{13}.$$
Finally, by substituting in equation (2), we find
$$h = \frac{360}{13}.$$

SECOND SOLUTION

Another solution uses the value of BD obtained in equation (1) to find the area T of isosceles triangle BCD. Once the area is known the value of the height h may be found from
$$T = \tfrac{1}{2} \times 39 \times h.$$
Can you see how to find T and so complete the solution?

REMARK

Triangle DYB is a '5, 12, 13' triangle.

7. Because PY is the fold line, triangle PXY is the reflection of triangle PQY in line PY. Hence $PX = PQ = \sqrt{2}$.

Applying Pythagoras' theorem to triangle PSX, we get
$$SX = \sqrt{PX^2 - PS^2} = \sqrt{2-1} = 1.$$
So $RX = \sqrt{2} - 1$. Also, since $SX = SP = 1$, triangle PSX is an isosceles right-angled triangle and $\angle SXP = 45°$.

Now angle PXY is the image under reflection of angle PQY and is therefore a right angle. So $\angle RXY = 180° - (90° + 45°) = 45°$ and we deduce that triangle RXY is also an isosceles right-angled triangle. So $RY = RX = \sqrt{2} - 1$.

It remains to find the length of XY. Because QY folds onto XY, we deduce that

$$XY = QY = QR - YR = 1 - (\sqrt{2} - 1) = 2 - \sqrt{2}.$$

8. Let the unknown side of the rectangle have length y and let one diagonal of the unshaded quadrilateral have length x, as shown below.

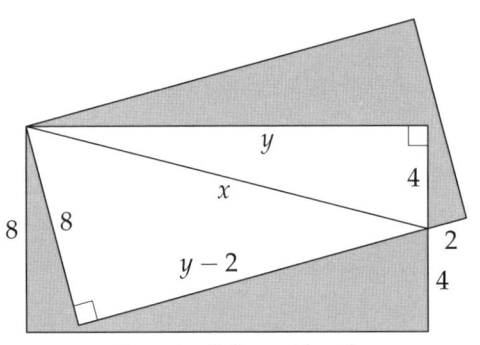

Exercise 3.3 question 8

Applying Pythagoras' theorem to the two unshaded right-angled triangles, we get

$$x^2 = 8^2 + (y-2)^2$$
$$\text{and} \quad x^2 = y^2 + 4^2.$$

We may eliminate x^2 from these equations to give

$$64 + (y-2)^2 = y^2 + 16,$$

that is,

$$64 + y^2 - 4y + 4 = y^2 + 16,$$

which may be rearranged to give

$$52 = 4y$$

and hence
$$y = 13.$$
Now the shaded area is equal to twice the area of one rectangle minus twice the area of the unshaded region, that is
$$2(8 \times 13) - 2\left(\tfrac{1}{2} \times 8 \times 11 + \tfrac{1}{2} \times 4 \times 13\right) = 68.$$
Hence the total shaded area equals 68.

Exercise 3.4

1. **FIRST SOLUTION**

   Let the width of the rectangle be l. Now region X is a triangle and region Y is a trapezium, so that area $X = \frac{1}{2}al$ and area $Y = \frac{1}{2}(a+2b)l$.

   Since area X : area $Y = 2 : 7$, we have
   $$\frac{\frac{1}{2}al}{\frac{1}{2}(a+2b)l} = \frac{2}{7}.$$
   Rearranging and simplifying, we get $5a = 4b$. Hence
   $$\frac{a}{b} = \frac{4}{5}$$
   so the ratio $a : b$ equals $4 : 5$.

   SECOND SOLUTION

   Since area X : area $Y = 2 : 7$ there is a positive number k such that area $X = 2k$ and area $Y = 7k$.

   Divide area Y into two parts, with areas X and $Y - X$, by drawing a line parallel to the base of the rectangle, as shown.

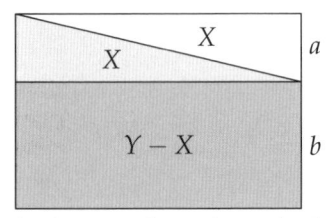

   Exercise 3.4 question 1 (second solution)

   The original rectangle has now been divided into two rectangles with equal width and with areas $2X$ and $Y - X$. Hence $a : b = 2X : Y - X$. Substituting for X and Y gives $a : b = 4k : (7k - 2k) = 4 : 5$.

2. Let the side length of the larger equilateral triangle be x units; this triangle therefore has a perimeter of length $3x$ units.

   Now consider the hexagon, which has sides of lengths 1, $x - 3$, 2, $x - 5$, 3 and $x - 4$ units. Hence the hexagon has perimeter length $3x - 6$ units.

Appendix C: Solutions to the exercises

Since the ratio of the perimeter lengths of the hexagon and the larger triangle is 5 : 7, we have

$$\frac{3x - 6}{3x} = \frac{5}{7}.$$

Rearranging to solve for x, we obtain

$$x = 7. \tag{1}$$

The four equilateral triangles in the problem are similar. Now the ratio of the areas of similar figures is equal to the ratio of the squares of their sides. Hence the four triangles have areas in the ratio $1^2 : 2^2 : 3^2 : 7^2 = 1 : 4 : 9 : 49$.

Hence the ratio of the areas of the hexagon and the larger triangle is $49 - (1 + 4 + 9) : 49 = 35 : 49 = 5 : 7$.

This may be illustrated by dividing the larger triangle into 49 small triangles, as shown.

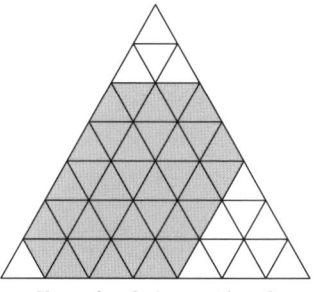

Exercise 3.4 question 2

REMARK

The observant reader will have noticed that the answer to this problem is surprising: the ratio of the areas is the same as the ratio of the perimeters. There is no reason to expect this to happen.

3. The centre of the large semicircular arc lies on AB, so we know that AB is a diameter of the large semicircle. But AB is 10 cm long, so the radius of the large semicircle is 5 cm.

Let the radii of the other three semicircles be r_1 cm, r_2 cm and r_3 cm. The centres of these arcs also lie on AB, so the sum of their diameters is equal to the length of AB. It follows that $2r_1 + 2r_2 + 2r_3 = 10$ and hence $r_1 + r_2 + r_3 = 5$.

Now the lengths, in cm, of the semicircular arcs are 5π, πr_1, πr_2 and πr_3. Therefore the perimeter of the figure has length, in cm,

$$5\pi + \pi r_1 + \pi r_2 + \pi r_3 = \pi(5 + r_1 + r_2 + r_3)$$
$$= \pi(5 + 5)$$
$$= 10\pi.$$

Hence the perimeter of the figure has length 10π cm.

4. Let CX have length $4x$ cm. Then $BX = 5x$ and $AB = 12x$, since $BX : CX = 5 : 4$ and $AB = 3 \times CX$.

Now from the area of triangle CXA, we get

$$\tfrac{1}{2} \times CX \times AB = 54 \tag{1}$$

and hence

$$\tfrac{1}{2} \times 4x \times 12x = 54. \tag{2}$$

Rearranging, we get

$$x^2 = \tfrac{9}{4}, \tag{3}$$

so that

$$x = \tfrac{3}{2} \tag{4}$$

since x is positive.

We may now proceed by using Pythagoras' theorem, or, more simply, by noting that triangles CBA and XBA are right-angled, with sides in the ratio $3 : 4 : 5$ and $5 : 12 : 13$. It follows that $AC = 15x$ and $AX = 13x$.

Hence the length of the perimeter of triangle CXA is $4x + 13x + 15x$ cm, that is, 48 cm.

5. The square is divided into five equal areas, so each is equal to 20 square units.

Considering the area of triangle ABP, we get

$$20 = \tfrac{1}{2} \times 10 \times BP.$$

Hence $BP = 4$. Similarly, $DS = 4$, $PQ = 4$ and $SR = 4$.

Hence $QC = CR = 2$.

Using Pythagoras' theorem, we obtain
$$QR^2 = QC^2 + CR^2$$
$$= 2^2 + 2^2$$
$$= 8$$
and therefore the length of QR is $2\sqrt{2}$ units.

6. FIRST SOLUTION

Consider each of the four unshaded triangles. The angle at the vertex of a square is $90°$ so each triangle is right-angled.

The marked angles in the left-hand diagram are both external angles of a regular octagon, so each is equal to $\frac{360°}{8} = 45°$. Hence each triangle is isosceles since 'sides opposite equal angles are equal'.

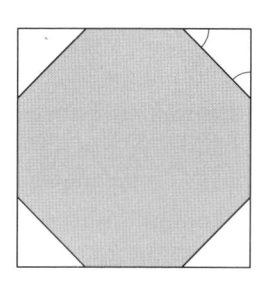

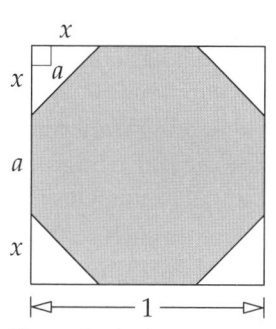

Exercise 3.4 question 6 (first solution)

Let the two equal sides of one of these triangles have length x, as shown in the right-hand diagram.

From Pythagoras' theorem, we obtain
$$x^2 + x^2 = a^2,$$
so that
$$2x^2 = a^2$$
and hence
$$x = \frac{a}{\sqrt{2}}.$$
Now the side of the square has length 1, therefore
$$a + 2x = 1,$$

that is,
$$a + a\sqrt{2} = 1,$$
or
$$a\sqrt{2} = 1 - a.$$

Squaring this equation, we get
$$2a^2 = 1 - 2a + a^2$$
and therefore
$$a^2 + 2a = 1.$$

SECOND SOLUTION

We derive an equation for a using

unshaded area + area of octagon = area of the square. (1)

Consider each of the four unshaded triangles. The angle at the vertex of a square is 90° so each triangle is right-angled.

The marked angles in the left-hand diagram are both external angles of a regular octagon, so each is equal to $\frac{360°}{8} = 45°$. Hence each triangle is isosceles since 'sides opposite equal angles are equal'.

Therefore each of the four unshaded triangles is isosceles and right-angled, with hypotenuse of length a, so the four triangles can be reassembled to form a square of side a (see the central figure). Hence the unshaded area is equal to a^2.

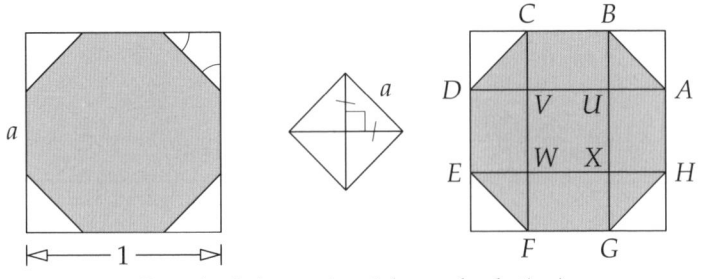

Exercise 3.4 question 6 (second solution)

Similarly, the four shaded triangles in the right-hand figure together have an area of a^2.

The octagon comprises these four shaded triangles together with two rectangles, $ADEH$ and $BCFG$, which overlap in the square $UVWX$.

Therefore the area of the octagon is

$$a^2 + \text{area } ADEH + \text{area } BCFG - \text{area } UVWX.$$

But the two rectangles each have area $a \times 1$ and the area of square $UVWX$ is $a \times a$, so that the octagon has area

$$a^2 + a + a - a^2 = 2a.$$

Finally, the square has area 1, so equation (1) gives

$$a^2 + 2a = 1.$$

7. Let the circles with diameters PQ and RS have radius x and the circle with diameter QR have radius y.

Then the radius of the circle with diameter PS is $y + 2x$, so that the shaded area is

$$\begin{aligned}\tfrac{1}{2}\pi(y+2x)^2 - \pi x^2 + \tfrac{1}{2}\pi y^2 &= \tfrac{1}{2}\pi(y^2 + 4xy + 4x^2) - \pi x^2 + \tfrac{1}{2}\pi y^2 \\ &= \tfrac{1}{2}\pi y^2 + 2\pi xy + 2\pi x^2 - \pi x^2 + \tfrac{1}{2}\pi y^2 \\ &= \pi y^2 + 2\pi xy + \pi x^2 \\ &= \pi(y^2 + 2xy + x^2) \\ &= \pi(y+x)^2,\end{aligned}$$

which is the area of a circle radius $x + y$.

But $MN = (y + 2x) + y = 2y + 2x$, so that the circle with diameter MN has radius $x + y$, as required.

REMARK

The shaded figure is known as a *salinon* and this result about its area appears in Archimedes, *Liber Assumptorum*, Proposition 14.

8. Consider the region of the big square which lies outside the circle. The lines in the figure divide the region into eight parts, four in the four corner squares, which are all identical by symmetry, and four in the four edge-centre squares, which are again all identical by symmetry.

The shaded area contains one part of each sort, and so takes up exactly a quarter of the difference between the big square and the circle, which we can work out.

The big square has area $9\,\text{cm}^2$, being made up of 9 squares each measuring $1\,\text{cm} \times 1\,\text{cm}$ squares.

By Pythagoras' theorem, the diagonal of a 1 cm × 1 cm square has length $\sqrt{2}$ cm. The radius of the circle is the length of one diagonal. Indeed, the radius is the distance from the centre of the middle square, to the centre of a corner square: two halves of a diagonal.

Hence the area of the circle is $\pi(\sqrt{2})^2 = 2\pi$.

Putting this all together, we see that the area outside the circle has area $9 - 2\pi$, and so the shaded region has area
$$\frac{9 - 2\pi}{4}.$$

9. Let $2r$ be the radius of the quarter-circle. Hence the radius of each semicircle is r. The diagram is divided into four regions; let their areas be X, Y, Z and T, as shown in the figure.

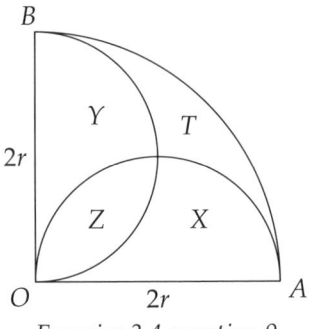

Exercise 3.4 question 9

The area of the quarter-circle is $\frac{1}{4}\pi(2r)^2 = \pi r^2$. The area of each semicircle is $\frac{1}{2}\pi r^2$. Hence $X + Z = \frac{1}{2}\pi r^2$.

However, the area inside the quarter-circle but outside one semicircle is $\pi r^2 - \frac{1}{2}\pi r^2 = \frac{1}{2}\pi r^2$. This means that $X + T = \frac{1}{2}\pi r^2$.

Therefore $X + T = X + Z$. We conclude that $T = Z$, so that the areas of the shaded regions are equal.

Thus the ratio of the area of the region shaded grey to the area of the region shaded black is $1 : 1$.

10. Let PQ be any straight line passing through point T.

The perimeter of the top two semicircles is $2 \times \frac{1}{2}(2\pi \times 1) = 2\pi$. The perimeter of the bottom semicircle is $\frac{1}{2}(2\pi \times 2)$, which also equals

Appendix C: Solutions to the exercises

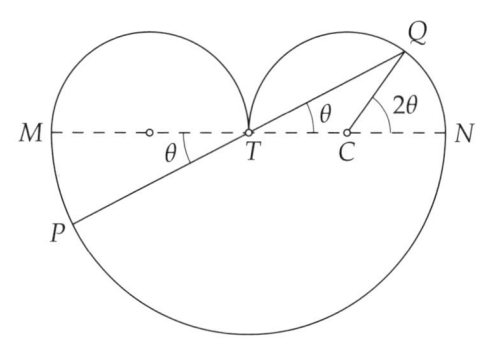

Exercise 3.4 question 10

2π. Therefore, in order to prove the required result, it is sufficient to show that the length of arc MP is equal to the length of arc QN.

Let $\angle MTP$ be $\theta°$. Then
$$MP = \frac{\theta}{360} \times 2\pi \times 2 = \frac{\theta\pi}{90}.$$

Now use the fact that in a circle, the angle subtended at the centre is twice the angle at the circumference. If point C is the centre of one of the smaller semicircles, as shown in the diagram, then $\angle QCN = 2\angle QTN = 2\theta$. Therefore
$$QN = \frac{2\theta}{360} \times 2\pi \times 1 = \frac{\theta\pi}{90}.$$
and so $MP = QN$, as required.

11. FIRST SOLUTION

Since the shaded area is one third of the area of the square, the area not shaded is two thirds. So each white triangle has an area of
$$\tfrac{1}{4} \times \tfrac{2}{3} \times 4a^2 = \tfrac{2}{3}a^2.$$

However, the base of a white triangle is $2a$, so the height h cm is given by $\tfrac{1}{2} \times 2a \times h = \tfrac{2}{3}a^2$. Hence $h = \tfrac{2}{3}a$.

Now the dashed line in the figure comprises two of these heights and a diameter of the circle. But the dashed line has a length of $2a$, the length of a side of the square. Thus the radius of the circle is $\tfrac{1}{3}a$.

SECOND SOLUTION

We first cut the star into eight congruent triangles, as shown.

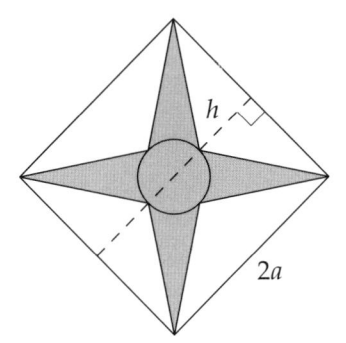

Exercise 3.4 question 11 (first solution)

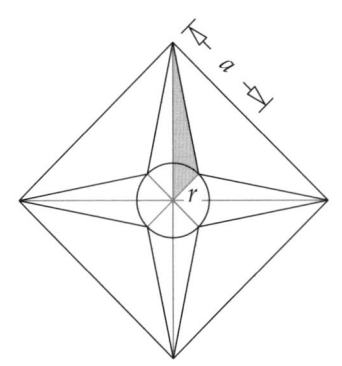

Exercise 3.4 question 11 (second solution)

Each triangle may be considered to have base r, the radius of the circle, and height a, as indicated for the shaded triangle.

Using the formula for the area of a triangle, and the fact that these eight triangles together have area one-third the area of the whole square, we get
$$8 \times \tfrac{1}{2} \times r \times a = \tfrac{1}{3} \times 4a^2,$$
which we solve to obtain $r = \tfrac{1}{3}a$.

12. The area of square S equals $(b-a)^2$.

    Let the side length of square T be $2x$. Consider the diagonal AD of the square of side b, shown dashed in the figure.

    This diagonal has three parts, the diagonal AB of the square of side a, a line BC crossing the square T, and the height CD of a small

Appendix C: Solutions to the exercises

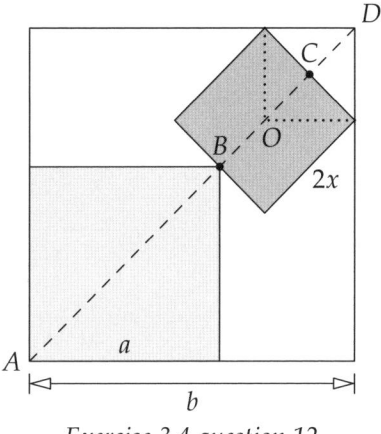

Exercise 3.4 question 12

triangle. That small triangle is congruent to one quarter of T, as indicated by the dotted lines.

We have $AD = b\sqrt{2}$ and $AB = a\sqrt{2}$ since these are diagonals of squares (using Pythagoras' Theorem). Also $BC = 2x$, and $CD = CO = x$, where O is the centre of the square T.

But $AD = AB + BC + CD$, so we have

$$b\sqrt{2} = a\sqrt{2} + 2x + x.$$

from which we deduce that $x = \frac{1}{3}\sqrt{2}(b-a)$.

Hence the area of T is

$$(2x)^2 = 4x^2 = 4 \times \tfrac{1}{9} \times 2(b-a)^2 = \tfrac{8}{9}(b-a)^2.$$

It follows that (area of S) : (area of T) = 9 : 8.

13. FIRST SOLUTION

Let $QT = x$, so that $PT = 2x$, since triangle PTQ is half an equilateral triangle.

Using Pythagoras' theorem in triangle PTQ, we get

$$\begin{aligned} PQ^2 &= PT^2 - QT^2 \\ &= (2x)^2 - x^2 \\ &= 3x^2 \end{aligned}$$

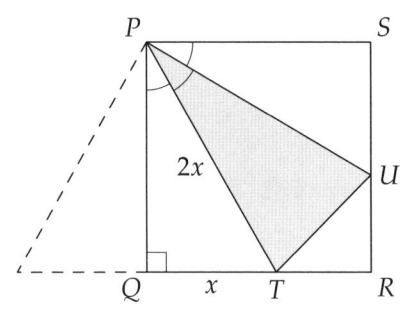

Exercise 3.4 question 13 (first solution)

and hence
$$PQ = \sqrt{3}x.$$

We may now find the areas of the three unshaded right-angled triangles.
$$\text{Area of triangle } PQT = \tfrac{1}{2} \times x \times \sqrt{3}x$$
$$= \frac{\sqrt{3}}{2}x^2.$$

Similarly,
$$\text{area of triangle } PSU = \frac{\sqrt{3}}{2}x^2.$$

Finally,
$$\text{area of triangle } TRU = \tfrac{1}{2} \times (\sqrt{3}x - x) \times (\sqrt{3}x - x)$$
$$= \tfrac{1}{2} \times (3x^2 - 2\sqrt{3}x^2 + x^2)$$
$$= 2x^2 - \sqrt{3}x^2.$$

Therefore the total unshaded area is
$$\frac{\sqrt{3}}{2}x^2 + \frac{\sqrt{3}}{2}x^2 + 2x^2 - \sqrt{3}x^2 = 2x^2.$$

However, the area of the square $PQRS$ is $\left(\sqrt{3}x\right)^2 = 3x^2$. It follows that the shaded area is x^2, which is one third of the area of the square.

SECOND SOLUTION

Let the sides of the square $PQRS$ have length x.

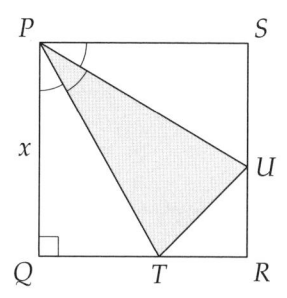

Appendix C: Solutions to the exercises

Exercise 3.4 question 13 (second solution)

Then, in triangle PQT, we have
$$\cos 30° = \frac{x}{PT}.$$
Hence
$$PT = \frac{x}{\cos 30°}.$$
Now by symmetry $PU = PT$ so that
$$\text{area of triangle } PTU = \tfrac{1}{2} PT \times PU \sin \angle TPU$$
$$= \tfrac{1}{2} x^2 \frac{\sin 30°}{\cos^2 30°}.$$
Now $\cos 30° = \frac{\sqrt{3}}{2}$ and $\sin 30° = \tfrac{1}{2}$. Therefore
$$\text{area of triangle } PTU = \tfrac{1}{2} x^2 \times \frac{\tfrac{1}{2}}{\tfrac{3}{4}}$$
$$= \tfrac{1}{3} x^2.$$

Hence the area of the triangle PTU is one third of the area of the square $PQRS$.

14. In the diagram, the line segments ED and DC represent two edges of the (possibly rotated) nonagon and AFG is the original equilateral triangle.

    The point B lies on AC so that EB is parallel to DC. Hence $BEDC$ is a parallelogram, since each pair of opposite sides is parallel.

    Now, opposite sides of a parallelogram are equal in length, so $EB + BC = ED + DC$. Therefore attaching the parallelogram to the nonagon creates a new polygon with the same perimeter length.

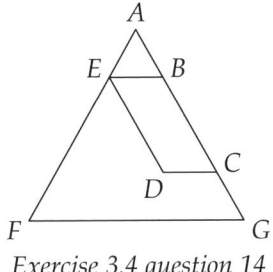

Exercise 3.4 question 14

Repeating this process at each of the three corners of the original triangle results in a hexagon with exactly the same perimeter length as the original nonagon.

Furthermore, DC is parallel to FG, so that EB is parallel to FG, and therefore the angles of triangle AEB are equal to those of triangle AFG. Since triangle AFG is equilateral it follows that triangle AEB is equilateral. But $EB = DC = 1$, so we deduce that $EA = 1$ and $AB = 1$.

Making similar deductions at the other corners of the original triangle, we can find the lengths of the sides of the hexagon, as shown.

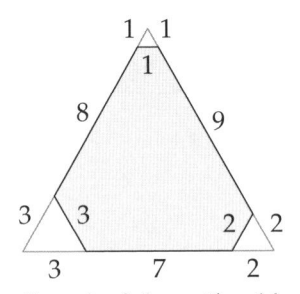

Exercise 3.4 question 14

The total perimeter of the hexagon, and therefore of the nonagon, is $1 + 8 + 3 + 7 + 2 + 9$, which equals 30.

15. Let F be the foot of the altitude from A in triangle ABC. Let D and E be the points where the required line parallel to the altitude AF meets the sides AB and BC, respectively.

    In appropriate units, let $BF = 18$, $FC = 7$, $BE = x$, $EC = 25 - x$, $DE = y$ and $AF = h$.

Appendix C: Solutions to the exercises

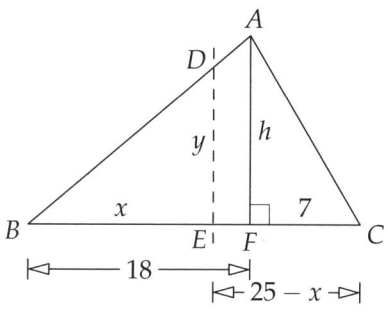

Exercise 3.4 question 15

The area of triangle ABC is

$$\tfrac{1}{2} \times 25 \times h = \frac{25}{2}h.$$

The area of triangle BED is half the area of triangle ABC, therefore

$$\tfrac{1}{2}xy = \tfrac{1}{2} \times \frac{25}{2}h$$

so that

$$2xy = 25h. \qquad (1)$$

Since $\angle DBE = \angle ABF$ and $\angle BED = \angle BFA$, triangles BED and BAF are similar with

$$\frac{y}{x} = \frac{h}{18}$$

so that

$$y = \frac{hx}{18}. \qquad (2)$$

Eliminating y from equations (1) and (2) we get

$$2x \times \frac{hx}{18} = 25h,$$

whence

$$x^2 = 9 \times 25$$

and so $x = 15$ since $x > 0$ here.

Therefore the base is divided in the ratio $15 : (25 - 15)$, which is $3 : 2$.

16. Notice that the shaded area is the intersection of the two triangles shown shaded in the following diagrams.

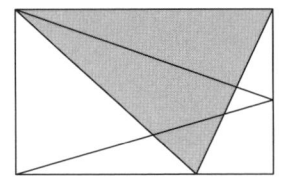

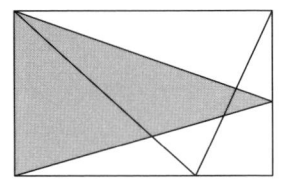

Exercise 3.4 question 16

The area of each of these triangles is half the area of the rectangle, since each has the same base and height as the rectangle. Therefore the total unshaded area within the rectangle in the right-hand figure is also half the area of the rectangle. In other words, the shaded area in the left-hand figure is equal to the total unshaded area in the right-hand figure.

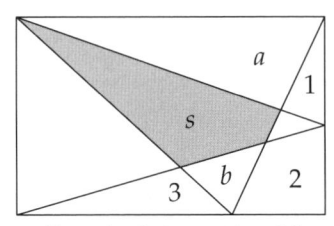

Exercise 3.4 question 16

Using the notation indicated, we therefore have $a + s + b = a + 1 + 2 + b + 3$ and hence $s = 1 + 2 + 3 = 6$. So the area of the shaded quadrilateral is 6.

REMARK

The result also applies if the rectangle is replaced by a parallelogram. Moreover, there is clearly nothing special about the values 1, 2 and 3.

Appendix C: Solutions to the exercises

Exercise 3.5

1. Let A, B, C be the centres of the circles and let D, E, F be the points where the circles touch each other. Let G, H be the points where the tangent touches two of the circles.

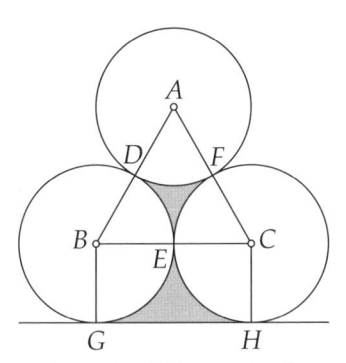

Exercise 3.5 question 1

Since each circle has radius 1, triangle ABC is an equilateral triangle of side 2. So each of the arcs DE, EF and FD has length
$$\tfrac{1}{6} \times 2\pi \times 1 = \frac{\pi}{3}.$$
Now consider quadrilateral $BGHC$. The sides BG and CH are both radii, so they have length 1 and are perpendicular to the tangent GH. Hence $BGHC$ is a rectangle. So each of the arcs GE and EH has length
$$\tfrac{1}{4} \times 2\pi \times 1 = \frac{\pi}{2}.$$
But the perimeter of the shaded region consists of arcs DE, EF, FD, GE, EH and line segment HG, which has length 2. So the required perimeter is
$$3 \times \frac{\pi}{3} + 2 \times \frac{\pi}{2} + 2,$$
which is $2\pi + 2$.

2. From the given information, the four circles are symmetrically arranged in the square and therefore joining the centres of the four circles we get a square of side two and area four.

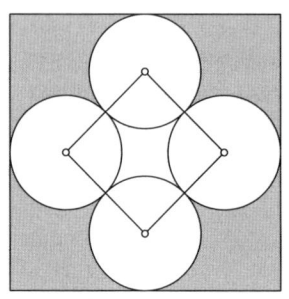

Exercise 3.5 question 2

The remaining unshaded area is made up of four three-quarter circles of total area

$$4 \times \tfrac{3}{4} \times \pi \times 1^2 = 3\pi.$$

Hence the unshaded area is $4 + 3\pi$.

By Pythagoras' theorem, the distance between the centres of two non-touching circles is

$$\sqrt{2^2 + 2^2} = 2\sqrt{2}.$$

Hence the given square has side $2\sqrt{2} + 2 \times 1$.

Therefore the shaded area is

$$(2 + 2\sqrt{2})^2 - (4 + 3\pi) = 4 + 8\sqrt{2} + 8 - 4 - 3\pi$$
$$= 8(1 + \sqrt{2}) - 3\pi.$$

3. Label the points common to the square and circle A, B, C, D and E, as shown. Label the remaining vertices of the square F, G and H. Let O be the centre of the circle. Finally, let CO (produced) meet AE at I and let DO (produced) meet AB at J.

Angles OCG and ODG are right angles since GC and GD are tangents to the circle at C and D respectively. Now angles OJA and ODG are alternate angles, so that angle OJA is a right angle. Similarly, angle OIA is a right angle. Angle IAJ is also a right angle and hence $AJOI$ is a rectangle.

Similarly, $GFJD$ and $GHIC$ are rectangles, so that $DJ = GF$ and $CI = GH$. But $FGHA$ is a square, so that $GF = GH$ and hence $DJ = CI$, and OC and OD are equal to 2, the radius of the circle.

Appendix C: Solutions to the exercises

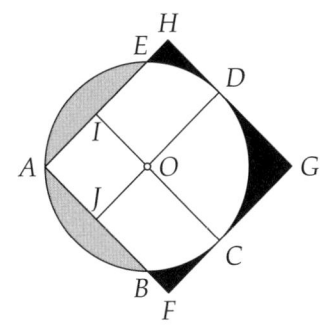

Exercise 3.5 question 3

Therefore $OJ = DJ - 2 = CI - 2 = OI$ and we deduce that rectangle $AJOI$ is a square. The diagonal, AO, of square $AJOI$ is equal to the radius of the circle and so the sides have length $\sqrt{2}$. Hence the length of the side of the square $AFGH$ is $2 + \sqrt{2}$.

If the region where the circle and square overlap has area Z then, using the notation in the question,

$$\text{(Area of the circle)} - \text{(Area of the square)} = (Y + Z) - (X + Z)$$
$$= Y - X,$$

which is the required quantity.

Hence

$$Y - X = \pi \times 2^2 - (2 + \sqrt{2})^2$$
$$= 4\pi - (4 + 4\sqrt{2} + 2)$$
$$= 4\pi - 6 - 4\sqrt{2}.$$

4. Let x be the radius of the circle, so that the square has side $2x$.

Let y be the width of the rectangle, so that the height of the rectangle is $2y$.

Applying Pythagoras' theorem to the triangle PQR, we have

$$x^2 = (x - 2y)^2 + (x - y)^2,$$

which we may rearrange to get

$$x^2 - 6xy + 5y^2 = 0.$$

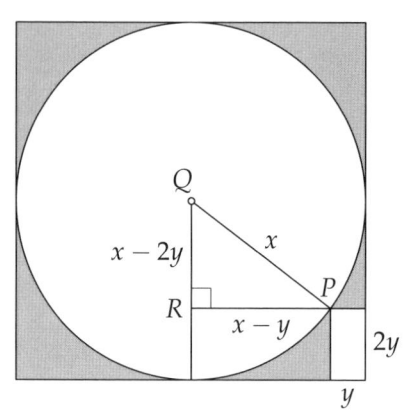

Exercise 3.5 question 4

Factorising the left-hand side, we obtain
$$(x - y)(x - 5y) = 0$$
and therefore $x = y$ or $x = 5y$.

However, $x = y$ is impossible since there would then be no circle.

When $x = 5y$ the ratio of the area of the square to the area of the rectangle is $(10y)^2 : 2y^2 = 50 : 1$.

5. Let r be the radius of the circle, so that the outer square has side length $2r$. Thus the total area between the circle and the outer square is
$$(2r)^2 - \pi r^2 = (4 - \pi)r^2.$$

Let the side of the inner square be s. Two radii and one side of this square form a right-angled triangle, as shown.

Applying Pythagoras' theorem to this triangle, we obtain $s^2 = r^2 + r^2 = 2r^2$. Thus the total area between the circle and the inner square is
$$\pi r^2 - s^2 = \pi r^2 - 2r^2 = (\pi - 2)r^2.$$

Since the figure has rotational symmetry of order four, the ratio of the darker to the lighter shaded area is therefore
$$\frac{(4 - \pi)r^2}{4} : \frac{(\pi - 2)r^2}{4} = (4 - \pi) : (\pi - 2).$$

Appendix C: Solutions to the exercises

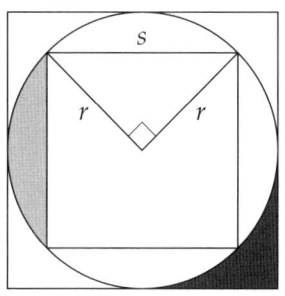

Exercise 3.5 question 5

6. In the rectangle $QRST$, we have $QR = TS$ and hence
$$a + b = c. \tag{1}$$

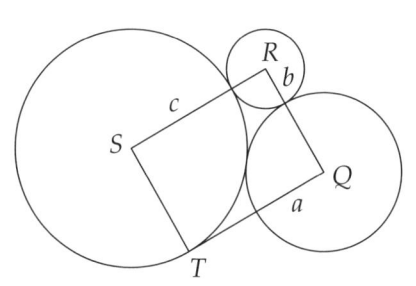

Exercise 3.5 question 6

In the right-angled triangle QRS, by Pythagoras' theorem, we have $QS^2 = QR^2 + RS^2$. But $QS = a + c$, $QR = a + b$ and $RS = b + c$, therefore
$$(a+c)^2 = (a+b)^2 + (b+c)^2 \tag{2}$$

Substituting for a from equation (1) into equation (2), we get
$$(2c - b)^2 = c^2 + (b+c)^2.$$

Thus
$$4c^2 - 4bc + b^2 = c^2 + b^2 + 2bc + c^2,$$

so that
$$2c^2 - 6bc = 0$$

and hence
$$c(c - 3b) = 0.$$

But $c \neq 0$ hence $c = 3b$.

Again from equation (1), $a + b = 3b$ and thus $a = 2b$.

Therefore the ratio $a : b : c = 2 : 1 : 3$.

7. Use the notation in the diagram.

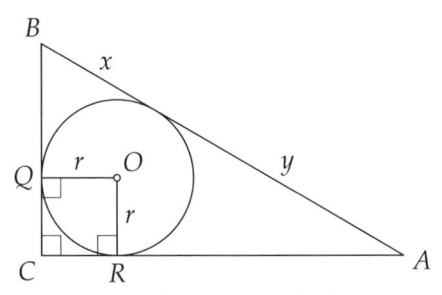

Exercise 3.5 question 7

Given any point on a circle, the two tangents from an external point are of equal length. Hence $AR = y$ and $BQ = x$.

Now OR and OQ are radii of the circle and AC and BC are tangents to the circle, so that $\angle ORC = 90°$ and $\angle OQC = 90°$. It follows that $OQCR$ is a square, and hence $CR = CQ = r$.

From Pythagoras' theorem applied to triangle ABC, we get

$$AB^2 = BC^2 + AC^2$$

and so

$$(x+y)^2 = (x+r)^2 + (y+r)^2,$$

which may be expanded and simplified to give

$$xy = xr + yr + r^2. \tag{1}$$

Now the area of the triangle is

$$\begin{aligned}\text{`}\tfrac{1}{2}\text{ base} \times \text{height'} &= \tfrac{1}{2} \times AC \times BC \\ &= \tfrac{1}{2}(y+r)(x+r) \\ &= \tfrac{1}{2}(xy + xr + yr + r^2) \\ &= \tfrac{1}{2}(xy + xy) \quad \text{from equation (1)} \\ &= xy,\end{aligned}$$

as required.

8. We add some labels and lines to the diagram, as shown: A, B and C are the centres; D, E and F are the points of contact of the circles and the straight line; and P is the foot of the perpendicular from B to AD.

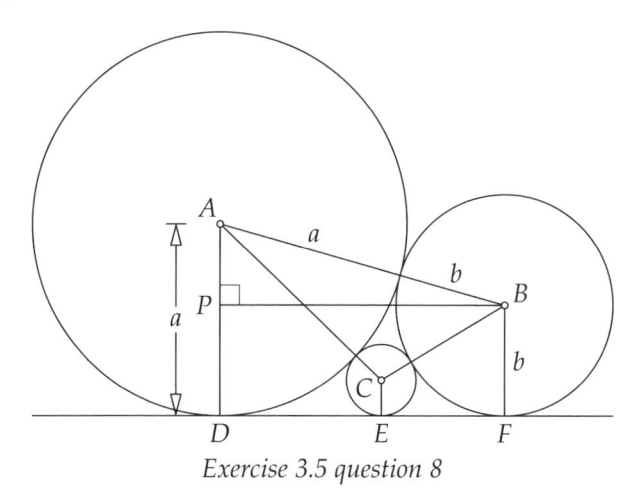

Exercise 3.5 question 8

Note first that AB, BC and CA, the lines of centres, pass through the points of tangency of the pairs of circles. Also, AD, CE and BF are perpendicular to the line DEF.

Then, by Pythagoras' theorem applied to triangle APB, we have
$$(a-b)^2 + PB^2 = (a+b)^2.$$
Therefore
$$PB^2 = (a+b)^2 - (a-b)^2$$
$$= 4ab.$$

Hence $DF = PB = 2\sqrt{ab}$. Similarly, $DE = 2\sqrt{ca}$ and $EF = 2\sqrt{bc}$. Since $DF = DE + EF$ we have
$$2\sqrt{ab} = 2\sqrt{ca} + 2\sqrt{bc}.$$
Dividing through by $2\sqrt{abc}$ gives the required result.

Exercise 3.6

1. FIRST SOLUTION

   Label the lines L_1, L_2, L_3 and L_4 in the order they appear in the question.

   We first find all the points of intersection between pairs of lines, by solving the corresponding pairs of equations simultaneously: L_1 and L_2 meet at $(4,4)$; L_2 and L_3 meet at $(2,0)$; L_3 and L_4 meet at $(-2,-2)$; and L_4 and L_1 meet at $(0,2)$.

   Call these points A, B, C and D respectively.

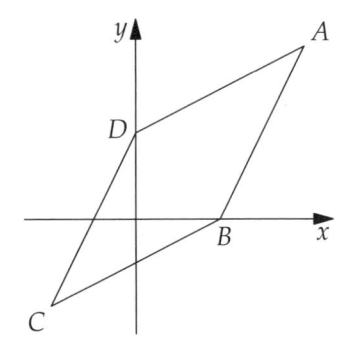

   Exercise 3.6 question 1 (first solution)

   Using Pythagoras' theorem, we can show that the lengths AB, BC, CD and DA are all equal to $\sqrt{20}$, that is, $2\sqrt{5}$. The quadrilateral enclosed is thus a rhombus and its area may be found by calculating $\frac{1}{2} \times$ (product of its diagonals).

   Using Pythagoras' theorem, we get
   $$AC^2 = 6^2 + 6^2$$
   $$= 72$$
   $$\text{and} \quad BD^2 = 2^2 + 2^2$$
   $$= 8.$$

   Therefore $AC = \sqrt{72} = 6\sqrt{2}$ and $BD = \sqrt{8} = 2\sqrt{2}$, so the area of the quadrilateral is $\frac{1}{2} \times 6\sqrt{2} \times 2\sqrt{2} = 12$.

SECOND SOLUTION

Using the notation shown in the diagram, as before we find that $A = (4,4)$, $B = (2,0)$ and also that $P = (-1,0)$.

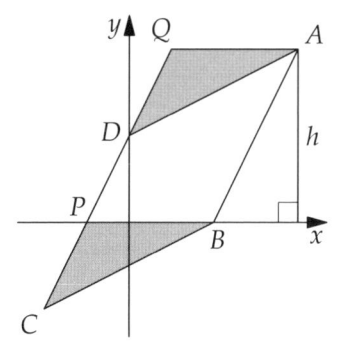

Exercise 3.6 question 1 (second solution)

Comparing the gradients of the lines, we see that each pair of opposite sides is parallel, so quadrilateral $ABCD$ is a parallelogram.

Let Q be the point for which $ABPQ$ is also a parallelogram. Then the two parallelograms $ABPQ$ and $ABCD$ have equal areas, because they have the same base AB and the same height.

Hence we have

$$\text{area } ABCD = \text{area } ABPQ = BP \times h = 3 \times 4 = 12.$$

2. The lines with equations $y = -x - 1$ and $y = 2x - 1$ intersect when

$$-x - 1 = 2x - 1,$$

from which

$$x = 0,$$

so that the lines meet at $(0, -1)$.

The line $y = k$ intersects the line $y = -x - 1$ when

$$k = -x - 1,$$

from which

$$x = -k - 1,$$

and it intersects the line $y = 2x - 1$ when

$$k = 2x - 1$$

from which
$$x = \tfrac{1}{2}(k+1).$$
Thus the three intersection points are
$$(0, -1), \ (-k-1, k) \ \text{and} \ \left(\tfrac{1}{2}(k+1), k\right).$$

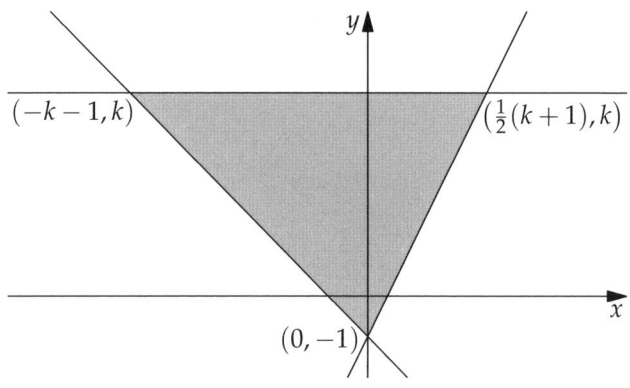

Exercise 3.6 question 2

Now the enclosed triangle has height $k+1$ and 'base' equal to
$$\tfrac{1}{2}(k+1) - (-k-1) = \tfrac{1}{2}(k+1) + k + 1$$
$$= \tfrac{3}{2}(k+1),$$
so the enclosed area is
$$\tfrac{1}{2} \times \tfrac{3}{2}(k+1) \times (k+1) = \tfrac{3}{4}(k+1)^2.$$
Therefore when the area equals 2008,
$$\tfrac{3}{4}(k+1)^2 = 2008,$$
so that
$$(k+1)^2 = \frac{8032}{3}$$
$$= 2667\tfrac{1}{3}.$$
Now $51^2 = 2601$ and $52^2 = 2704$ so that $k + 1 < 52$, that is, $k < 51$. We are told that k is a positive integer, so the possible values of k are given by $1 \leq k \leq 50$.

Exercise 3.7

1. FIRST SOLUTION

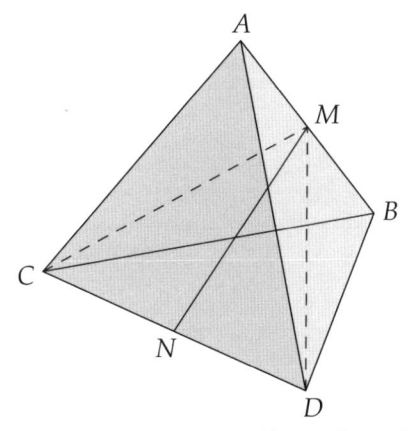

Exercise 3.7 question 1 (first solution)

Consider triangle ABC, one face of the tetrahedron. The triangle is isosceles and AM is a median, so that $\angle AMC = 90°$. Similarly, in triangle ABD, we have $\angle AMD = 90°$.

Now we apply Pythagoras' theorem to the triangles AMC and AMD to get

$$CM^2 = AC^2 - AM^2$$
$$= 2^2 - 1^2$$
and $$DM^2 = AD^2 - AM^2$$
$$= 2^2 - 1^2.$$

Hence $CM = \sqrt{3}$ and $DM = \sqrt{3}$, so triangle CMD is isosceles.

Because triangle CMD is isosceles and MN is a median it follows that $\angle CNM = 90°$.

Then, by Pythagoras' theorem in triangle CNM, we have

$$MN^2 = CM^2 - CN^2$$
$$= 3 - 1.$$

Therefore $MN = \sqrt{2}$.

Second solution

A tetrahedron may be formed by joining face diagonals of a cube, as shown.

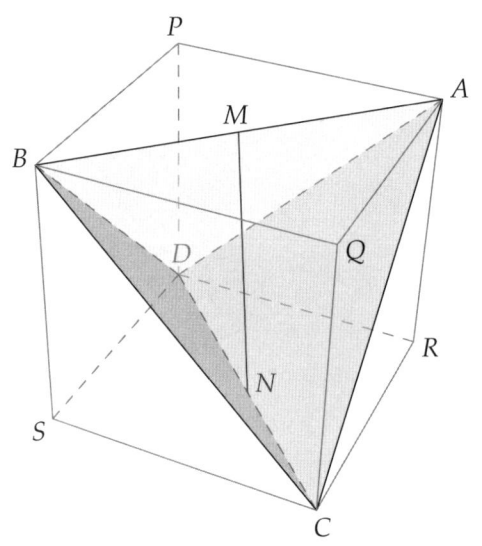

Exercise 3.7 question 1 (second solution)

Since the faces of the cube are congruent squares the face diagonals have equal length and so the tetrahedron is regular.

Now M and N are midpoints of opposite edges of the tetrahedron. Therefore they are midpoints of opposite face diagonals of the cube, that is, centres of opposite faces of the cube. Hence $MN = AR$.

Letting the sides of the cube have length a, from Pythagoras' theorem in triangle ARC we get

$$AC^2 = AR^2 + RC^2$$

so that

$$2^2 = a^2 + a^2$$
$$= 2a^2.$$

Hence $a = \sqrt{2}$ and therefore $MN = \sqrt{2}$.

2. Let the large cuboid have dimensions x, y and z, as shown.

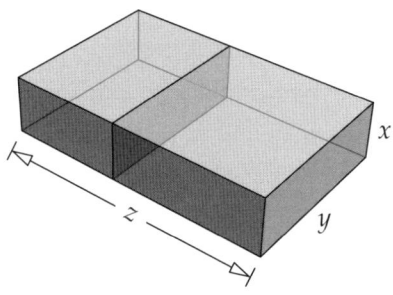

Exercise 3.7 question 2

Now the sum T of the surface areas of the original two cuboids is equal to the surface area of the large cuboid added to the area of the two faces which are joined together. But the surface area of the large cuboid is $\frac{3}{4}T$, hence the area of the two faces which are joined together is $\frac{1}{4}T$, that is, $\frac{1}{3}$ of the surface area of the large cuboid.

Therefore
$$2xy = \tfrac{1}{3}(2xy + 2yz + 2zx)$$
so that
$$6xy = 2xy + 2yz + 2zx$$
and hence
$$2xy = yz + zx.$$

Dividing by xyz we obtain, as required,
$$\frac{2}{z} = \frac{1}{x} + \frac{1}{y}.$$

3. Let A, B and C be the points $(4,0,3)$, $(6,4,1)$ and $(2,8,5)$. Using Pythagoras' theorem, we can calculate the distances between pairs of points: $AB = \sqrt{24}$, $BC = \sqrt{48}$ and $AC = \sqrt{72}$.

Consider the eight vertices of a cube. There are only three possible lengths of distances between pairs of points, namely those given by an edge, a face diagonal and a space diagonal. These lengths are in the ratio $1 : \sqrt{2} : \sqrt{3}$.

By considering the relative sizes of the lengths we have calculated we conclude that AB is an edge, BC is a face diagonal and AC is a space diagonal, as shown.

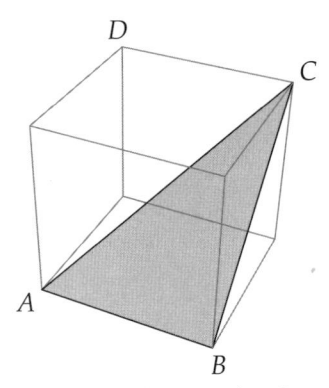

Exercise 3.7 question 3

We notice from the diagram that the face diagonal AD is parallel to BC, but on the opposite side of the cube. Thus the translation that takes us from B to C will also take us from A to D. This translation is -4 in the x-direction, $+4$ in the y-direction, and $+4$ in the z-direction.

Hence the coordinates of D are $(4-4, 0+4, 3+4)$, that is $(0,4,7)$.

REMARK

Using a more sophisticated argument, it is possible to show that the coordinates of the remaining four vertices are $(4,6,3) \pm \sqrt{6}(1,0,1)$ and $(2,2,5) \pm \sqrt{6}(1,0,1)$.

4. FIRST SOLUTION

Consider any two adjacent faces along which the ant moves and unfold them as shown.

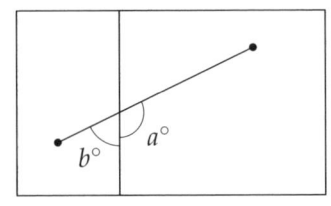

Exercise 3.7 question 4 (first solution)

Since the ant takes the shortest possible path between any two points, on the unfolded diagram the path will be a straight line. It follows that the path, when it crosses an edge, always forms a pair of supplementary angles, such as $a°$ and $b°$ in the diagram.

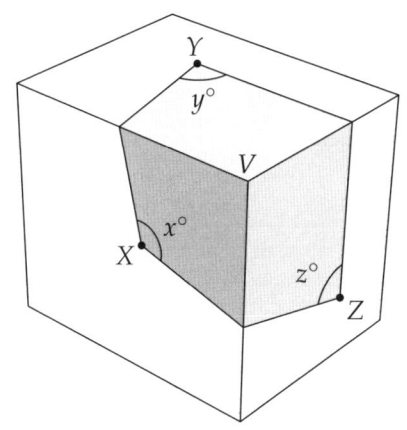

Exercise 3.7 question 4 (first solution)

Now consider the three quadrilaterals, shown shaded, which are bounded by the ant's path and which have one vertex V of the cuboid in common.

The angle sum of each quadrilateral is $360°$ and so the sum of the angles in all three quadrilaterals is $3 \times 360° = 1080°$.

This sum comprises:

> the three angles $x°$, $y°$ and $z°$;
> three pairs of supplementary angles, as described above; and
> three right angles at the vertex V.

We thus obtain the equation

$$x + y + z + 3 \times 180 + 3 \times 90 = 1080$$

and hence

$$x + y + z = 270,$$

as required.

SECOND SOLUTION

Consider a net of three faces of the cuboid, drawn on a sheet of paper. There is more than one way to draw such a net; the figure shows two ways. On each net, one section of the ant's path is disconnected.

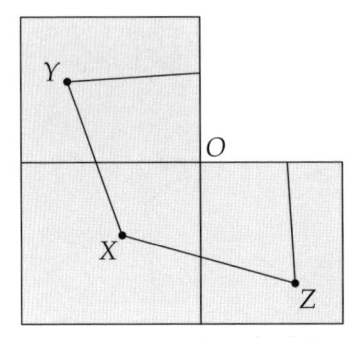

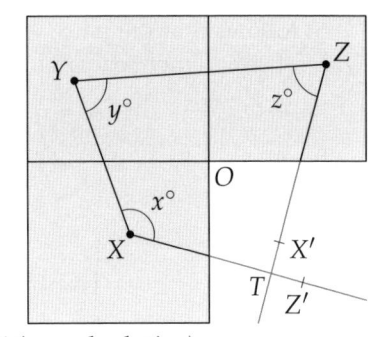

Exercise 3.7 question 4 (second solution)

Consider the second net. Rotating the right-hand rectangle clockwise through 90° about O, we obtain the first net. In the process, the line segment ZX' rotates to $Z'X$, where the point Z' corresponds to the position of Z in the first net.

Let the lines ZX' and $Z'X$ meet at T. Then the angle XTZ is a right angle, and we may use the fact that the sum of the angles in the quadrilateral $ZYXT$ is 360° to complete the proof.

5. Let the radius of the smallest cylinder be r. Then the total volume of the sandcastle is

$$\pi r^2 \times r + \pi(2r)^2 \times r + \pi(3r)^2 \times r = \pi r^3 + 4\pi r^3 + 9\pi r^3$$
$$= 14\pi r^3.$$

Let the smaller radius of the bucket be R. To calculate the volume of the bucket, consider the frustum to be the difference between two cones.

Referring to the diagram and noting that the shaded triangles are congruent, we have $h = 2R$. The volume of the bucket is therefore

$$\tfrac{1}{3}\pi(2R)^2 \times 4R - \tfrac{1}{3}\pi R^2 \times 2R = \frac{16}{3}\pi R^3 - \frac{2}{3}\pi R^3$$
$$= \frac{14}{3}\pi R^3.$$

Appendix C: Solutions to the exercises

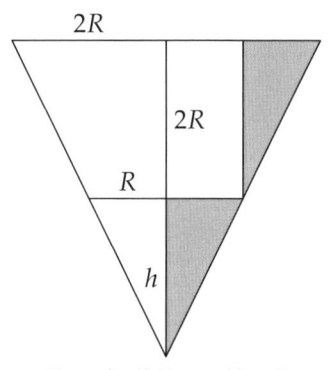

Exercise 3.7 question 5

As the bucket was filled 24 times to make the sandcastle, we have

$$14\pi r^3 = 24 \times \frac{14}{3}\pi R^3,$$

which may be simplified to give $r^3 = 8R^3$, and so $r = 2R$.

The total height of the sandcastle is $3r$ and the height of the bucket is $2R$, so the required ratio is $3r : 2R = 3 : 1$.

Exercise 3.8

1. FIRST SOLUTION

    In the figure, the shaded right-angled triangle is similar to the triangle forming the upper-right half of the rectangle and so the ratios of corresponding sides are equal.

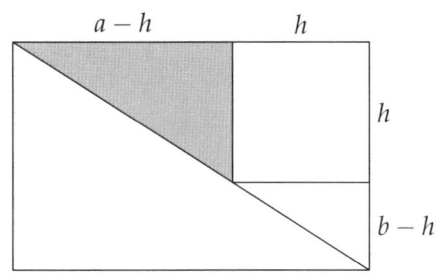

    Exercise 3.8 question 1 (first solution)

    Therefore
    $$\frac{a-h}{h} = \frac{a}{b},$$
    and so
    $$b(a-h) = ah.$$
    Expanding the brackets and simplifying, we get
    $$ab = bh + ah.$$
    If we now divide throughout by abh, we arrive at the desired result.

    SECOND SOLUTION

    In the figure, a diagonal XT of the square has been drawn.

    This creates two triangles XYT and XZT. The sum of the areas of these two triangles equals half the area of the rectangle. Therefore
    $$\tfrac{1}{2}bh + \tfrac{1}{2}ah = \tfrac{1}{2}ab.$$
    Dividing throughout by $\tfrac{1}{2}ab$, we get the desired result.

2. FIRST SOLUTION

    We add some labels to the diagrams and let the dimensions of the rectangle be $x \times y$, as shown.

Appendix C: Solutions to the exercises

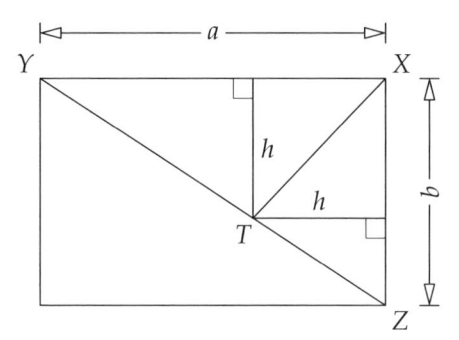

Exercise 3.8 question 1 (second solution)

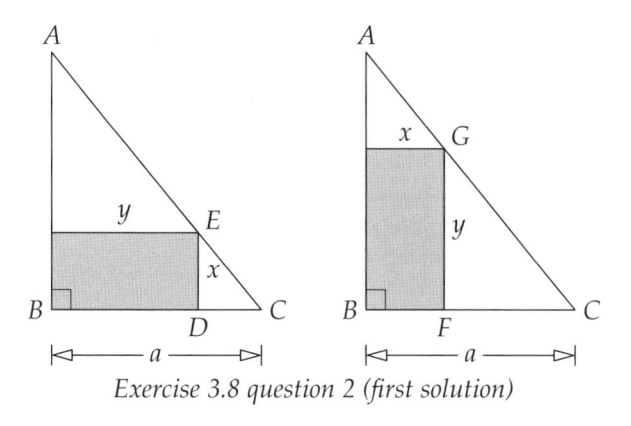

Exercise 3.8 question 2 (first solution)

The triangles DCE and FCG are similar, so
$$\frac{x}{a-y} = \frac{y}{a-x},$$
which may be rearranged to give
$$x(a-x) = y(a-y),$$
that is,
$$a(x-y) = x^2 - y^2$$
$$= (x-y)(x+y).$$

Since $x - y \neq 0$ (because there are two *different* ways of fitting the rectangle) this implies that $a = x + y$. Thus the perimeter of the rectangle is $2x + 2y = 2a$.

SECOND SOLUTION

Superimpose the two orientations of the rectangle inside the triangle, as shown. Once again we have added some labels and have let the dimensions of the rectangle be $x \times y$.

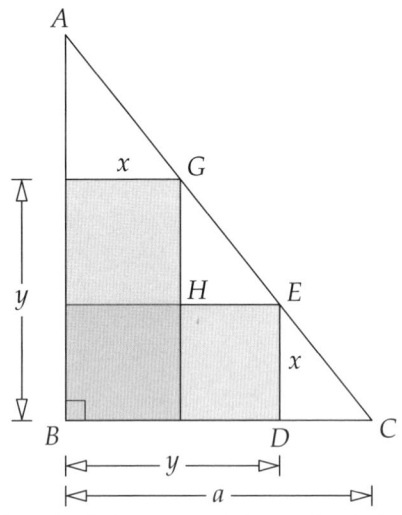

Exercise 3.8 question 2 (second solution)

Now we have $GH = y - x$ and $HE = y - x$, so that triangle GHE is isosceles. But $\angle GHE = 90°$ and hence $\angle HEG = \angle EGH = 45°$. Since the opposite sides of a rectangle are parallel, CD and EH are parallel, and so are ED and GH (they are both parallel to AB). It follows that $\angle DCE = 45°$ and $\angle CED = 45°$, and so $ED = DC$ (sides opposite equal angles). Hence $DC = x$.

Therefore $BC = BD + DC = y + x$, so that $a = y + x$. Thus the perimeter of the rectangle is $2y + 2x = 2a$.

3. We begin with a diagram showing the information given in the question. The three marked angles are equal.

FIRST SOLUTION

Since AB is parallel to DC, the alternate angles $\angle DCP$ and $\angle CPB$ are equal. Hence the two triangles $\triangle CDP$ and $\triangle PCB$ are similar.

Exactly the same argument shows that $\triangle DPA$ is also similar to $\triangle PCB$. We therefore have three similar triangles. Notice that we

Exercise 3.8 question 3

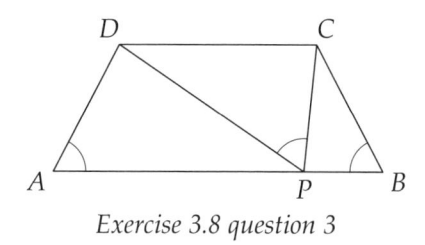

have been careful to describe the triangles in the correct order of vertices, so that the ratios of sides can now be read off conveniently.

Now corresponding sides are in the same ratio, so we have

$$\frac{PB}{PC} = \frac{PC}{DC} \quad \text{and} \quad \frac{AP}{PD} = \frac{PD}{DC},$$

and it follows that

$$PC^2 = PB \times DC \quad \text{and} \quad PD^2 = AP \times DC.$$

Adding these two equations, we obtain

$$PC^2 + PD^2 = (AP + PB) \times DC$$
$$= AB \times DC.$$

SECOND SOLUTION

This proof starts by using the converse of the alternate segment theorem. Because $\angle DAB = \angle CPD$ it follows that CP is a tangent at P to the circumcircle of $\triangle DAP$.

Similarly, DP is a tangent at P to the circumcircle of $\triangle BCP$.

Let DC (extended) meet the two circles at X and Y, as shown.

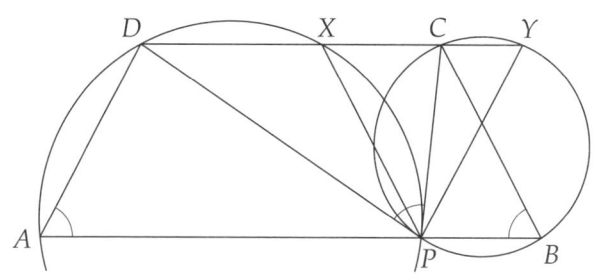

Exercise 3.8 question 3 (second solution)

Now $\angle CXP = \angle DAP$, by the external angle of a cyclic quadrilateral, and also $\angle CXP = \angle XPA$, by alternate angles. Hence $\angle XPA = \angle DAP = \angle CBP$ and so XP is parallel to CB and $PBCX$ is a parallelogram. Similarly, $APYD$ is a parallelogram. In particular, $CX = PB$ and $DY = AP$.

Now we use the tangent-secant theorem for each circle. This gives
$$CP^2 = CX \times CD$$
$$= PB \times CD$$

and
$$DP^2 = DC \times DY$$
$$= DC \times AP.$$

The last stage of the proof proceeds in the same way as the first solution.

REMARK

When the three marked angles are right angles the result reduces to Pythagoras' theorem.

4. FIRST SOLUTION

Let O be the centre of the circle, so that $OA = OB = OC = 2$, and let chord AC and radius OB meet at X.

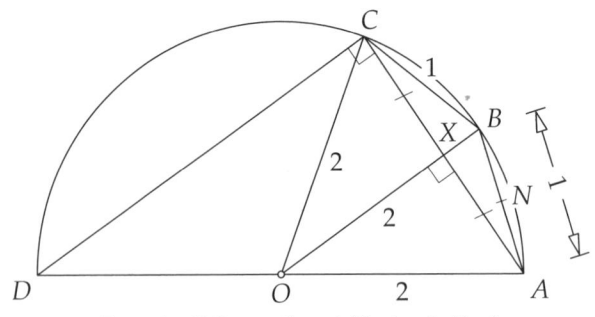

Exercise 3.8 question 4 (first solution)

Triangle OAC is isosceles and OB bisects angle AOC (because the chords AB and BC are equal and so subtend equal angles at the centre). Hence OB is the perpendicular bisector of the base AC of the isosceles triangle OAC. In other words, $AX = XC$ and $\angle AXO = 90°$, as shown.

Appendix C: Solutions to the exercises

Since angle ACD is $90°$ (angle in a semicircle) triangle ACD is a right-angled triangle with CD, the length we have to find, as one side. We know $AD = 4$, so can find CD, using Pythagoras' theorem, from
$$CD^2 = AD^2 - AC^2, \tag{1}$$
provided we can find the length of AC. We shall do this by using areas, but there are other methods.

Now consider isosceles triangle OAB and let N be the midpoint of AB, so that OA is a median and so triangle ANO is right-angled. Then, from Pythagoras' theorem, $NO^2 = 2^2 - \left(\frac{1}{2}\right)^2 = \frac{15}{4}$, so that $NO = \frac{\sqrt{15}}{2}$. Hence the area of triangle OAB is $\frac{1}{2} \times AB \times NO = \frac{\sqrt{15}}{4}$. But the area of triangle OAB is also $\frac{1}{2} \times OB \times AX$. Therefore $AX = \frac{\sqrt{15}}{4}$ and so $AC = 2AX = \frac{\sqrt{15}}{2}$. Using this value in equation (1), we get
$$CD^2 = AD^2 - AC^2 = 4^2 - \frac{15}{4} = \frac{49}{4}$$
and hence $CD = \frac{7}{2}$.

SECOND SOLUTION

Let P be the intersection of AB produced and DC produced.

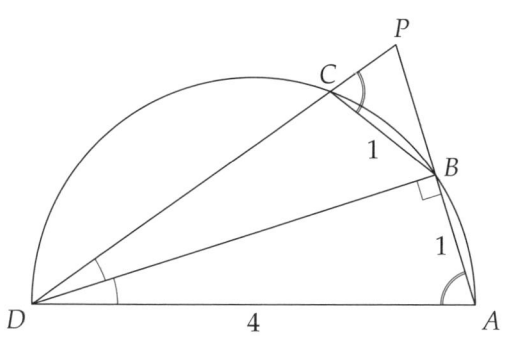

Exercise 3.8 question 4 (second solution)

Now angles ADB and BDC are both angles at the circumference subtended by chords of length 1. These angles are therefore equal. Also, $\angle ABD = 90°$ (angle in a semicircle). Therefore triangles ABD and PBD are congruent (ASA). Hence $BP = 1$ and $PD = 4$.

Further, in triangles BCP and DAP, angle P is common and $\angle BCP = \angle DAP$ (exterior angle of cyclic quadrilateral). These triangles are therefore similar and hence $PC : 1 = 2 : 4$.
So $PC = \frac{1}{2}$ and $CD = PD - PC = 4 - \frac{1}{2} = 3\frac{1}{2}$.

5. Using Pythagoras' theorem, $CB = 10\,\text{cm}$.

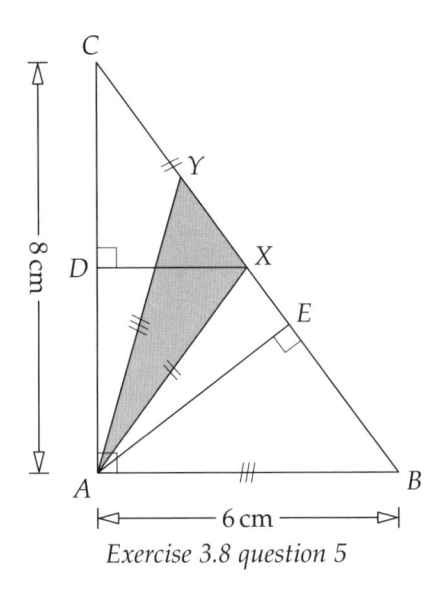

Exercise 3.8 question 5

Let E be the midpoint of BY. Then AE is a median of isosceles triangle ABY so that $\angle AEB = 90°$.

Triangles EBA and ABC are similar since they both include a right angle and the angle at B is common to both triangles. The ratio of sides is $BA : BC = 3 : 5$ and hence the ratio of their areas is $3^2 : 5^2 = 9 : 25$. So

$$\text{area } ABY = 2 \times \text{area } ABE$$
$$= 2 \times \frac{9}{25} \times \text{area } ABC$$
$$= 2 \times \frac{9}{25} \times 24\,\text{cm}^2$$
$$= \frac{432}{25}\,\text{cm}^2.$$

Now let D be the midpoint of AC. Then XD is a median of isosceles triangle ACX so that $\angle CDX = 90°$.

Triangles XCD and BCA are similar since they both include a right angle and angle C is common. The ratio of sides is $CD : CA = 1 : 2$ and hence $XD = \frac{1}{2}AB = 3$ cm. So area $ACX = \frac{1}{2} \times 8 \times 3 = 12\,\text{cm}^2$.

Putting this all together, we have

$$\text{area } AXY = \text{area } ABY + \text{area } ACX - \text{area } ABC$$
$$= \frac{432}{25} + 12 - 24 \text{ cm}^2$$
$$= \frac{132}{25} \text{ cm}^2.$$

6. Let O_1 and P_1 be the original positions of O and P. When the disc reaches the corner at A, let O_2 be the position of the centre and let Q_1 and Q_2 be the points of contact with AB and AF. Finally, when the disc has revolved exactly once, let O_3 be the centre, let Q_3 be the point of contact and let P_2 be the final position of P.

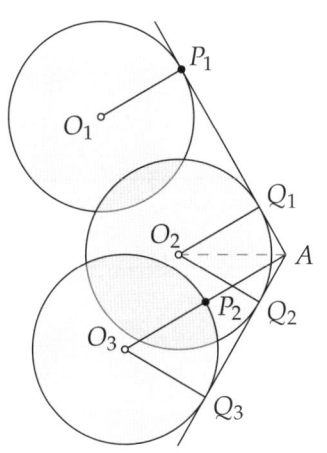

Exercise 3.8 question 6

Now $\angle Q_2 A Q_1 = 120°$ and $O_2 Q_1 = 3$, so $AQ_1 = AQ_2 = \sqrt{3}$. Since the circle has completed one revolution without slipping $P_1 Q_1 + Q_2 Q_3 = 6\pi$.

Also O_3A is perpendicular to AP_1, so $\angle O_3AQ_3 = 30°$. Hence $AQ_3 = 3\sqrt{3}$. Letting $P_1A = a$ and putting all of this together, we obtain
$$P_1Q_1 + Q_2Q_3 = \left(a - \sqrt{3}\right) + \left(3\sqrt{3} - \sqrt{3}\right) = 6\pi$$
and so $a = 6\pi - \sqrt{3}$.

Therefore the length $2a$ of the side of the hexagon $2a$ is $12\pi - 2\sqrt{3}$.

REMARK

Notice that part of the circle (the arc Q_2Q_1) is never in contact with the hexagon. But, because the circle makes one complete revolution, this means that part of the circle (the arc Q_3P_2) actually makes contact with the hexagon twice.

7. FIRST SOLUTION

First note that the length of an arc of a circle is proportional to the angle subtended at the centre. Hence, by appropriate choice of radius, we can arrange that the arc lengths are actually equal to these angles. (If this is not done, the calculation proceeds in the same way, but there is some cancelling to do at the end.)

The diagram shows these four angles at the centre of the circle.

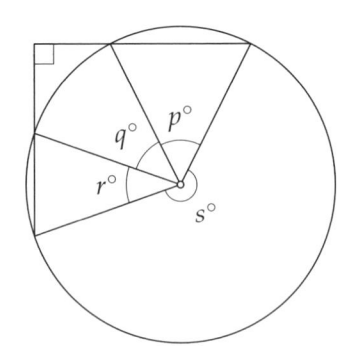

Exercise 3.8 question 7 (first solution)

Now there are two relationships between p, q, r and s. First there is the obvious one
$$p + q + r + s = 360°. \tag{1}$$
We also have the angle sum of a quadrilateral; one of the angles is $90°$, one is $p + q + r$, and the others can be calculated in terms of p

Appendix C: Solutions to the exercises 217

and r using the fact that there are two isosceles triangles. This gives
$$(p+q+r) + (90° - \tfrac{1}{2}p) + 90° + (90° - \tfrac{1}{2}r) = 360°$$
and so
$$p + 2q + r = 180°.$$
Hence, from (1),
$$p + q + r + s = 2p + 4q + 2r$$
and so
$$s = p + 3q + r.$$

SECOND SOLUTION

We construct the two radii perpendicular to the two given chords, as shown in the diagram.

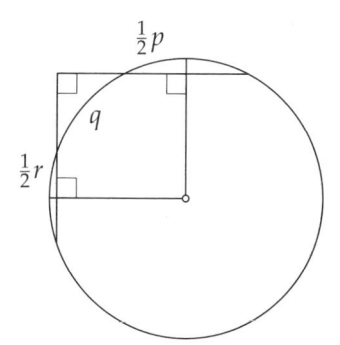

Exercise 3.8 question 7 (second solution)

Since a radius perpendicular to a chord bisects the chord, it also bisects the corresponding arc. So we have arcs of length $\tfrac{1}{2}p$ and $\tfrac{1}{2}r$, as shown.

Now the diagram contains a quadrilateral with three right angles, so the fourth angle is also a right angle and therefore the two radii are perpendicular. Hence the radii determine a quarter of the circle, and so
$$p + q + r + s = 4 \times (\tfrac{1}{2}p + q + \tfrac{1}{2}r),$$
which gives
$$s = p + 3q + r.$$

8. Let O be the centre of the circular arc.

Exercise 3.8 question 8

In the figure, the points A, B, D, E and F correspond to points on the original diagram, so that $BE = 9$, $AE = 27$ and $DF = 10$. The point C is the point obtained by drawing a line from B, perpendicular to the line OF.

Let the radius of the circular arc be r, so that $OA = OB = OF = r$. Furthermore, $OC = r - 1$ and $OD = r - 10$.

Finally, let $ED = BC = x$, so that $AD = 27 + x$.

We now apply Pythagoras' theorem to triangles OCB and ODA in turn.

In triangle OCB,
$$x^2 + (r-1)^2 = r^2,$$
which may be expanded and simplified to give
$$x^2 = 2r - 1 \qquad (1)$$

In triangle ODA,
$$(x+27)^2 + (r-10)^2 = r^2,$$

from which we get
$$x^2 + 5x - 20r + 829 = 0.$$
Now replace r in this equation with
$$r = \frac{x^2 + 1}{2}$$
from equation (1) to obtain
$$x^2 + 54x + 829 - 10x^2 - 10 = 0,$$
which may be simplified to give
$$x^2 - 6x - 91 = 0.$$
Factorising the left-hand side, we get
$$(x - 13)(x + 7) = 0$$
and so either $x = 13$ or $x = -7$. Of course, x has to be positive and so we discard the negative solution.

The width of the tunnel at ground level is therefore $2 \times (27 + 13) = 80$ feet.

Exercise 4.2

1. In the "letter sum", label the units column (1), the tens column (2), and so on, as shown in the left-hand figure.

$$
\begin{array}{ccccc}
(5) & (4) & (3) & (2) & (1) \\
S & E & V & E & N \\
 & & O & N & E \\
\hline
E & I & G & H & T \\
\end{array}
\qquad
\begin{array}{ccccc}
(5) & (4) & (3) & (2) & (1) \\
8 & 9 & V & 9 & N \\
 & & O & N & 9 \\
\hline
9 & I & G & H & T \\
\end{array}
$$

Exercise 4.2 question 1

In column (5), since different letters represent different digits, then S cannot be equal to E. This shows that a '1' is carried from column (4) to column (5). Therefore $E = 9$ and $S = 8$. Rewriting the sum with these values gives the right-hand figure.

Consider column (1). If $N = 0$ then $T = 9$ and so $T = E$, which contradicts the statement that different letters represent different digits. Hence N is non-zero and a '1' is carried from column (1) to column (2).

Comparing columns (1) and (2) shows that $H = T + 1$, since the columns are identical except for the '1' carried to column (2). However, column (1) shows that $N + 9 = T + 10$, so that $T = N - 1$. Hence $H = (N - 1) + 1 = N$, which contradicts the statement that different letters represent different numbers.

Therefore there are no solutions to this "letter sum".

2. (a) To answer the question, it is only necessary to find one number with the required property and the corresponding value of k. Here, we will find all such numbers and show that k has the same value in all cases.

   The number 'ab' equals $10a + b$. We require $10a + b = 4(a + b)$, which may be simplified to give $2a = b$.

   Therefore, any two digit number which has a units digit equal to twice its tens digit will satisfy the required condition. There are four possibilities for such a number: 12, 24, 36 and 48.

   Now we note that, in each case, the reversed number equals 7 times the sum of the digits, for example, $84 = 7(4 + 8)$.

Appendix C: Solutions to the exercises

Hence $k = 7$.

(b) Notice that $10a + b$ and $10b + a$ add up to $11(a+b)$, that is, 11 times the sum of the digits (of either number). Hence, if one of the numbers is n times the digit sum, the other is $11 - n$ times the digit sum.

Hence $k = 11 - n$.

3. Let the three-digit number be 'abc', where 'abc' $= 100a + 10b + c$.

   The six two-digit numbers which can be formed are $10a + b$, $10a + c$, $10b + a$, $10b + c$, $10c + a$ and $10c + b$. These numbers have sum $22(a+b+c)$, thus 'abc' $= 22(a+b+c)$.

   Equating the two expressions for 'abc' we get the equation
   $$100a + 10b + c = 22(a+b+c). \tag{1}$$
   Thus $78a - 12b - 21c = 0$, or, more simply, $26a - 4b - 7c = 0$, which we may rewrite in the form
   $$4b + 7c = 26a.$$
   Since b and c are at most 9, the left-hand side of this equation is at most $4 \times 9 + 7 \times 9$, which is 99, and so a can be at most 3.

   Subtracting $a + b + c$ from each side of equation (1), we get
   $$99a + 9b = 21(a+b+c),$$
   that is,
   $$3(11a + b) = 7(a+b+c).$$
   Hence 7 divides $11a + b$.

   Therefore, if $a = 1$, then $b = 3$ and so $c = 2$; if $a = 2$, then $b = 6$ and $c = 4$; if $a = 3$, then $b = 2$ or 9 and so $c = 10$ or 6. Clearly $c = 10$ is invalid.

   So the solutions are 132, 264 and 396.

4. For a positive integer with less than four digits, adding a 5 at each end increases the number by less than 59 995. Similarly, a number with more than four digits increases by more than 5 000 005. Since the required number is increased by 518 059, it therefore has four digits.

Let x be the required four-digit number. Then adding a 5 to each end gives the number $500\,005 + 10x$. Hence
$$500\,005 + 10x = x + 518\,059,$$
that is,
$$9x = 518\,059 - 500\,005$$
$$= 18\,054,$$
so that
$$x = 2006.$$
Therefore the positive integer is 2006.

5. For ease of reference, label the columns (0) to (5) as shown.

```
      (0) (1) (2) (3) (4) (5)
           M   A   T   H   S
      +    M   A   T   H   S
      ─────────────────────────
       C   A   Y   L   E   Y
```
Exercise 4.2 question 5

From column (5), we see that Y is even. Hence, since the greatest possible 'carry' is 1, looking at column (2) there can be no carry from column (3) and so $T < 5$. Also, comparing columns (2) and (5), A and S differ by 5.

From column (0) we know that $M \geq 5$ and $C = 1$.

Now consider columns (1) and (2). If $A > 5$, then there is a carry from column (2) to column (1), so that A is odd. If $A < 5$ then there is no such carry and A is even. Note that $A \neq 5$ since then there is no possible value for S.

Thus there are four cases to consider, with $A = 2, 4, 7$ or 9. We shall investigate two cases and leave the other two for the reader.

If $A = 9$, using the information found above we can start to complete the sum as shown in the left-hand figure. But now there is no possible value for M, since 9 is already allocated.

Each of the cases $A = 2$ and $A = 7$ proceeds in a similar way. Though more progress can be made, in each case you should be able to show that there is no solution.

If $A = 4$, we can proceed as far as shown in the right-hand figure. There is a carry from column (5), so we conclude that E is odd and

Appendix C: Solutions to the exercises

$$\begin{array}{r} M\,9\,-\,-\,4 \\ +\,M\,9\,-\,-\,4 \\ \hline 1\,9\,8\,-\,-\,8 \end{array} \qquad \begin{array}{r} 7\,4\,T\,H\,9 \\ +\,7\,4\,T\,H\,9 \\ \hline 1\,4\,8\,L\,E\,8 \end{array}$$

Exercise 4.2 question 5

there are only two options, $E = 3$ or 5, since all other odd digits are allocated. Both values of E lead to a solution. Can you complete the analysis and so find the two solutions?

Exercise 4.3

1. The sum of all five odd digits is $1 + 3 + 5 + 7 + 9 = 25$.

   Subtracting 1, 3, 5, 7 and 9 in turn we get 24, 22, 20, 18 and 16, only one of which is a multiple of 9, namely $18 = 25 - 7$. Since the sum of the digits of a multiple of 9 is also a multiple of 9, it follows that the four digits can only be 1, 3, 5 and 9.

   The number of arrangements of these four digits is $4 \times 3 \times 2 \times 1 = 24$.

   Hence there are 24 four-digit multiples of 9 that consist of four different odd digits.

2. We note that being divisible by 15 is the same as being divisible by 3 and 5.

   We also note that a number is divisible by 5 if, and only if, the units digit is 0 or 5.

   However, our number cannot end in a 0. Indeed, every number begins with a non-zero digit. A palindrome has equal first and last digits, so the last digit is non-zero.

   Hence we seek a particular six-digit palindrome which begins and ends in 5, and which is divisible by 3.

   The largest six-digit palindromes beginning and ending in 5 have the form '59dd95', for some digit d. This is divisible by 3 when the digit-sum is a multiple of 3 and therefore $5 + d$ is divisible by 3. Hence $d = 1, 4$ or 7. Thus the number required is 597 795.

3. Note that all five-digit integers are divisible by 1.

   Next, notice that if a number is divisible by 2 and 5, then it is divisible by 10 and hence has last digit t equal to 0. Since all the digits are different, that means all the other digits are non-zero.

   Among five-digit numbers, those that begin with 1 are smaller than all those which don't. So if we find a number of the required form with first digit 1, then it will be smaller than numbers with larger first digits.

   Similarly, those with first two digits 12 are smaller than all other numbers with distinct non-zero digits. And, in fact, those with first three digits 123 are smaller than all others. Hence if we find such a number with the required properties, it will be smaller than all others.

Appendix C: Solutions to the exercises 225

So let us try to find a number of the form '123s0'.

A number is a multiple of four only if its last two digits form a multiple of four. So we need consider only the case where s is even.

Similarly, a number is a multiple of three if and only if the sum of its digits is a multiple of three. Since $1 + 2 + 3 + s + 0 = 6 + s$, we only need consider the case where s is a multiple of three.

Thus 12360 is the only number of the form '123s0' which is divisible by 1, 2, 3, 4 and 5, and as we've explained along the way, it's the smallest number with the required divisibility properties.

4. The required number is divisible by 12, so it is also divisible by 3 and by 4.

    Since the number is divisible by 3 the sum of its digits is a multiple of 3. But the digits are all 0 or 1, hence at least three of the digits are 1.

    Since the number is divisible by 4 the only possible final two digits are 00.

    Hence the smallest number of the required form is 11 100.

5. (a) If N is divisible by 2, then its unit digit is even, so in this case it is 2.

    Since N is divisible by 3, the sum of its digits is a multiple of 3. Hence the number of twos which N contains is itself a multiple of 3, since the only other digits N contains are threes. So the smallest possible integer N contains 1 three and 3 twos.

    Since N ends in 2, its value is 2232.

    (b) If M is divisible by 8, then its last three digits form a multiple of 8. In this case it means that the last three digits are 888 as no other three digit arrangement of eights and/or nines gives a multiple of 8.

    Since M is a multiple of 9, the sum of its digits must be a multiple of 9. Hence the number of eights which M contains is itself a multiple of 9, since the only other digits M contains are nines. So the smallest possible integer M contains 1 nine and 9 eights.

    Since M ends in 888, its value is 8 888 889 888.

6. Since '$p543q$' is a multiple of 36 it is a multiple of both 9 and 4.

The sum of the digits of a multiple of 9 is also a multiple of 9, hence $p + 5 + 4 + 3 + q$ is a multiple of 9. But $5 + 4 + 3 = 12$ and each of p and q is a single digit, so that $p + q = 6$ or $p + q = 15$ are the only possibilities.

Since '$p543q$' is a multiple of 4 and '$p5400$' is always divisible by 4, it follows that '$3q$' is divisible by 4. The only possible values for '$3q$' are 32 and 36, so that $q = 2$ or $q = 6$.

If $q = 2$, then $p + q = 15$ is not possible since p is a single digit. Hence $p + q = 6$ and so $p = 4$.

If $q = 6$, then $p + q = 6$ is not possible since '$p543q$' is a five-digit number and therefore the digit p cannot be zero. Hence $p + q = 15$ and so $p = 9$.

Therefore $p = 4$, $q = 2$ and $p = 9$, $q = 6$ are the only possible values of the digits p and q.

7. As the required number is a multiple of 35 it is also a multiple of 5 and so has units digit, and hence every other digit, equal to 0 or 5.

   Clearly the digits must be non-zero and so the required number is of the form '$55\ldots5$'.

   Division by 5 will give a number '$11\ldots1$' that is divisible by 7.

   We now take successive numbers of the form '$11\ldots1$' and try dividing by 7. We want the smallest such number that leaves no remainder. The numbers 111, 1111, 11 111 leave remainders of 6, 5 and 2 when divided by 7, but $111\,111 = 7 \times 15873$, so 111 111 is the smallest such number that is a multiple of 7.

   The required number is therefore 555 555.

8. Since 3 is a factor of '$xyxyx$' we know that 3 is a factor of the digit sum $3x + 2y$ and hence of $2y$. But 2 is coprime to 3, so 3 is a factor of y.

   The integer '$yxyxyxy$' is even, so y is even. Hence we deduce that $y = 6$, the only even digit that has 3 as a factor.

   Now 9 is a factor of '$6x6x6x6$' and so it is also a factor of the digit sum $24 + 3x$, and hence of $6 + 3x$. Thus $x = 1$, 4 or 7, the only digits for which this is the case.

9. Since the required number has four digits, it is between 1000 and 9999.

Appendix C: Solutions to the exercises

Let the number be N. We know that N is a perfect square, and also that $N - 1$ is divisible by 2, 3, 4, 5, 6, 7, 8 and 9. Hence $N - 1$ is divisible by the lowest common multiple of these numbers, which is $8 \times 9 \times 5 \times 7 = 2520$.

There are therefore only three possible values for N in the range, namely 2521, 5041 and 7561, and of these only the middle one is a perfect square, being 71^2.

Hence Miko's PIN is 5041.

Exercise 4.4

1. The number 'sss' equals $s \times 111 = s \times 3 \times 37$. Now 37 is prime, so one of the two numbers 'pq' and 'rq' is 37 or 74.

   The case 74 is not possible, since then $q = 4$, giving $s = 6$ and so 'sss' equals 9×74, which is not of the required form 'pq' $\times$ 'rq'.

   The case 37 gives $q = 7, s = 9$ and 'sss' $= 27 \times 37$, so that $p, r = 2, 3$, in either order.

2. The area of the polygon is 12 square units so that fitting together four copies of the polygon will create a rectangle with an area of 48 square units. The only possible integer dimensions for such a rectangle are 1×48, 2×24, 3×16, 4×12 and 6×8. Since the polygon has a height of 3 units and a length of 6 units, the first two rectangles are impossible. The figure shows that the other three are possible.

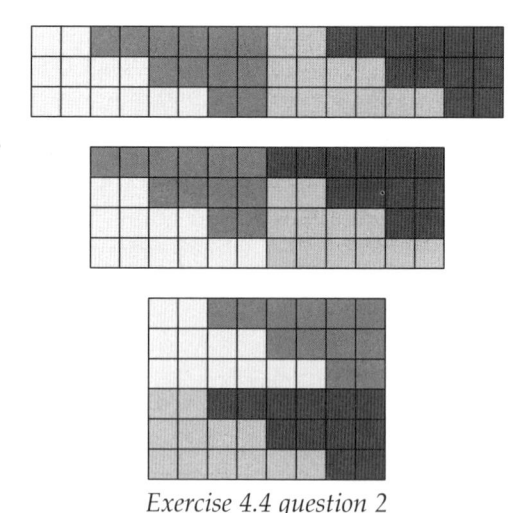

   Exercise 4.4 question 2

   Hence three different rectangles can be made.

3. Let the number in the bottom left-hand block be n.

   By rule A the other values on the bottom row are $2n$, $4n$ and $8n$.

   By rule B the values in the second row are $3n$, $6n$ and $12n$, those on the third row are $9n$ and $18n$, and the fourth row is $27n$. Hence the sum of all ten numbers is $90n$.

Appendix C: Solutions to the exercises 229

Since $90 = 2 \times 3^2 \times 5$ the smallest value of n for which $90n$ is a cube is $2^2 \times 3 \times 5^2 = 300$.

4. Let the number of consecutive integers which sum to 75 be n. We consider separately the cases when n is odd and when n is even.

   If n is odd, then let the middle number be k. Then k is the average of all the numbers, that is, $75 \div n$. It follows that $nk = 75$. Because n is greater than 1 and odd, the possible values of (n,k) are $(3,25)$, $(5,15)$, $(15,5)$, $(25,3)$ and $(75,1)$.

   If $n = 3$, then we have $24 + 25 + 26 = 75$. If $n = 5$, then we have $13 + 14 + 15 + 16 + 17 = 75$. If $n = 15$, then we have $(-2) + (-1) + 0 + 1 + 2 + 3 + \cdots + 12 = 75$, but not all of these are positive integers. Similarly, when $n = 25$ and when $n = 75$, the sequence contains negative integers.

   So there are two different ways for which the number of consecutive positive integers is odd.

   If n is even, then let the middle two numbers be $k - 1$ and k. Then the average of the middle two numbers, $\frac{1}{2}\{(k-1) + k\}$, is the average of all the numbers, that is, $75 \div n$. It follows that $n(2k - 1) = 150$. Because n is greater than 1 and even, the possible values of (n,k) are $(2,38)$, $(6,13)$, $(10,8)$, $(30,3)$, $(50,2)$ and $(150,1)$.

   If $n = 2$, then we have $37 + 38 = 75$. If $n = 6$, then we have $10 + 11 + 12 + 13 + 14 + 15 = 75$. If $n = 10$, then we have $3 + 4 + 5 + 6 + 7 + 8 + 9 + 10 + 11 + 12 = 75$. When $n = 30$, when $n = 50$ and when $n = 150$, the sequence contains negative integers.

   So there are three different ways for which the number of consecutive positive integers is even, giving five different ways overall.

5. Let x be the smallest positive integer in the sequence.
   From the information given,
   $$x^2 + (x+1)^2 + (x+2)^2 = (x+3)^2 + (x+4)^2,$$
   which may be rearranged to give
   $$x^2 - 8x - 20 = 0.$$
   Hence
   $$(x - 10)(x + 2) = 0$$
   so that $x = 10$ or $x = -2$.

But x is positive and therefore $x = 10$ is the only solution.
This proves that there is exactly one such sequence.

6. We may multiply every term in the equation
$$\frac{2}{15} = \frac{1}{a} + \frac{1}{b}$$
by $15ab$ in order to clear the fractions. We obtain
$$2ab = 15b + 15a.$$
We now rearrange this equation, first writing it in the form
$$4ab - 30a - 30b = 0,$$
then adding 225 to both sides to give
$$4ab - 30a - 30b + 225 = 225,$$
that is,
$$(2a - 15)(2b - 15) = 225.$$
Therefore $2a - 15$ is a divisor of $225 = 3^2 \times 5^2$, so that $2a - 15 = 1$, 3, 5, 9, or 15. Larger values are not possible since $a \leq b$ and so $2a - 15 \leq 2b - 15$. Also, negative values are not possible since then $2a - 15$ would be at most -15, but $a > 0$ so that $2a - 15 > -15$.
Each of the corresponding values of a and b is an integer:
$$(a, b) = (8, 120), (9, 45), (10, 30), (12, 20), \text{ or } (15, 15).$$
Hence there are five ways to express $\frac{2}{15}$ in the required form.

7. Let
$$N + 74 = x^2 \tag{1}$$
$$\text{and} \quad N - 15 = y^2, \tag{2}$$
where x and y are different positive integers.
Subtracting equation (2) from equation (1) gives $89 = x^2 - y^2$. Hence
$$89 = (x - y)(x + y). \tag{3}$$
Now x and y are integers, so equation (3) gives a factorisation of 89. But 89 is a prime number, so the only possible factors are 1 and 89.

Appendix C: Solutions to the exercises

Since $x + y > x - y$ we therefore have
$$x + y = 89$$
$$\text{and} \quad x - y = 1.$$
Adding these equations gives $2x = 90$, thus $x = 45$.
Substituting for x in equation (1), we obtain $N = 45^2 - 74 = 2025 - 74 = 1951$.

REMARK

As a check, we may also find $y = 44$ and substitute in equation (2), to obtain $N = 44^2 + 15 = 1936 + 15 = 1951$.

8. Assume, without loss of generality, that $x \leq y$. Then
$$\frac{1}{x} + \frac{1}{y} \leq \frac{2}{x}$$
so that
$$\frac{5}{11} \leq \frac{2}{x}$$
and hence
$$5x \leq 22.$$
Therefore $x \leq 4$ since x is an integer.

Can you see how to proceed?

REMARK

A *unit* fraction has numerator 1. An *Egyptian fraction* is constructed by adding *different* unit fractions together, for example,
$$\frac{5}{11} = \frac{1}{3} + \frac{1}{11} + \frac{1}{33}.$$
In ancient Egypt fractions were written like this.

It is possible to write any given fraction as an Egyptian fraction, but finding the smallest number of unit fractions needed is not easy—this problem shows that $\frac{5}{11}$ requires more than two.

9. Notice that the right-hand side $9b^2$ is always positive, since the square b^2 is always positive. However, the left-hand side $5a - ab = a(5 - b)$ is only positive for $b \leq 4$. So, given that b is a positive integer, we can consider four cases separately, namely $b = 1, 2, 3$ and 4.

If $b = 1$, then the equation becomes $(5 - 1)a = 9 \times 1^2$, that is, $4a = 9$. This has no solution for a positive integer a.

If $b = 2$, then the equation becomes $(5 - 2)a = 9 \times 2^2$, that is, $3a = 36$, so that $a = 12$. This gives the solution $a = 12, b = 2$.

If $b = 3$, then the equation becomes $(5 - 3)a = 9 \times 3^2$, that is, $2a = 81$. This has no solution for a positive integer a.

If $b = 4$, then the equation becomes $(5 - 4)a = 9 \times 4^2$, that is, $a = 144$. This gives the solution $a = 144, b = 4$.

Thus the solutions are $a = 12, b = 2$ and $a = 144, b = 4$.

10. (a) If we add the two given equations, taking $(x - y)$ out as a common factor, then we obtain the equation

$$(x - y)((y - z)(z + x) + (y + z)(z - x)) = -48,$$

which may be simplified to give

$$(x - y)(yz + yx - z^2 - zx + yz - yx + z^2 - zx) = -48.$$

Hence

$$(x - y)(2yz - 2zx) = -48.$$

Taking out $2z$ as a factor and then dividing throughout by -2, we obtain the required result.

(b) Note that we are told that x, y and z are positive integers. If the equations are added in pairs as in part (a), the following system of equations is obtained.

$$z(x - y)^2 = 24 = 2^2 \times 3 \tag{1}$$
$$y(z - x)^2 = 9 = 3^2 \tag{2}$$
$$x(y - z)^2 = 75 = 3 \times 5^2. \tag{3}$$

Considering equation (2), $(z - x)^2$ is a square integer and so equals either 1 or 9. Consequently, y equals 9 or 1.

Similarly, by considering equation (3), we conclude that x equals 75 or 3. This means there are four possibilities for the value of $(x - y)^2$: $66^2, 74^2, 6^2$ or 2^2. The only one of these which is consistent with equation (1) is 2^2, from which we conclude that the value of z is $2 \times 3 = 6$.

The full solution is $x = 3, y = 1$ and $z = 6$.

11. Let the white bag contain y green balls. Then it will contain ky red balls, where k is a positive integer.

Hence the black bag contains $140 - y$ green balls and $140 - ky$ red balls, so that
$$140 - y = 2(140 - ky),$$
which may be rearranged to give
$$y = \frac{140}{2k - 1}.$$
We conclude that $2k - 1$ is a factor of 140.

Now the odd factors of 140 are 1, 5, 7 and 35, so the only possible values of k are 1, 3, 4 and 18. The corresponding values of y are 140, 28, 20 and 4.

But if $y = 140$ then the black bag is empty, which is not possible. We may check that each of the other values leads to a solution:

Black bag		White bag	
Red	Green	Red	Green
56	112	84	28
60	120	80	20
68	136	72	4

Exercise 4.5

1. The sum of the cubes of the positive integers in the problem is 251, which is less than $7^3 = 343$, hence none of the integers is greater than 6.

   Now $\frac{251}{3} = 83\frac{2}{3} > 64 = 4^3$, therefore at least one of the integers is 5 or more.

   If one of the integers is 5, then the other two cubes add up to $251 - 5^3 = 251 - 125 = 126$. Now
   $$1^3 = 1, \ 2^3 = 8, \ 3^3 = 27, \ 4^3 = 64 \text{ and } 5^3 = 125, \qquad (1)$$
   so that $5^3 + 1^3 = 125 + 1 = 126$ is the only possibility. Also, $5 + 5 + 1 = 11$ so that 5, 5 and 1 is a possible triple of numbers.

   If one of the integers is 6, then the other two cubes add up to $251 - 6^3 = 251 - 216 = 35$. From list (1), we see that $3^3 + 2^3 = 27 + 8 = 35$ is the only possibility. Also, $6 + 3 + 2 = 11$ so that 6, 3 and 2 is a possible triple of numbers.

   Hence 1, 5, 5 and 2, 3, 6 are the triples of numbers satisfying the given conditions.

2. If an integer leaves a remainder of 31 when divided into 2011, then it divides exactly into $2011 - 31 = 1980$. Also, in order to leave a remainder of 31, the integer itself needs to be greater than 31.

   Now $1980 = 2^2 \times 3^2 \times 5 \times 11$. Hence any divisor of 1980 may be obtained by choosing one term from each of the following four lists and multiplying them together:
   $$1, 2, 2^2;$$
   $$1, 3, 3^2;$$
   $$1, 5;$$
   $$1, 11.$$
   There are $3 \times 3 \times 2 \times 2 = 36$ ways of choosing the terms and therefore 1980 has 36 divisors.

   The divisors of 1980 which are less than or equal to 31 are
   $$1, 2, 3, 4, 5, 6, 9, 10, 11, 12, 15, 18, 20, 22, \text{ and } 30,$$

Appendix C: Solutions to the exercises

that is, 15 divisors in all. Hence the number of divisors of 1980 which are greater than 31 is $36 - 15 = 21$.

Therefore there are 21 positive integers which leave a remainder of 31 when divided into 2011.

3. Firstly, it is clear that the three-digit number 'ODD' lies between 100 and 999. Therefore, since 'EVEN' = 2 × 'ODD', we have

$$200 < \text{'EVEN'} < 1998.$$

Hence the first digit E of 'EVEN' is 1 since it is a four-digit number. We are left with the problem shown in the left-hand figure.

$$\begin{array}{r} O\,D\,D \\ +\,O\,D\,D \\ \hline 1\,V\,1\,N \end{array} \qquad \begin{array}{r} O\,5\,5 \\ +\,O\,5\,5 \\ \hline 1\,V\,1\,0 \end{array}$$

Exercise 4.5 question 3

Now the same numbers are added in the tens and units columns, but $N \neq 1$, otherwise N and E would be equal. The only way for different totals to occur in these columns is for there to be a 'carry' to the tens column, and the greatest possible carry is 1, so that $N = 0$.

There are two possible digits D that give $N = 0$, namely 0 and 5. But 0 is already taken as the value of N, so that $D = 5$. The problem is therefore as shown in the right-hand figure.

Now, the digit O has to be big enough to produce a carry, but cannot be 5, which is already taken as the value of D. So the possibilities are $O = 6, 7, 8$ or 9.

Can you see how to deal with each of these in turn? You should find that two values work and two do not, so there are two possible solutions of the 'word sum'.

4. We may place the numbers from 1 to 99 into three categories, determined by how they are transformed when they are reversed:

A) single digit numbers '*a*' are unchanged;
B) a two digit number '*ab*', where neither *a* nor *b* is zero, is transformed to the two digit number '*ba*'; and
C) a multiple of 10 such as '*a*0' is transformed to '0*a*' = *a*, a single digit number.

Thus there is a correspondence between the numbers in N and M, as shown in the table.

N	M
'a'	'a'
'aa'	'aa'
'ab' and 'ba'	'ba' and 'ab'
'$a0$'	'a'

Exercise 4.5 question 4

Single digit numbers are unchanged; two-digit numbers with a repeated digit are unchanged; pairs of two-digit numbers, with different digits and neither digit zero, are unchanged as a pair; the multiples of 10 in N are replaced by single-digit numbers in M.

Thus when we divide N by M all the common terms cancel and we are left with

$$\frac{N}{M} = \frac{10 \times 20 \times \cdots \times 90}{1 \times 2 \times \cdots \times 9}$$
$$= 10^9.$$

5. Firstly, the answer to 2 Down has to be one of 198, 297, 396, 495, 594, 693, 792, 891 or 990. In all of these cases, the sum of the digits is the same: the answer to 2 Across is thus 18.

Knowing the first digit is 1 immediately allows us to narrow down 2 Down to 198. Also, 3 Down begins with an 8 and is the square of 4 Across, an integer which ends in 9. The number $19^2 = 361$ is too small, and 39^2 and subsequent squares have four or more digits. Hence 4 Across is 29 and 3 Down is 841.

We now use the clue for 5 Across: we get

$$'x1' + 18 + 841 = 'y81',$$

where x is the missing top left-hand digit and y is the missing bottom left-hand digit. Clearly y is 8, since even if x were 9 it would not be big enough to give a total of 981.

We can then subtract to find the answer to 1 Down: it is given by

$$881 - 841 - 18 = 22.$$

Appendix C: Solutions to the exercises

We have uniquely identified values for all nine digits, using the clues, as shown.

2	1	8
2	9	4
8	8	1

Exercise 4.5 question 5

In checking, we observe that we have not used the clue for 1 Down; however $22 = 2 \times 11$, so it does indeed work.

6. The pattern suggested by the three equations has the general form
$$\underbrace{111\ldots 11}_{2k \text{ digits}} - \underbrace{222\ldots 22}_{k \text{ digits}} = (\underbrace{333\ldots 33}_{k \text{ digits}})^2. \qquad (1)$$

We may prove that the generalisation in equation (1) is correct by letting $U = \underbrace{111\ldots 11}_{k \text{ digits}}$. Then

$$\underbrace{222\ldots 22}_{k \text{ digits}} = 2U,$$

$$\underbrace{333\ldots 33}_{k \text{ digits}} = 3U$$

and $\underbrace{999\ldots 99}_{k \text{ digits}} = 9U.$

Also
$$\underbrace{111\ldots 11}_{2k \text{ digits}} = U \times \underbrace{100\ldots 001}_{k+1 \text{ digits}}$$
$$= U(10^k + 1).$$

Hence
$$\underbrace{111\ldots 11}_{2k \text{ digits}} - \underbrace{222\ldots 22}_{k \text{ digits}} = U(10^k + 1) - 2U$$
$$= U(10^k - 1)$$
$$= U \times \underbrace{999\ldots 99}_{k \text{ digits}}$$

$$= U \times 9U$$
$$= (3U)^2$$
$$= (\underbrace{333\ldots 33}_{k \text{ digits}})^2,$$

as required.

7. If $x^2 + y^2 = x^3$, then $y^2 = x^2(x-1)$ and therefore, since $x > 0$,

$$\frac{y^2}{x^2} = x - 1. \tag{1}$$

We know that $x - 1$ is an integer. We deduce from equation (1) that $x - 1$ is a perfect square. Let $x - 1 = n^2$ for some non-negative integer n.

Now $0 < x < 2011$, so that $-1 < n^2 < 2010$ and hence $0 \leq n \leq 44$. But when $n = 0$ we have $x = 1$ and so $y = 0$, which is not allowed. Each other value of n gives a unique value of x, and therefore of y since $y > 0$.

Hence there are 44 solutions to the given equation in positive integers.

8. Firstly, note that it is possible to tile both a 6×2 and a 6×3 rectangle, as shown in the left-hand figure. It is clearly not possible to tile a 6×1 rectangle.

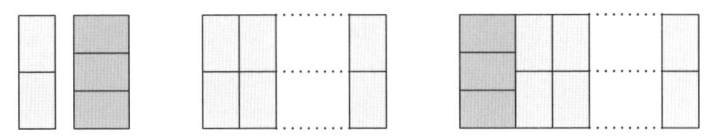

Exercise 4.5 question 8

We claim that a $6 \times m$ rectangle may be tiled for any $m > 1$. If m is even, use repeated copies of the 6×2 tiling, as shown in the central figure. If m is odd, use one copy of the 6×3 tiling and then use repeated copies of the 6×2 tiling, as shown in the right-hand figure.

Since a $6k \times m$ rectangle may be divided into k copies of a $6 \times m$ rectangle, it follows that it is possible to tile any $6k \times m$ rectangle, provided $m > 1$ and $k > 0$.

9. (a) Let the number of integers in the list be n. Then considering the total of all the numbers we get $47n = 329$ and therefore $n = 7$.

Let X be the largest possible value for a number in the list. Since the list has a fixed sum, the maximum value of X occurs when the other numbers are as small as possible, that is, when the list is 1, 2, 3, 4, 5, 97, X (remembering that the numbers are distinct, positive integers). But the total is 329, so $X = 217$.

(b) Let Y be the largest number in the list of positive integers. We wish to maximise Y and yet maintain an average of 47.

Form a new list by subtracting 47 from every number in the original list. Then the average of the numbers in the new list is zero and therefore

(the sum of the positive numbers)
$$+ \text{(the sum of the negative numbers)} = 0.$$

Since $Y - 47$ is one of the positive numbers in the new list, to maximise Y the new list needs to have as many negative numbers as possible (thereby making the sum of the positive numbers as large as possible), but as few positive numbers as possible (thereby making Y as large as possible).

In other words, the original list needs to have as many integers as possible less than 47 and as few integers as possible greater than 47. One such list of numbers is 1, 2, 3, 4, ..., 45, 46, 97, Y. Since there are 48 integers in this list and the average is 47, their sum is $48 \times 47 = 2256$ and hence Y is 1078.

Note that other such lists are possible, which include the same numbers as the one considered but also include 47 any number of times. These all give the same value for Y.

10. To help to understand this problem, it is natural to test the first few numbers to see which small numbers are qprime, and which are not:

> 1 is not a qprime since it has no prime factors.
> 2 and 3 are not qprimes since they are prime.
> 4 is not qprime since it is 2×2.
> 5 is not qprime, since it is prime.
> $6 = 2 \times 3$ is the first qprime number.
> 7 is not qprime.
> 8 is not qprime, since it is $2 \times 2 \times 2$.
> 9 is not, since it is 3×3.
> $10 = 2 \times 5$ is another qprime.

11 is not.
12 is not, since it is $2 \times 2 \times 3$.

Of course, we cannot prove a general result just by continuing the list, but it can guide us to a proof, such as the one that follows.

We note that no multiple of 4 is ever qprime, since a multiple of 4 is a multiple of 2×2. This means that a string of consecutive qprime numbers can be at most of length three, because any sequence of four or more consecutive integers includes a multiple of 4.

We are therefore led to ask whether any strings of three consecutive qprime numbers exist. We have looked as far as 12 and not found any, but we will continue searching, using the fact that none of the numbers is a multiple of 4.

13, 14, 15: the number 13 is prime and so not qprime.
17, 18, 19: 17 is not qprime (nor are the others).
21, 22, 23: 23 is not qprime.
25, 26, 27: 25 is not qprime (nor is 27).
29, 30, 31: 29 is not qprime (nor are the others).
33, 34, 35: all three are qprime (being 3×11, 2×17, and 5×7).

So we have found a sequence of three consecutive qprimes, and have also proved that no sequence of four (or more) consecutive qprimes exists.

Thus the the longest possible sequence of consecutive integers all of which are qprime numbers has length 3.

11. All multiples of 12 are even, so each digit of 5 ACROSS is 2, 4, 6 or 8. Now 5 ACROSS is a multiple of 21 so it is also a multiple of 3, and we know that a number is a multiple of 3 if, and only if, the sum of the digits is also a multiple of 3. But $2 + 4 + 6 + 8 = 20$, so that the only possibilities are not to use 2, or not to use 8. Hence the digits of 5 ACROSS are 4, 6 and 8, or 2, 4 and 6, in some order. We deduce that 5 ACROSS is 246, 264, 426, 462, 624, 642, 468, 486, 648, 684, 846 or 864. But 5 ACROSS is a multiple of 21 so it is also a multiple of 7. By checking them, we see that only 462 is divisible by 7. Thus 5 ACROSS is 462.

Now $12 = 4 \times 3$, so that all the DOWN answers are multiples of 4, and the number formed by the last two digits of a multiple of 4 is itself divisible by 4. Hence the last two digits of 1 DOWN are 24, 44,

64 or 84. But 2, 4 and 6 have already been placed, therefore the last two digits of 1 Down are 84.

The first digit of 4 Across is therefore 8. Now the multiples of 21 between 800 and 900 are 819, 840, 861 and 882. Once again, since 2, 4 and 6 have already been placed 4 Across can only be 819. The last two digits in the Down columns are now 84, 16 and 92, all of which are divisible by 4.

Finally, 1 Down is a multiple of 3, so it is 384, 684 or 984. But 6 and 9 have already been placed so 1 Down is 384. Likewise, 2 Down is 516 and 3 Down is 792.

Therefore the completed crossnumber can only be as shown and we may check that all the clues are satisfied.

3	5	7
8	1	9
4	6	2

Exercise 4.5 question 11

In particular, we observe that we have not used clue 1 Across, so we need to check that 357 is divisible by 21.

Thus there is exactly one solution to the crossnumber.

12. (a) The only factors of a prime number are 1 and the number itself. Therefore $S(p) = 1$ for every prime number p and so no prime number is abundant.

It is an easy task to check the factors of the first few remaining positive integers:

$$S(4) = 1 + 2 = 3;$$
$$S(6) = 1 + 2 + 3 = 6;$$
$$S(8) = 1 + 2 + 4 = 7;$$
$$S(9) = 1 + 3 = 4;$$
$$S(10) = 1 + 2 + 5 = 8;$$
$$S(12) = 1 + 2 + 3 + 4 + 6 > 12.$$

Therefore, 12 is the smallest abundant positive integer. (Note that $S(1)$ is not defined, since by definition, we must include 1 but not include the number itself, which in this case is also 1, clearly a contradiction.)

(b) Since p and q are prime, the only factors of the number are 1, p, q and pq. Therefore $S(pq) = 1 + p + q$. It is now necessary to compare the size of $1 + p + q$ with that of pq.

If we assume, without loss of generality, that $p < q$, then $p \geq 2$ and $q \geq 3$. Hence $pq \geq q + q \geq 1 + p + q$ and so $S(pq) \leq pq$. Thus pq is not abundant.

(c) If m has factors $1, m_1, m_2, \ldots, m_k$ and m, then

$$S(m) = 1 + m_1 + m_2 + \cdots + m_k$$

and, since m is abundant, $1 + m_1 + m_2 + \cdots + m_k > m$. The number pm will have the same factors as m and the additional factors $p, pm_1, pm_2, \ldots, pm_k$ and pm (since p is not a factor of m, these are all new factors.)

Therefore

$$\begin{aligned} S(pm) &= 1 + m_1 + m_2 + \cdots + m_k \\ &\quad + p + pm_1 + pm_2 + \cdots + pm_k + m \\ &= (1+p)(1 + m_1 + m_2 + \cdots + m_k) + m \\ &> (1+p)m + m \\ &= (2+p)m, \end{aligned}$$

which is the required result.

13. Without any loss of generality, we may suppose that the sheet of paper measures $\sqrt{2}$ units by 1 unit. Let the width of the margin be m units and let the $g \times (g+1)$ grid be composed of squares with sides of length d units, as shown.

The length of the sheet is

$$d(g+1) + 2m = \sqrt{2}$$

and the width of the sheet is

$$dg + 2m = 1.$$

Eliminate d from this pair of equations to yield the relationship

$$2m = g + 1 - g\sqrt{2}.$$

Appendix C: Solutions to the exercises

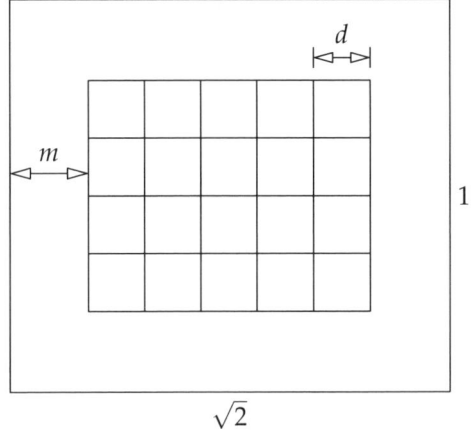

Exercise 4.5 question 13

We now use the fact that m has to be positive to obtain
$$0 < g + 1 - g\sqrt{2}$$
and hence
$$(\sqrt{2} - 1)g < 1,$$
so that
$$g < \frac{1}{\sqrt{2} - 1}$$
$$= \frac{1}{\sqrt{2} - 1} \times \frac{\sqrt{2} + 1}{\sqrt{2} + 1}$$
$$= \sqrt{2} + 1.$$

Restricting our solutions to positive integers, we deduce that there are only two possibilities: $g = 1$ or $g = 2$.

If $g = 1$, then from equations (2) and (1) we find that
$$2m = 2 - \sqrt{2} > 0$$
and
$$d = 1 - (2 - \sqrt{2})$$
$$= \sqrt{2} - 1$$
$$> 0,$$

so that the arrangement is indeed possible for a 1×2 grid. Similarly, if $g = 2$, then
$$2m = 3 - 2\sqrt{2} > 0$$
and
$$2d = 1 - (3 - 2\sqrt{2})$$
$$= 2\sqrt{2} - 2$$
$$> 0,$$
so that the arrangement is also possible for a 2×3 grid.

Hence the arrangement is possible for grids of size 1×2 or 2×3 but impossible for any other grids of the form $g \times (g+1)$.

14. Let the integers be a, b and c, where $0 < a < b < c$. Hence $a + b < 2c$, but c is a factor of $a + b$, so $a + b = c$.

Thus the integers are a, b and $a + b$.

Now we also require b to divide $2a + b$. It follows that b divides $2a$. But $2a < 2b$ so $b = 2a$, and therefore $c = 3a$. But then the condition that a divides $b + c$ automatically holds.

Hence there is an infinite number of solutions: $(a, b, c) = (k, 2k, 3k)$, where k is any positive integer.

REMARK

For any $n \geq 3$, there exists a list of n different positive integers such that each of them divides the sum of the remaining $n - 1$ numbers. However, classifying all solutions for general n is an unsolved problem. One possible list is
$$1,\ 2,\ 3 \times 2^0,\ 3 \times 2^1,\ \ldots,\ 3 \times 2^{n-3}.$$
Can you prove that this list has the desired property?

Exercise 5.2

1. FIRST SOLUTION

   Consider the possible right angles at a vertex. A right angle may be formed by two edges (in 3 ways), or by an edge and a face diagonal (in 3 ways). This is the same for each of the eight vertices.

   Hence the total number of triangles is $8 \times 6 = 48$.

   SECOND SOLUTION

   Consider all possible rectangles whose vertices are vertices of the cube. There are 6 faces and 6 diagonal rectangles. Each diagonal of such a rectangle determines two right-angled triangles, so each rectangle corresponds to 4 right-angled triangles.

   Hence the total number of triangles is $12 \times 4 = 48$.

2. That 'the angle in a semicircle is 90°' is well known: given a diameter AB of a semicircle and another point C on the circumference, as shown on the left, then $\angle BCA = 90°$. This is *Thales' theorem*.

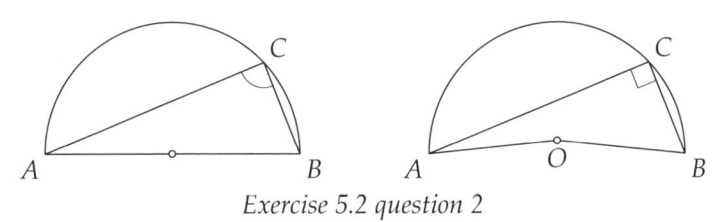

   Exercise 5.2 question 2

   The converse result is also true, but may be less well known: given a right-angled triangle ABC with hypotenuse AB, then AB is a diameter of the circle through A, B and C.

   To see why this is true, join A and B to the centre O of the circle (see the right-hand figure). Then, using 'the angle at the centre is twice the angle at the circumference', we obtain $\angle AOB = 2 \times \angle BCA = 2 \times 90° = 180°$. It follows that AOB is a straight line, as required.

   Now consider triangles formed by joining three of the eight points given in the question. The first result shows that the triangle will be right-angled when one side is a diameter, and the second result shows that this is the only way to obtain a right-angled triangle. So we may find the number of right-angled triangles by counting the number of ways of choosing two points at the ends of a diameter, and then choosing the third point.

Now there are 4 ways to choose a diameter connecting the given points: AE, BF, CG and DH.

For a given choice of diameter, there are 6 different ways to choose the third point to form a triangle. For example, diameter AE forms a right-angled triangle with each of the points B, C, D, F, G and H.

Hence altogether there are $4 \times 6 = 24$ ways to form a right-angled triangle.

3. Let there be n existing stations before any additional stations are added to the network. Starting at any station, it is possible to travel to any of the remaining $n - 1$ stations. Thus a total of $n(n - 1)$ different tickets are needed. Note that this takes into account the fact that the ticket from station A to station B is different from that from station B to station A.

Suppose we add m new stations to the network. This will require a further $m(m - 1)$ tickets for travel between the new stations and $2mn$ tickets for travel between the old stations and the new stations.

So we are required to find values of m and n for which

$$(m(m - 1)) + 2mn = 200.$$

This relationship can be rewritten as

$$(m(m + 2n - 1)) = 200,$$

so that m is a factor of 200 and, rearranging, we get

$$2n - 1 = \frac{200}{m} - m.$$

Possible values for m are 1, 2, 4, 5, 8, 10, 20, 25, 40, 50, 100 and 200, of which only 1, 5 and 8 yield integer values for n, namely 200, 40 and 25.

Thus there are three different combinations of the number of existing stations and the number of new stations for which 200 new types of ticket will be required.

Appendix C: Solutions to the exercises

4. (a) Let there be q ways of making N p. Simply adding a 1 p stamp to each of these ways will result in a way of making $(N+1)$ p. Hence there are at least q ways of making $(N+1)$ p.
   (b) We show that there is at least one way of making $(N+1)$ p that does not require the use of a 1 p stamp.

   If $N+1$ is even, then make up the amount using only 2 p stamps. If $N+1$ is odd, then use one 3 p stamp and all the rest 2 p.

   Since all the ways of making $(N+1)$ p in part (a) involved the use of a 1 p stamp, we have shown that there exists at least one further way of making $(N+1)$ p.

   Hence the number of ways of making $(N+1)$ p is always strictly greater than the number of ways of making N p.

Exercise 5.3

1. Let us write a, b, c, d, e, f for the six values in the outer circles, as shown, and write S for the common sum of the three lines.

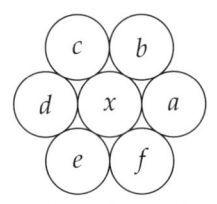

Exercise 5.3 question 1

The given conditions then say that
$$a + x + d = S,$$
$$b + x + e = S,$$
$$\text{and} \quad c + x + f = S.$$

If we add these equations together, we get
$$a + b + c + d + e + f + 3x = 3S.$$

However, the sum $a + b + c + d + e + f + x$ is equal to 28, since the numbers are 1, 2, 3, 4, 5, 6 and 7 in some order. So, rewriting, we get
$$2x + 28 = 3S,$$

which says that $2x + 28$ is a multiple of 3.

We can quickly check that this happens only when $x = 1, 4$ or 7. Hence all other values of x are impossible.

In order to complete the solution, it is necessary to demonstrate with three examples that each of these three values of x is possible. Can you find an example for each of $x = 1$, $x = 4$ and $x = 7$?

2. (a) The total of the numbers 1 to 9 is 45. Let the numbers placed at the vertices of the triangle be a, b and c.

    The numbers along each side of the triangle add up to T, so that adding the three sides together gives $3T$. This total includes all nine numbers, but with a, b and c included twice. Therefore we have
    $$3T = 45 + a + b + c. \tag{1}$$

Now the smallest value for $a+b+c$ is $1+2+3 = 6$ and the largest value is $7+8+9 = 24$. Hence $45+6 \leq 3T \leq 45+24$ and so $17 \leq T \leq 23$.

(b) When $T = 23$ we know from equation (1) that 7, 8 and 9 are placed at the vertices. Can you find a solution in that case?

(c) We have $a+b+c = 15$ and so the only possible choices for the values of a, b and c are:

$$9, 5, 1; \quad 9, 4, 2; \quad 8, 6, 1; \quad 8, 5, 2;$$
$$8, 4, 3; \quad 7, 6, 2; \quad 7, 5, 3; \quad 6, 5, 4.$$

Each of these may lead to a solution and some may not, but we can conclude that there are at most these 8 possible choices.

3. Let C be the sum of the four corner numbers. Now the sum of the numbers 1 to 10 is 55, so that the sum of the numbers in the two rows and two columns is $55 + C$ and therefore

$$4T = 55 + C. \tag{1}$$

(a) When $T = 20$, from equation (1) we have $4 \times 20 = 55 + C$ so that $C = 25$. Can you find a solution in that case?

(b) The smallest sum of four of the ten numbers is $1+2+3+4 = 10$. Therefore $C \geq 10$ so that $4T \geq 55 + 10$, from equation (1), and hence $T > 16$.

Suppose $T = 17$. From equation (1) we have $4 \times 17 = 55 + C$ so that $C = 13$. Let the middle numbers in the two columns be x and y. Then the sum of these columns is $2T = C + x + y$. Hence $x + y = 2T - C = 2 \times 17 - 13 = 21$, which is impossible since $x + y$ is at most $9 + 10$..

However, when $T = 18$ we have $C = 17$ and $x + y = 19$ so that x and y are 9 and 10. Can you find a solution in that case?

Once you have found a solution when $T = 18$, since we have ruled out any smaller values of T we may deduce that the minimum possible value of T is 18.

4. Let T be the common total and let the numbers in the circles be a to j, as shown in the figure. Note that a, b, c d are the numbers which occur in three lines.

Finding the sum of the six lines of three numbers, we obtain

$$3(a+b+c+d) + (e+f+g+h+i+j) = 6T. \tag{1}$$

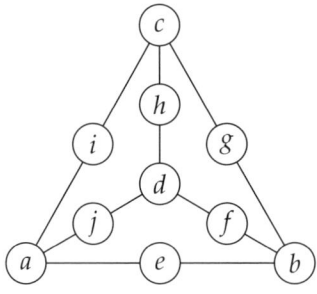

Exercise 5.3 question 4

Now the sum of all the numbers from 1 to 10 equals 55, so that
$$(a+b+c+d) + (e+f+g+h+i+j) = 55.$$
Hence equation (1) may be rewritten
$$2(a+b+c+d) + 55 = 6T. \qquad (2)$$
But 55 is odd and the other two terms in equation (2) are even, which is not possible. We deduce that Sam's task is impossible.

5. The total of the numbers in the grid is $1 + 2 + \cdots + 9 = 45$.

   Let the central number be x, let the four middle numbers along the sides be a, b, c, d and let the four corner numbers be p, q, r, s, as shown in the left-hand figure.

p	a	q
b	x	c
r	d	s

4	3	5
8	9	7
1	6	2

1	6	3
9	8	7
2	5	4

Exercise 5.3 question 5

Now add up the totals of the numbers in the four 2×2 blocks in two ways to show that
$$4T = 4x + 2(a+b+c+d) + (p+q+r+s)$$
$$= 45 + 3x + (a+b+c+d).$$
Since $x \leq 9$ and $x + a + b + c + d \leq 9 + 8 + 7 + 6 + 5 = 35$ we have $4T \leq 45 + 18 + 35 = 98$. Therefore $T \leq 24$.

Appendix C: Solutions to the exercises 251

However, it is possible to achieve this value in several ways. Two examples are shown on the right of the figure.

We deduce that the maximum value of T is certainly 24.

REMARK

Notice that it is possible to achieve the maximum T using 8 in the central cell, somewhat counter-intuitively.

Exercise 5.4

1. It is possible to complete a table showing the numbers of pupils in each category in the following way.

   There are 300 children, 60% of them play tennis and 40% play badminton, so 180 play tennis and 120 play badminton.

   Also, 30% of the tennis players swim, so there are 54 tennis players who swim. Hence there are $180 - 54 = 126$ tennis players who play hockey.

   Now 56% of the hockey players play tennis, so 56% of the number of hockey players is 126, therefore the number of hockey players is

   $$126 \times \frac{100}{56} = 225.$$

   Hence the number of hockey players who play badminton is $225 - 126 = 99$ and so the number of badminton players who swim is $120 - 99 = 21$.

	hockey	swimming	total
tennis	126	54	180
badminton	99	21	120
total	225		300

2. Team A lost all their matches, scoring 2 goals and having 3 goals scored against them. Since each lost match leads to at least one more 'goal against' a team than the number of 'goals for', team A can have played only one match, with a score of 2 – 3. Now B only had one goal scored against them and G did not win any matches, so A's opponents were C and the result was A 2 C 3.

   Team G drew one match. Now neither A nor B drew any matches, so G's opponents were C, which completes C's list of two matches played. Team C scored 4 goals in all, of which 3 were against A, and hence the result of this match was C 1 G 1.

   Team B played at least one match, since they had one goal scored against them, but can only have played against G and hence played exactly one match. Team G has 4 'goals against' unaccounted for, so the result was B 4 G 1.

The completed table is:

Team	Played	Won	Lost	Drawn	Goals for	Goals against
A	1	0	1	0	2	3
B	1	1	0	0	4	1
C	2	1	0	1	4	3
G	2	0	1	1	2	5

3. (a) Team A won all three games and so beat teams B, C and D.

   Of the three games that team C played, the one that was lost can only have been against team A. Therefore team C drew against teams B and D.

   If we consider the three games that team B played, the game against team A was lost, the game against team C was a draw and so the remaining game, that team B won, was against team D.

   In summary:

   A beat B, A beat C, A beat D;
   B drew with C, B beat D; and
   C drew with D.

   (b) Consider the following table in which the rows give the number of goals scored *for* each team and the columns give the number of goals *against* each team.

   | | | \multicolumn{5}{c}{Goals against} |

		A	B	C	D	All
Goals for	A	–		$z+1$		5
	B		–	x	t	2
	C	z	x	–	y	5
	D			y	–	3
	All	1	2	6	6	15

   We have let the number of goals scored by team C against team B be x, so that the number of goals scored by team B against team C is also x, since their match was a draw. Similarly, we have let the number of goals scored by team C against team D be y, so that this is also the number scored by team D against team C.

Furthermore, we have let the number of goals scored by team C against team A be z, so that the number of goals scored by team A against team C is $z + 1$ since the difference between the number of goals scored and conceded by team C is 1.

Finally, we have let the number of goals scored by team B against team D be t. Then t is at least 1 since B beat D.

We observe that the row for C now means that $x + y + z = 5$ (which agrees with the column for C).

From the column for A we see that z is at most 1, since the total in that column is 1. Similarly, from the row for D we see that y is at most 3, and from the row for B we see that x is at most 1 since t is at least 1.

But we have $x + y + z = 5$, so that the only possibilities are $x = 1$, $y = 3$ and $z = 1$. It follows that $t = 1$.

Therefore the table is:

Goals against

	A	B	C	D	All
A	–		2		5
B		–	1	1	2
C	1	1	–	3	5
D			3	–	3
All	1	2	6	6	15

Goals for

We may now complete the table by, for example, first noting that all other entries in the column for A are 0, and then filling in the rows from the bottom. Can you do this and hence find the scores in each match?

4. (a) To find the minimum number of triangles visited, consider the straight lines across the diagram. There are seven horizontal lines, and three lines in each diagonal direction. This makes a total of 13 straight lines. The bug wishes to cross all of them, so must cross at least 13 edges of triangles. In crossing 13 edges, the bug must visit at least 14 triangles.

Appendix C: Solutions to the exercises 255

The route shown in the figure alongside illustrates that it is possible to visit exactly 14 triangles.

Hence 14 is the minimum number.

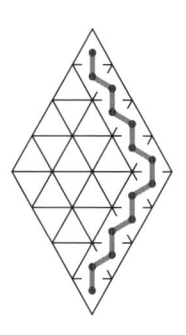

(b) Notice that the bug visits upward- and downward-pointing triangles alternately. Therefore a path that visits only 14 triangles will visit 7 downward-pointing triangles, one of which is B. But the downward-pointing triangles appear in exactly 7 rows. It follows that a shortest path has to move down from one such row to the next in every two steps.

We now count the number of different ways of reaching each downward-pointing triangle in a shortest route.

Clearly there is only one way to reach the top downward-pointing triangle, the one below T.

For every other downward-pointing triangle, the bug must first reach one of the downward-pointing triangles which touches it and which is in the row above. So the number of different ways of reaching each downward-pointing triangle is the number of ways of reaching it from above and to the left, plus the number of ways of reaching it from above and to the right.

Continuing from the top triangle in this way, we get the table of numbers shown in the figure alongside.

Hence the number of ways of reaching the bottom cell is 20.

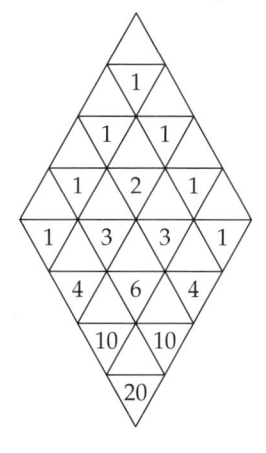

5. In any rotation or reflection, adjacent faces remain adjacent, and opposite faces remain opposite. We know that face 1 is adjacent to face 2, and can therefore be opposite to 3, 4, 5 or 6. Without loss of generality we may take 1 as the base. Now consider the four possible top faces in turn.

3 at the top: Then 2, 4, 5, 6 form the sides. Now 5 has to be adjacent to 4 and 6, and hence is opposite 2, so there is only one such cube possible.

4 at the top: Then 2, 3, 5, 6 form the sides. Now 2 and 3 are adjacent, as are 5 and 6, so there are two possible cubes, because we can have 2, 3, 5, 6 (with 2 opposite 5) or 2, 3, 6, 5 (with 2 opposite 6) in order round the cube.

5 at the top: Then 2, 3, 4, 6 form the sides. Since 3 is adjacent to 2 and 4, and hence opposite 6, there is just one possibility.

6 at the top: Then 2, 3, 4, 5 form the sides. We must have 2 opposite 4, and 3 opposite 5, so there is just one possibility.

Thus there are five distinct ways that a cubical die can be numbered from 1 to 6 so that consecutive numbers are on adjacent faces. The corresponding nets are:

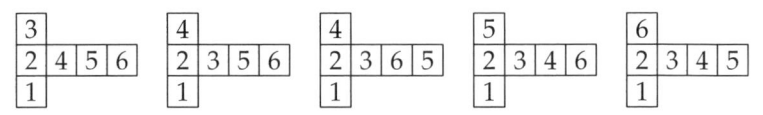

3			
2	4	5	6
1			

4			
2	3	5	6
1			

4			
2	3	6	5
1			

5			
2	3	4	6
1			

6			
2	3	4	5
1			

Exercise 5.4 question 5

6. Whenever a cell is shaded, one is added to all the cells with which it shares an edge or corner. So consider an alternative numbering system: in each shaded cell write the number of cells with which it shares an edge or corner; leave each unshaded cell blank. For example, for the shading pattern given in the question we obtain the numbers shown in the figure.

This is equivalent to the original numbering system; in particular, the total of all the numbers is the same.

Now a shaded corner cell has 3 adjacent cells; a shaded outer middle cell has 5 adjacent cells; the shaded inner middle cell has 8 adjacent cells. Thus the total of all the numbers for a shading pattern is made up solely by adding multiples of 3, 5 and 8.

Appendix C: Solutions to the exercises 257

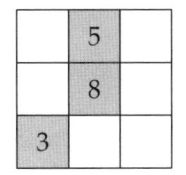

Exercise 5.4 question 6

For a 3×3 diagram the available numbers are therefore: four 3s, four 5s and one 8.

If the 8 is used, a remaining total of $17 - 8 = 9$ is required. The only way to attain 9 is to use three 3s.

If the 8 is not used, since 17 is not a multiple of 3 at least one 5 is needed. Now $17 - 1 \times 5 = 12$, $17 - 2 \times 5 = 7$ and $17 - 3 \times 5 = 2$, but neither 7 nor 2 is a multiple of 3. So the only possibility is to use one 5 and then a remaining total of 12 is required. The only way to attain 12 is to use four 3s.

Thus the only possibilities are: 3, 3, 3, 3, 5 and 3, 3, 3, 8. It turns out that both of these are possible using the available numbers. For each set of numbers, can you find all the corresponding shading patterns and so complete the solution?

7. It is worth observing that, for the purposes of this question, we can replace the numbers on the balls by their remainders when they are divided by 3. This is because, for any two numbers a and b, their sum $a + b$ is a multiple of 3 if, and only if, the sum of their remainders is divisible by 3. To prove this, suppose that, when divided by 3, a has remainder r and b has remainder s. Then we can write $a = 3m + r$ and $b = 3n + s$, for some integers m and n. Therefore

$$a + b = 3m + 3n + r + s$$
$$= 3(m + n) + r + s$$

and this is divisible by 3 if, and only if, $r + s$ is divisible by 3.

Using this idea, any selection of five balls will result in a set of five numbers, each of which is 0 or 1 or 2.

If three of the balls have the same number, then their sum will be divisible by 3, and we are done.

If not, then there is one pair of numbers equal to x, another pair equal to y and a fifth number equal to z, where x, y and z are 0, 1 and 2, in some order. This means that there are three balls numbered 0, 1 and 2, and the sum of these numbers is divisible by 3.

Hence, in either case, we have a choice of three of the five balls whose sum is a multiple of 3.

8. We shall use the notation $\binom{n}{r}$ for the number of ways of choosing r objects from n. This is a *binomial coefficient*, sometimes written ^nC_r. We have
$$\binom{n}{r} = \frac{n!}{r!(n-r)!} = \frac{n(n-1)\cdots(n-r+1)}{1 \times 2 \times \cdots \times r}.$$

We give three different methods, all of which create a plan for the next eleven days by constructing a line of Cs and Hs.

FIRST METHOD

We create a plan for the next eleven days by constructing a line of Cs and Hs from two types of tile, $\boxed{\text{C}}$ or $\boxed{\text{HC}}$, which ensures that two Hs are never placed together. There are various possibilities, determined by the number of $\boxed{\text{C}}$ tiles which are used, which can be 11, 9, 7, 5, 3 or 1.

Eleven $\boxed{\text{C}}$ tiles can be placed in just one way, or $\binom{11}{0}$ ways.

Nine $\boxed{\text{C}}$ tiles and one $\boxed{\text{HC}}$ tile can be placed in $\binom{10}{1}$ ways, the number of ways of choosing the position of one $\boxed{\text{HC}}$ tile in a row of 10 tiles.

Seven $\boxed{\text{C}}$ tiles and two $\boxed{\text{HC}}$ tiles can be placed in $\binom{9}{2}$ ways, the number of ways of choosing the position of two $\boxed{\text{HC}}$ tiles in a row of 9 tiles.

Continuing in this way, we see that the total number of ways is

$$\binom{11}{0} + \binom{10}{1} + \binom{9}{2} + \binom{8}{3} + \binom{7}{4} + \binom{6}{5}$$
$$= 1 + 10 + 36 + 56 + 35 + 6$$
$$= 144.$$

However, placing tiles in this way always ends the line with a C, so does not allow for the possibility of ending with an H. But if the line ends with an H, then the remainder of the line has ten letters and ends with a C. We may count the number of ways for this in a similar way to the above, but with a total of 10 letters instead of 11:

$$\binom{10}{0} + \binom{9}{1} + \binom{8}{2} + \binom{7}{3} + \binom{6}{4} + \binom{5}{5}$$
$$= 1 + 9 + 28 + 35 + 15 + 1$$
$$= 89.$$

Therefore the total number of ways altogether is $144 + 89 = 233$.

SECOND METHOD

We create a plan for the next eleven days by starting with k Cs in a line, where $k \leq 11$, and adding some Hs (possibly none) to construct a line of Cs and Hs. There are $k + 1$ slots into which a single H may be placed—at either end or between two Cs. We need to place $11 - k$ Hs so that each H is in a *different* slot, so we have to choose $11 - k$ of the $k + 1$ slots; there are $\binom{k+1}{11-k}$ ways in which this can be done.

Now we cannot add more Hs than the number of available slots, so $11 - k \leq k + 1$, that is, $k \geq 5$.

Therefore the total number of ways is the sum of $\binom{k+1}{11-k}$ for $5 \leq k \leq 11$, in other words

$$\binom{6}{6} + \binom{7}{5} + \binom{8}{4} + \binom{9}{3} + \binom{10}{2} + \binom{11}{1} + \binom{12}{0}$$
$$= 1 + 21 + 70 + 84 + 45 + 11 + 1$$
$$= 233.$$

Sources of the problems

Every problem in this book, whether used as an example or in an exercise, is taken from one of the IMOK Olympiad papers for the years 2003–2012.

The following tables give the sources of all the problems. The symbols C, H and M stand for Cayley, Hamilton and Maclaurin. In the few cases where a problem appeared on more than one paper, only the first paper is given.

Examples			
2.2	2007	C	2
2.3	2005	M	2
2.4	2004	H	4
2.5	2006	H	5
3.2	2003	C	2
3.3	2003	H	5
3.4	2007	H	5
3.5	2006	M	3
3.6	2005	M	5
3.7	2003	M	2
4.2	2008	M	1
4.3	2005	C	4
4.4	2003	H	1
4.5	2005	H	4
5.2	2005	M	3
5.3	2006	H	6

Exercise 2.2			
1.	2005	C	1
2.	2009	C	1
3.	2005	C	2
4.	2009	C	3
5.	2011	C	3
6.	2009	M	1
7.	2010	C	4
8.	2004	H	3
9.	2006	C	5
10.	2006	C	6
11.	2004	H	5
12.	2006	M	5

Exercise 2.3			
1.	2004	C	2
2.	2011	H	1
3.	2012	C	3
4.	2006	H	3
5.	2012	H	3
6.	2006	M	2
7.	2009	H	4
8.	2009	M	3
9.	2010	M	3
10.	2008	H	6
11.	2004	M	4
12.	2005	H	6
13.	2007	M	6

Exercise 2.4

1. 2004 C 4
2. 2010 H 3
3. 2003 H 3
4. 2007 M 1

Exercise 2.5

1. 2005 H 3
2. 2008 H 3
3. 2004 M 2
4. 2011 M 2
5. 2009 C 5
6. 2003 H 4
7. 2007 H 4
8. 2012 M 3
9. 2012 M 4

Exercise 3.2

1. 2004 C 1
2. 2010 C 2
3. 2011 C 2
4. 2012 C 2
5. 2006 C 3
6. 2008 C 3
7. 2004 H 2
8. 2006 H 2
9. 2010 H 2
10. 2011 H 2
11. 2012 H 2
12. 2008 M 2
13. 2010 M 2
14. 2012 M 2
15. 2005 C 5
16. 2007 C 5

Exercise 3.3

1. 2004 C 3
2. 2003 H 2
3. 2009 C 4
4. 2009 H 3
5. 2010 C 5
6. 2008 C 5
7. 2005 H 5
8. 2008 H 5

Exercise 3.4

1. 2006 C 1
2. 2008 C 2
3. 2009 C 2
4. 2005 C 3
5. 2007 C 3
6. 2008 H 2
7. 2003 C 4
8. 2011 C 4
9. 2010 H 4
10. 2003 M 3
11. 2012 C 6
12. 2012 H 5
13. 2009 H 5
14. 2006 M 4
15. 2007 M 4
16. 2010 M 5

Exercise 3.5

1. 2005 H 2
2. 2007 H 3
3. 2007 M 2
4. 2006 H 4
5. 2011 H 4
6. 2010 H 5
7. 2008 M 4
8. 2011 M 5

Exercise 3.6

1. 2004 M 1
2. 2008 H 4

Exercise 3.7

1. 2008 C 6
2. 2009 H 6
3. 2007 M 5
4. 2008 M 5
5. 2005 M 6

Exercise 3.8

1. 2004 M 3
2. 2011 M 3
3. 2009 M 4
4. 2010 M 4
5. 2004 H 6
6. 2012 M 5
7. 2009 M 6
8. 2004 M 6

Sources of the problems

Exercise 4.2

1. 2006 C 2
2. 2003 M 1
3. 2005 M 1
4. 2006 C 4
5. 2004 C 6

Exercise 4.3

1. 2008 C 1
2. 2011 C 1
3. 2012 C 1
4. 2006 H 1
5. 2004 H 1
6. 2009 H 2
7. 2006 M 1
8. 2012 M 1
9. 2009 M 2

Exercise 4.4

1. 2003 C 1
2. 2007 C 1
3. 2007 H 1
4. 2005 H 1
5. 2007 H 2
6. 2010 M 1
7. 2011 H 3
8. 2008 M 3
9. 2011 C 5
10. 2003 M 4
11. 2004 M 5

Exercise 4.5

1. 2010 C 1
2. 2011 M 1
3. 2010 C 3
4. 2008 C 4
5. 2012 C 5
6. 2005 M 4
7. 2011 M 4
8. 2005 C 6
9. 2007 C 6
10. 2010 C 6
11. 2012 H 6
12. 2003 M 5
13. 2008 M 6
14. 2012 M 6

Exercise 5.2

1. 2007 C 4
2. 2012 H 4
3. 2007 M 3
4. 2006 M 6

Exercise 5.3

1. 2012 C 4
2. 2003 C 5
3. 2007 H 6
4. 2011 H 6
5. 2011 M 6

Exercise 5.4

1. 2003 C 3
2. 2004 C 5
3. 2009 C 6
4. 2011 C 6
5. 2011 H 5
6. 2010 H 6
7. 2009 M 5
8. 2010 M 6

Index

1001, factorisation of ~, 88
111, factorisation of ~, 88

alphametic, 77
areas of similar triangles, 50

binomial coefficient, 258

cases
    dealing with a lot of ~, 4
    special ~, 11, 102
    working with ~, 102
Cayley, Arthur, 117
checking, 11, 28, 79, 103
circles, touching ~, 58
circular cone, 69
conditions, given ~, 102
cone, circular ~, 69
cuboid, 69

deriving equations, 9
diagrams, 33, 102
digits, 79
Diophantine equation, 88
divisibility, 83
division by zero, 10

Egyptian fraction, 231
equations
    deriving ~, 9
    labelling ~, 10
    proving given ~, 9

exterior angle
    ≈ of a polygon, 36
    ≈ of a triangle, 35

factorial, 104
factorisation
    ~ of 1001, 88
    ~ of 111, 88
    standard ~s, 16
facts, using standard ~, 35
Fibonacci sequence, 22
fraction, Egyptian ~, 231

given
    ~ conditions, 102
    proving ~ equations, 9
    working towards a ~ result, 35

Hamilton, William Rowan, 118
Hamiltonian circuit, 119

integers, sum of ~, 22, 107
intercepts, line ~, 64
isosceles, median of an ~ triangle, 44

labelling equations, 10
line
    ~ intercepts, 64
    perpendicular ~s, 64

Maclaurin, Colin, 119

median of an isosceles triangle, 44
multiples, 85

naming triangles, 34
natural numbers, sum of ≈, 22, 107
nature of the solutions, 8
notation, 7, 34, 78

patterns and proof, 11, 101
perpendicular lines, 64
polygon
    exterior angle of a ∼, 36
    regular ∼, 37
proof, patterns and ∼, 11, 101
proving given equations, 9
Pythagoras' theorem, 43

radius, tangent and ∼, 58
regular polygon, 37
results table, 113
right-angled triangle, 44

salinon, 181
sequence, Fibonacci ∼, 22
sides opposite equal angles, 35
simplifying, 10

solutions, nature of the ∼, 8
solve, meaning of ∼, 8
sum
    ∼ of integers, 22, 107
    ∼ of natural numbers, 22, 107

tangent and radius, 58
tetrahedron, 69
Thales' theorem, 245
touching circles, 58
triangle
    ∼ numbers, 22
    areas of similar ∼s, 50
    exterior angle of a ∼, 35
    median of an isosceles ∼, 44
    naming ∼s, 34
    right-angled ∼, 44
trisection, points of ∼, 52
Trisectrix of Maclaurin, 120

valid arguments, 78

working towards a given result, 35

zero, division by ∼, 10